Popular
PATRON SAINTS

DON SHARKEY

AND

SISTER LORETTA CLARE, S.C.

THE BRUCE PUBLISHING COMPANY • Milwaukee

NIHIL OBSTAT:

John F. Murphy, S.T.D.
Censor librorum

IMPRIMATUR:
✠ William E. Cousins
Archbishop of Milwaukee
October 16, 1959

Library of Congress Catalog Card Number: 60–7175

© 1960 The Bruce Publishing Company
MADE IN THE UNITED STATES OF AMERICA

To Mary,
Queen of All Saints

How to Use This Book

This is a book of patron saints, but you will find that it has a wider use than merely looking up your particular patron or the patrons of your relatives and friends.

What is a patron saint? Jessie Corigan Pegis in her *Practical Catholic Dictionary* gives this definition: "A saint chosen to be the special advocate for a person, country, diocese, or church, or for a particular occupation in life." In this book, the emphasis is on personal patrons, although other patrons are listed in a special table at the end of the book (pp. 223–226).

"One's own patron saint," Mrs. Pegis continues, "is usually the saint whose name has been given to him in Baptism or whose name he has taken in Confirmation." In order to include the patrons of as many persons as possible, the authors of this book first compiled a list of the most common Christian names and then wrote about a saint for each name, as many as space would allow. A few names, such as Isaac, Perpetua, Felicity, are not so common, but they were included for special reasons.

It has been possible to tell the story of only one saint for each name. Other saints of the same name, however, are listed at the end of the sketch. The field is further broadened by the fact that most of these common names have a number of equivalents. Thus, it is entirely possible that a person who has a name that is not so common might still be able to find his patron here. A person named Carroll, for example, can look up his name in the index (p. 227), and when he turns to the page given there he will find that his name-patron is St. Charles.

The book should be valuable to everyone who wishes to know more about his patron and the patrons of others. It should also be valuable to anyone who wishes to find a saint's name to use in Baptism or in Confirmation.

But the book should have a wider value than that. We are interested in all God's saints, whether or not they are our special patrons. A collection such as this makes interesting and inspiring reading. It shows that there have been saints in all centuries including our own, and from all countries including our own. It shows that saints have come from all walks of life; powerful kings have become saints, and so have lowly peasants.

The book has been divided into three sections: Saints of the First Five Centuries, Saints of the Middle Ages, and Saints of Modern Times. Each section has its own short introductory note. This has been done because conditions have varied so much in the different periods. It is easier to appreciate a saint if we know something about the world in which he lived. The best way to read this book is straight through from beginning to end, including the introductions to each section. Read in this way, the book will show that the history of the Church has been reflected largely in the lives of her saints.

The story of a saint is the only true success story, the only story with a truly happy ending. It is the story of a person who, like ourselves, was born in original sin and with an inclination toward evil. But the saints had such great love for God, and co-operated with His graces to such a great extent, that they were able to overcome sin and attain eternal union with God in heaven.

That should be our ambition — our only ambition: to love God so much and to serve Him so faithfully that we will be united with Him in heaven. If we co-operate with God's graces we shall succeed. The saints have already succeeded. They will help us succeed if we will let them.

CONTENTS

HOW TO USE THIS BOOK vii

SAINTS OF
THE FIRST FIVE CENTURIES

Grandparents of Jesus
ST. ANNE and ST. JOACHIM 3

Universal Patron
ST. JOSEPH 7

Fisherman
ST. JAMES THE GREATER 12

Prince of the Apostles
ST. PETER 16

Apostle of the Gentiles
ST. PAUL 21

Manager of the Household
ST. MARTHA 26

Girl Martyrs of the Early Church
SS. PERPETUA and FELICITY 30
ST. CECILIA 34
ST. BARBARA 35
ST. AGATHA 35
ST. AGNES 35
ST. LUCY 35
ST. DOROTHY 36

God's Soldier
    ST. MARTIN OF TOURS   37

Model Wife and Mother
    ST. MONICA   41

Apostle of Ireland
    ST. PATRICK   45

Other Early Saints
    ST. MICHAEL THE ARCHANGEL   51
    ST. GEORGE   52
    ST. HELENA   52
    POPE ST. LEO I   53
    ST. GENEVIEVE   54
    ST. EUGENIUS   55

SAINTS OF THE MIDDLE AGES

Queen and Empress
    ST. ADELAIDE   59

King of England
    ST. EDWARD THE CONFESSOR   63

Embattled Bishops
    ST. HUGH OF LINCOLN   67
    ST. RICHARD OF CHICHESTER   67

Missionary to Mohammedans
    ST. RAYMOND OF PENAFORT   73

CONTENTS

God's Troubador
ST. FRANCIS OF ASSISI 78

Poor Lady
ST. CLARE OF ASSISI 83

Hammer of the Heretics
ST. ANTHONY OF PADUA 88

Scientist
ST. ALBERT THE GREAT 91

Princess and Pauper
ST. ELIZABETH OF HUNGARY 95

King of France
ST. LOUIS 101

God's Ambassador
ST. BRIDGET OF SWEDEN 105

Girl Warrior
ST. JOAN OF ARC 111

Savior of Switzerland
ST. NICHOLAS VON FLÜE 117

Other Medieval Saints

ST. MATILDA 123

ST. HENRY THE EMPEROR 124

ST. STEPHEN 125

ST. GREGORY VII 125

ST. GILBERT OF SEMPRINGHAM 127

ST. DANIEL OF MOROCCO 128

SAINTS OF MODERN TIMES

Pioneer of Teaching Nuns
ST. ANGELA MERICI 131

King's Chancellor
ST. THOMAS MORE 136

Defender of the Faith
ST. ROBERT BELLARMINE 141

Grandfather and Grandson
BL. PHILIP HOWARD 146
BL. WILLIAM HOWARD 146

Apostle of Organized Charity
ST. VINCENT DE PAUL 151

First American Saint
ST. ROSE OF LIMA 157

North American Martyrs
ST. ISAAC JOGUES, S.J. 162
ST. CHARLES GARNIER, S.J. 162

Saint of the Sacred Heart
ST. MARGARET MARY 168

Patron of Mothers
ST. GERARD MAJELLA 174

Model of Reparation
BL. JULIE BILLIART 179

Guardian of the Queen's Secret
ST. CATHERINE LABOURÉ 184

CONTENTS

Friend of Boys
    ST. JOHN BOSCO 191

Peasant Girl of Lourdes
    ST. BERNADETTE SOUBIROUS 198

United States Citizen
    ST. FRANCES XAVIER CABRINI 205

Saint of the Little Way
    ST. THÉRÈSE OF LISIEUX 210

Child Martyr of Our Century
    ST. MARIA GORETTI 215

Other Modern Saints
    ST. BENEDICT THE MOOR 218
    ST. VERONICA GIULIANI 219
    ST. LEONARD OF PORT MAURICE 220
    ST. CLEMENT HOFBAUER 221

Patron Saints of Special Works and Groups 223
Patron Saints of Industries and Occupations 223
Patron Saints of Countries 225

INDEX 227

POPULAR PATRON SAINTS

SAINTS OF THE
FIRST FIVE CENTURIES

The saints in this section reflect the beginning of Christ's Church, its persecution by the pagan Roman Empire, and its triumphant emergence from that persecution.

God chose Anne and Joachim, of all the people who had ever lived or ever would live, to be the grandparents of His Son, the promised Redeemer. He chose Joseph to be the protector and guardian of His Son.

The Redeemer came, and He knew that the time of His public life would be short. He chose Apostles who would carry on the work of His Church. Among the Apostles were James and Peter. The latter was to become the first pope. Jesus, of course, had many friends who were not Apostles; among these was Martha who often entertained Jesus in her house and who demonstrated her great devotion to Him.

Jesus brought a message of love into the world, but He was met by fanatical hatred, and He died nailed to a cross. The persecution that began with Jesus continued for His Church. For three centuries, the Church fought for its very existence in the pagan Roman Empire. Peter and all the popes who followed him for 250 years were martyrs. James and all the other Apostles except John were martyrs. Paul began as a fierce persecutor of the Church, became one of its greatest defenders, and then died a martyr. The "Girl Martyrs of the Early Church" are typical of thousands of both sexes who died for their faith in the Roman persecutions.

The "blood of the martyrs" proved to be "the seed of Christians," and the Church grew during the persecutions. Then, in 313, the Emperor Constantine, published his Edict of Toleration and the

1

Church was free. In this era we find Monica praying for her son Augustine who was to become a great bishop and doctor of the Church. We find Martin of Tours, first as a hermit then as a great bishop. And we find Patrick carrying the word of Christ to Ireland, which was beyond the limits of the Roman Empire.

The Church had survived the persecution and was spreading even beyond the outermost limits of the Empire.

Grandparents of Jesus

ST. ANNE and ST. JOACHIM,
First Century B.C.

Feast of St. Anne: July 26
Feast of St. Joachim: August 16

EQUIVALENTS OF ANNE: Ann, Anna, Annabel, Annabelle, Anita, Anitra, Annina, Annette, Anusia, Grace, Hanna, Nan, Nann, Nannette, Nancy, Nina, Ninette, Nanna

EQUIVALENTS OF JOACHIM: Joaquin. FEMININE: Joachima, Joaquina

---

Little is known for certain about the lives of Joachim and Anne, but one great fact sets them apart from all other human beings: they were the parents of the Blessed Virgin Mary, the Mother of God.

According to a story which dates from about A.D. 150, Joachim and Anne had long been childless. Among the Jews this was a disgrace and was taken as a sign of God's disapproval. Joachim took a handsome gift to the temple but the priests in charge rejected the gift because it came from a man considered unworthy in the sight of God. Joachim grieved over the rejection of his gift. Instead of returning home he retired to the fields to pray and to fast and to perform other acts of penance. Anne, hearing of the rejection, also turned to penance and begged God to take away the reproach of childlessness.

One day as Anne prayed earnestly in the garden of their home, an angel appeared and said: "Anne, thy prayer is heard; a child shall be born to thee, and this child shall be called blessed throughout the world. And not thy prayer only is heard, but the prayer of Joachim,

3

thy husband. He comes to thee now, by way of the golden gate, having learned through me the gracious designs of God toward him and thyself."

Anne's sorrow was turned to joy, and she hastened to meet Joachim by the golden gate. The couple promised God that their child, whether son or daughter, should be given entirely to Him to serve in His holy temple.

With inexpressible happiness Anne welcomed her child into the world. Joyfully she wrapped the little one in swaddling clothes. With loving care she performed each motherly act for her.

The daughter of Joachim and Anne was the only creature ever conceived without original sin. Her intellect was not clouded and she had not the slightest inclination toward evil. Joachim and Anne probably did not know about the Immaculate Conception, but they could not help seeing that there was something most unusual about their child, something that set her far above other creatures. Anne is reported to have said: "She is a blessing, not only to us, but to all Israel."

It takes but a little stretch of the imagination to hear Anne exclaiming: "Look, Joachim, our child prays without being taught!"

The joyful time of Mary's infancy passed quickly for Anne and Joachim. When she was three years old the time had come for her parents to fulfill their promise. Mary was to be taken to the temple. It would be difficult for any parents to give up their three-year-old child. For Joachim and Anne the parting must have been especially difficult. Mary was their only child and had come to them late in life. And such a very extraordinary child! But she belonged to God more than she did to them, and they willingly made the sacrifice.

Tradition tells us that Joachim and Anne placed their little daughter on the first step of the temple and that she quickly climbed the fifteen steps leading to the altar; there the high priests waited to receive her and bless her. The parents returned home thankful that their child had entered the temple so willingly and had not wished to turn back even to them. But how lonesome that home must have seemed without Mary!

There is no record of Joachim and Anne after Mary was presented in the temple. They undoubtedly visited her from time to time and were happy to see her advance in age and grace and wisdom. When Mary was betrothed to Joseph, the marriage arrangements were made by the priests of the temple, not by her father. Nor do we find any mention of Anne at that time. Perhaps both parents were dead by then. Did God grant these holy parents a foreknowledge of the Annunciation and the birth of our Lord? We do not know. Joachim and Anne lived in obscurity and they died in obscurity.

Through the centuries, Catholics have venerated St. Anne and, to a lesser extent, St. Joachim. They have felt that this couple must have been very close to God in order to be selected as the grandparents of the Son of God. The Church, which is guided by the Holy Spirit in such matters, has looked favorably upon the popular devotion and has assigned a feast to each of the parents of Mary. God Himself has honored St. Anne by performing many wonders, both spiritual and physical, through her intercession.

One of the best known shrines to St. Anne is in d'Auray, in the section of France known as Brittany. The people of this region have been devoted to St. Anne ever since their conversion to Christianity. The chapel of St. Anne d'Auray has been destroyed several times through the centuries but has always been replaced. Numerous miracles have taken place before the statue there. In 1868 Pope Pius IX granted the miraculous statue the privilege of being crowned.

The French who came to the New World brought with them their devotion to St. Anne. At the village of Beaupre, twenty-one miles from the city of Quebec, a chapel dedicated to St. Anne was begun on March 13, 1658. On that day, a man named Louis Grimont, badly crippled from rheumatism, insisted upon placing three stones in the foundation. As he did so he was immediately cured of his illness. Marvelous cures have been taking place at St. Anne de Beaupre from that day till our own, and the shrine is often called "the Lourdes of America."

St. Anne de Beaupre resembles Lourdes in another way: there are numerous spiritual cures which are even greater than the bodily cures. Many come begging St. Anne for a cure; they leave still suffering from their infirmities, but with a great difference. They have learned from St. Anne the value of suffering in patience. With changed hearts they thank God for not curing them!

In 1947 a young man seriously afflicted wrote upon his return from Beaupre:

"Wherever I go, I wish always to be the grandson of St. Anne. My very weakness entitles me in a special way to her love. Henceforward, St. Anne will be for me a good, kind, generous grandmother. . . . My health has remained good in spite of the paralysis which deprives me of the use of half of my body. But it is especially my soul that has gained. Now I see quite clearly that the highest perfection and the purest happiness lie in willing all that God wills. What difference does it make whether the body can walk or not, if the soul is paralyzed?"

St. Joachim does not have any great shrines, but he too is ready to help us. As the grandparents of Jesus, Joachim and Anne are also our grandparents. When we go to them they are ready to listen to us with the love of a grandfather and a grandmother.

OTHER SAINTS OF THE SAME NAMES:

St. Anne, or Susanna, of Constantinople, d. 918. A nun for fifty years. Feast, July 23.
Bl. Ann of St. Bartholomew, 1549–1626. A companion of St. Teresa of Avila. Feast, June 7.
Bl. Anna Maria Taigi, 1796–1837. Wife, mother, housekeeper. Feast, June 9.
Bl. Joachim of Siena, 1259–1305. Remarkable for humility and for charity to the poor. Feast, April 16.
Bl. Joachima, 1783–1854. Widow; foundress of the Carmelites of Charity. Feast, May 22.

Universal Patron

ST. JOSEPH
Feasts: March 19, May 1

EQUIVALENTS: Jose, Josef, Giuseppe. FEMININE: Josephine, Josepha, Giuseppa

---

God selected Joseph to be the foster father of Christ and the man nearest to Christ on earth. God also selected Joseph to be the husband of the Blessed Virgin Mary, the holiest creature that the world has ever known. God makes no mistakes; since He chose Joseph for these unique duties and honors, Joseph must have been, of all the men in the world, the one most worthy of them.

The marriage between Mary and Joseph, as was usual among the Jews, must have been arranged by relatives on both sides, or by the priests in the temple. At a very early age Mary had made a vow of perpetual virginity. In justice she must have made known this fact to her future husband. He had to impose a like obligation upon himself before he could marry her. They were married and made their home in Nazareth.

After the espousals, and before the formal wedding, the angel Gabriel appeared to Mary and told her that she was to be the mother of the Messias, the Redeemer long expected by the Jews. Before she gave her consent, she was assured that her virginity would be preserved. After the angel's visit Mary went off to visit her cousin Elizabeth in the hill country of Judea. She remained several months.

The mystery of the Incarnation had been revealed to Elizabeth, but it had not yet been revealed to Joseph. His anguish must have been great when Mary returned to Nazareth and he saw that she

7

was with child. Mary must have suffered for Joseph, but she was not at liberty to tell her secret. He resolved to put her away quietly. Then an angel appeared to Joseph and told him that the Child had been conceived by the Holy Spirit and should be called Jesus because He would save His people from their sins. And Joseph's anguish must have turned to great joy.

Other trials and other joys were ahead. Emperor Augustus decreed that a census of the whole Empire should be taken. Every man would be required to register in the city of his ancestors. Joseph and Mary were of the house of David, so they had to go to Bethlehem. Mary was nearing the end of her time and we can imagine how anxious Joseph was about her and what good care he took of her on the four day journey. We can imagine his anxiety, too, when he could find no place for Mary to stay in Bethlehem. The only place he could find was a cave that had been used as a stable. How humiliating this must have been to Joseph. He was the man of the family, and he could not provide better quarters for Mary and for the Messias who was soon to come. We may be sure that he worked hard to make the cave as presentable and as comfortable as possible.

In that cave Mary brought forth her Son, and Joseph was the first man to look upon the newborn Saviour, and the first to worship Him. Joseph heard the songs of the angels and he received the Child's first human visitors, the shepherds who had been invited to the cave by the angels.

It was Joseph who arranged for the circumcision of the Child, and it was he who, according to the directions of the angel, gave him the name Jesus.

Joseph took Jesus to the Temple, as was required by law, and presented Him to God the Father. Here, he and Mary heard the prophecies of the holy old man, Simeon. We are told that a sword of sorrow pierced Mary's heart when she realized the sufferings that were in store for her Son. We are not told what the effect was on Joseph, but his heart was certainly pierced by a sword of sorrow also when he realized the suffering in store for his foster Son and his wife.

When the census had been taken and the crowds had left Bethlehem, Joseph was able to find a better home for his little family. To this home came the Magi, and Joseph witnessed the adoration of these men who had come from afar to see the newborn King.

After the Magi had left, an angel told Joseph to take the Child and His mother and to flee into Egypt because King Herod wished to kill Jesus. Joseph guided the little group on the long difficult journey. And then in a foreign land he had to find a home for his family, and he had to find work so he could support them. After several years in exile the angel told Joseph that it was safe to return to their own country. At the end of another long difficult journey the family finally settled in its home in Nazareth.

In Nazareth Joseph resumed his work as an artisan, and he also taught Jesus what was suitable for a boy of his years and strength. Joseph advanced in holiness day by day, for he was always living in the presence of God and serving Him in the person of His Son.

The little home in Nazareth was the most perfect home in all the world for in it lived the perfect Child, the perfect mother, and a husband worthy of his God-given office. The early years in Nazareth must have been happy years for Joseph and Mary, but they were sad years too. Both knew that this peace and quiet would not last forever, and both knew that the future held great suffering for Jesus.

When Jesus was twelve, the family made the yearly trip to Jerusalem for the Feast of the Passover. On the return trip the pilgrims had made a day's journey and were preparing to camp for the night when Joseph met Mary. She had traveled with the women, he with the men. Then they discovered that Jesus was missing. Each had assumed that he was with the other. The anguish of their loss cannot be imagined. Night had fallen and they had to wait till daylight before they could start back to Jerusalem. Then there was a whole day of traveling. Relief came on the third day when they found Jesus in the Temple with the Doctors who were "astonished at His wisdom and His answers."

As mothers of all ages have done in their effort to impress a son, Mary said: "Thy father and I have sought thee sorrowing." From this, it seems evident that when Mary was speaking to Jesus about Joseph, she referred to the latter as "your father."

Jesus returned with Joseph and Mary to Nazareth and the Gospel tells us that He was subject to them. He, the God-Man, was subject to Mary and subject to Joseph.

After that incident Joseph is not mentioned again. Since he is not mentioned during the public life of Jesus while Mary is mentioned a number of times, it seems safe to assume that Joseph died before our Lord's public life began. We may be sure that during his last illness and at his death, Joseph was attended by the Lord of heaven and earth and by the Queen of saints and angels. No wonder that Joseph is venerated everywhere as the patron of a happy death. He is also venerated as the patron of the Christian family.

On December 8, 1870, when the Church was beset by many powerful enemies, Pope Pius IX named Joseph Patron of the Universal Church. His successor, Leo XIII, issued an encyclical on Joseph as Patron of the Universal Church.

In 1920, Pope Benedict XV, who had said that the loss of the workingman to the Church was the scandal of the nineteenth century, named Joseph Patron of Workingmen. Pope Pius XII inaugurated a new Feast of Joseph the Working Man which was celebrated for the first time on May 1, 1955.

In 1937 Pope Pius XI designated Joseph as the patron of all those who fight atheistic Communism.

The Church has conferred signal honors on Joseph. He has a litany of his own; he has two feasts; he has a special preface in the Mass of his feasts. The last is a privilege shared only by our Blessed Lady and the Apostles.

Many saints have had great devotion to St. Joseph. St. Teresa of Avila said: "I do not remember to this day ever having asked him for anything he did not grant me. The Lord seems to have given other saints grace to help in some troubles, but I know by experience that this glorious saint helps in all."

OTHER SAINTS OF THE SAME NAME:

St. Joseph of Leonessa, 1556–1612. Capuchin missionary in Turkey. Feast, February 4.

St. Joseph of Oriel, 1650–1702. Spanish priest devoted to the poor. Feast, March 23.

St. Joseph Benedict Cottolengo, 1786–1842. "Italian St. Vincent de Paul." Feast, April 30.

ST. JAMES THE GREATER, d. 43
Feast: July 25

EQUIVALENTS: Diago, Diego, Iago, Jacques, Jacob, Jago, Jamine, Jamek, Jamnik, Seamus, Seumas, Shamus. FEMININE: Jacqueline, Jacquetta, Jacquette, Jaculin

---

Jesus, walking along the shore of the Lake of Galilee, saw the two brothers Peter and Andrew fishing. He called them to come with Him saying that He would make them fishers of men. Going a little farther He saw two other brothers who were also professional fishermen, James and John. They were in a boat with their father Zebedee and some hired men. Jesus also called to them. They left their boat and their nets and followed Him. These were the first four disciples that Jesus called. All four were to be included among the Twelve Apostles who would be the companions and helpers of Jesus during His public life and who would carry on the work of His Church after His Ascension.

Here we are concerned with James, son of Zebedee and brother of John. This James was called the Greater to distinguish him from another Apostle of the same name who is called James the Less. The names do not imply any difference in rank or ability. They simply mean that James the Greater was older than the other James.

The Jews who listened to our Lord's preaching and teaching did not realize that His mission on earth was entirely spiritual. Even those who accepted Him as the promised Redeemer expected Him to re-establish the glorious Jewish kingdom of David and Solomon. James and John shared in this belief for a time. One day their mother, Salome, said to Jesus: "Say that these my two sons may sit, the one on thy right hand and the other on thy left, in thy kingdom." The brothers joined their mother in urging this.

Jesus said to Salome: "You know not what you ask." Then turning to the brothers, He said: "Can you drink the chalice I shall drink?"

Promptly they replied: "We can."

"My chalice indeed you shall drink," Jesus said, and they understood that it was to be a chalice of suffering. "But to sit on my right hand or on my left is not mine to give you, but them for whom it is prepared by my Father."

Because of their impetuous natures, James and John were called by our Lord "Boanerges," sons of thunder. When a town of the Samaritans refused to give Jesus hospitality, James and John asked: "Lord, wilt thou that we command fire to come down from heaven and consume them?" Jesus replied: "You know not of what spirit you are. The Son of Man came not to destroy souls but to save."

James is linked so closely with Peter and John that it is impossible to tell his story separately. These three were the favored Apostles; they were often with Jesus when the others were absent. Peter, James, and John were present when Jesus cured Peter's mother-in-law. The same three were present when the daughter of Jairus was brought to life. These three saw the Transfiguration of our Lord on Mount Thabor when He appeared in His glory with Moses and Elias beside Him, and they heard a voice out of the cloud saying: "This is my beloved Son; hear him." It was Peter, James, and John who accompanied Jesus to the Garden of Gethsemani after the Last Supper. While He underwent the terrible Agony in the Garden, they waited a short distance away. Three times Jesus interrupted His prayer to come to the three, and each time He found them sleeping. In later years they must have thought often of His sorrowful reproach: "Could you not watch one hour with me?"

After the descent of the Holy Spirit, the Apostles went their separate ways to do their Lord's work. There is a strong tradition that James went to Spain and established the Church in that land. There is also a tradition that Mary, the Mother of Jesus, appeared to him while he was in Saragossa, Spain. She was standing on a pillar of jasper, with angels all about her, and beautiful music came from the angelic choir. James readily recognized Mary, for he knew her well, but he was puzzled because he knew that she was still alive and living in the home of his brother John in Jerusalem. Mary reassured James. She told him she wished a chapel built where she stood, for she knew the people of this region would always be faithful to her. Then she vanished and the angels with her. This was the origin of the devotion to Our Lady of the Pillar, which is very popular in Spain. The church which encloses the shrine today has an altar on the gospel side that is dedicated to St. James.

After a long missionary journey James returned to Jerusalem and was active in that city. Herod Agrippa, who ruled Jerusalem, sought to please both the Jews and the Romans by putting James to death for preaching the Christian religion. According to an old story, James was betrayed by a man named Josias. While James and Josias were on their way to the place of execution James cured a poor paralytic. Josias was so impressed by this, and by the serenity of James, that he asked to be baptized. James baptized him. Then, the story concludes, the two were beheaded together. Scripture tells us simply that Agrippa "killed James, the brother of John, with a sword." This was in the year 43. Except for the traitor Judas, James was the first of the Apostles to die.

James was buried in Jerusalem. Tradition tells us that his remains were taken to Spain where they were eventually enshrined in the Cathedral of Compostello. During the Middle Ages the burial place became one of the greatest of Christian shrines.

Some scholars say that it is doubtful that St. James ever went to Spain. They also tell us that it is not certain that the remains at Compostello are actually those of St. James the Greater. But there is no doubt about the affection of the Spanish people for St. James. They invoked him repeatedly during their seven-centuries struggle against the Moors and gave him much of the credit for their eventual victory. They also invoked him in their exploration and conquest of the New World. We can see evidences of their devotion today in the many places in Latin America that are named Santiago and in the name they gave to San Diego in our state of California.

OTHER SAINTS OF THE SAME NAME:

St. James the Less, first century. Apostle. Feast, May 1.
St. James of the Marches, 1389–1479. Franciscan missionary. Feast, November 28.
St. James Philippi, 1444–1483. Italian Servite. Feast, May 25.

ST. PETER, d. about 67

Feast: June 29

EQUIVALENTS: Pearce, Peadar, Peder, Pedro, Petro, Piers, Pierce, Peirce, Perrin, Perry, Pierson, Pierre, Petroc, Petrus, Parnell.
FEMININE: Petra, Petronella

Peter was selected by our Lord Himself to be the chief of His Apostles and the Head of His Church. His name was Simon, but our Lord, on first meeting him, told him that he would be called Cephas, which means rock. The English form is Peter.

Simon was born in Bethsaida. He and his brother Andrew had been disciples of John the Baptist. It was Andrew who brought Simon to the first memorable meeting with Christ. From that moment till the end of his life Peter occupied a place of pre-eminence among the followers of Christ. He was present at all the important events of Christ's public life, beginning with the marriage feast at Cana. After this initial gathering of the Apostles they went back for a time to their occupations until the final call to be fishers of men.

For Peter, the final call was a dramatic one. The crowds were pressing about our Lord near the Lake of Genesareth. He saw two boats nearby. He got into the one that was Peter's and did His preaching from the boat. When He had finished speaking He told Peter and his companions to go out into the deep water and to lower their nets. The astonished Peter said: "Master, the whole night through we have toiled and have taken nothing, but at thy word I will lower the net." The result was an immense catch that filled both boats so that they were almost sinking.

When Peter saw what had happened he fell at the feet of Jesus and said: "Depart from me, for I am a sinful man, O Lord."

Jesus reassured Peter, saying: "Do not be afraid; henceforth thou shalt catch men."

Peter and his companions — Andrew, James, and John — brought their boats to shore, left all things, and followed Him.

Much of Peter's nature is shown in the words he used on this occasion: "Depart from me, for I am a sinful man, O Lord." In these words we find impetuosity, humility, and self-sacrificing love. The last thing in the world that Peter really wanted was for our Lord to depart, but he was so aware of his own unworthiness that the words just tumbled out.

As Peter was first among the Apostles in so many other respects, so he was also the first to recognize the divinity of Christ.

"But who do you think that I am?" our Lord asked him.

Without hesitation, Peter answered: "Thou art Christ, the Son of the living God."

Our Lord replied with these solemn words: "Blessed art thou Simon Bar-Jona, because flesh and blood hath not revealed it to thee, but my Father who is in heaven. And I say to thee, that thou art Peter, and upon this rock I will build my Church, and the gates of hell shall not prevail against it: and I will give to thee the keys of the kingdom of heaven; and whatever thou shalt bind on earth, it shall be bound in heaven; and whatever thou shalt loose on earth, it shall be loosed in heaven."

Once when our Lord spoke to the crowd about the Blessed Sacrament He said He would give them His body to eat and His blood to drink. Many in the crowd found this disgusting and unbelievable, and they turned away from Christ. Our Lord then said to Peter: "Will you go also?"

Peter's faith and his matchless loyalty are seen in his reply: "Lord, to whom shall we go? Thou hast the words of eternal life."

When Jesus foretold His approaching passion, Peter would have none of it. "Lord, be it far from thee," he exclaimed. "This shall not be to thee."

Our Lord rebuked Peter for opposing God's plans. Peter accepted the rebuke, but he was not cured of his impetuosity.

At one time, after a day of hard work, the Apostles had put to sea at the command of the Lord. A terrible storm came up and it seemed that the boat would sink. When they saw Jesus coming to them over the water, the impetuous Peter called out: "Lord, if it be thou, bid me come to thee over the water." Then he plunged into the overpowering waves in his eagerness to reach his Lord.

After the Transfiguration, the enthusiastic Peter cried out: "Lord, let us build here three tabernacles: one for thee, one for Moses, and one for Elias." Jesus restrained him with the words: "Tell the vision to no man. . . ."

At the Last Supper when Christ was about to wash the feet of the Apostles, Peter was shocked and said: "Thou shalt never wash my feet." When our Lord said that this was necessary if they were to continue their companionship, Peter exclaimed: "Not only my feet, but also my hands and my head."

After the Last Supper, when our Lord sorrowfully announced: "This night all you will be scandalized in me," Peter was quick with a reply: "Although all should deny thee, I will never deny thee."

In the Garden of Gethsemani that night, when the soldiers came to arrest Jesus, it was the impetuous Peter who drew a sword and struck off the ear of Malchus. Our Lord restored the ear.

Later that night, after all his protestations of loyalty, Peter vehemently denied that he knew Jesus. Then he shed such bitter tears of repentance that furrows were worn in his cheeks. Some years later Peter insisted that St. Mark include the story of the denial, with all its humiliating details, in the Gospel that Mark was writing. This was an act of self-imposed penance on the part of the contrite Apostle.

Peter knew he had sinned grievously in denying Christ, but his faith was too great for him to despair of our Lord's mercy. Our Lord, in turn, loved Peter too much to deprive him of his privileges. Peter was the first to enter the empty tomb on Easter morning and he was the first of the Apostles to whom the Lord appeared. After the descent of the Holy Spirit it was Peter, inspired by the marvels that had just taken place, who preached the first sermon. Three thousand Jews were converted as a result. It was also Peter who performed the first miracle in the newly founded Church; to a cripple who asked alms he said: "Gold and silver, I have none, but what I have I will give you. In the name of Jesus Christ, arise and walk." And the cripple rose and leaped for joy.

After a second sermon, which resulted in the conversion of 5000, Peter was arrested, along with John, and was ordered to preach no more. Peter replied: "Whether it be just to obey you rather than God, be yourselves the judges." The prisoners were dismissed.

Peter went to Antioch where he remained as bishop for seven years. Then he went back to Jerusalem where he was arrested, put into prison, and heavily chained. An angel released Peter from his chains and opened the prison doors for him.

It seemed only natural that Peter, the first of the Apostles, should eventually make his headquarters in Rome, the first city of the Empire. For the remainder of his life he was the Bishop of Rome, and ever since then the Bishop of Rome, as the successor of St. Peter, has been the visible head of the Church.

He preached as boldly in Rome as he had in Jerusalem, and there were many converts. A persecution broke out, and the Catholics of Rome begged Peter to leave the city while there was yet time. They told him that he must save himself because the young Church needed his leadership. According to a beautiful legend, Peter half-heartedly directed his steps from the city. He had not gone far when he beheld Christ coming toward him. Peter exclaimed: "Master, whither goest thou?" Our Lord answered: "To Rome to be crucified again." Then he disappeared. Peter realized that Christ was being crucified in His Church and that he should stand by the Church. He turned around and went back into Rome.

Peter was captured, put into prison, and sentenced to death. Tradition says that he was sentenced to be crucified and that, at his own request, he was crucified upside down because he was not worthy to die in the same manner as his Saviour.

What a welcome to heaven the divine Master must have accorded to this courageous, humble, contrite, devoted Apostle!

OTHER SAINTS OF THE SAME NAME:

St. Peter Celestine, 1215–1296. Pope. Feast, May 19.

St. Peter Thomas, died 1366. Carmelite preacher who worked for the reunion of the Greek and Latin Churches. Feast, January 6.

St. Peter Canisius, 1521–1597. Jesuit who combated Protestantism. Feast, April 27.

Bl. Peter Julian Eymard, 1811–1868. Founder of the Fathers of the Blessed Sacrament. Feast, August 3.

Apostle of the Gentiles

ST. PAUL, d. about 67
Feasts: January 25 and June 29

EQUIVALENTS: **Pablo, Paulus.** FEMININE: **Paula, Pauline, Paulette**

Paul was one of the most extraordinary men who ever lived. Physically he was small; mentally and spiritually he was a giant. From early life Paul was wholehearted in his devotion to a cause. With him there were no such things as half measures or selfish considerations. Early in his life he threw all of his tremendous energy into an attempt to wipe out Christ's Church. Later, he used that same great energy in behalf of the Church. He reached such a pinnacle of spirituality that he could say: "I live now not I, but Christ liveth in me."

The man who was to become the Apostle of the Gentiles was a Jew of the tribe of Benjamin. At his circumcision on the eighth day after his birth he was given the honored Jewish name of Saul. His home was the city of Tarsus and he was a Roman citizen. His fervent Jewish parents trained him at home and then sent him to Jerusalem to be instructed in the law of Moses. He joined the Pharisees who were the strictest of all Jews in observing the letter of the law.

When his schooling was completed Saul went back to Tarsus. He was there while our Lord was preaching and teaching in and around Jerusalem. Saul never met Jesus.

Some time after our Lord had ascended into heaven, Paul was back in Jerusalem. Being a dedicated Pharisee, he was enraged by the new Church which had sprung up in Jerusalem and the surrounding country. These people who called themselves Christians were departing from Jewish laws and traditions! He felt that this Church must be wiped out, and he felt that he was serving the cause of God when he tried to wipe it out. He was one of those who were present when Stephen, the first martyr, was stoned to death. Saul himself did not throw a stone but he looked after the garments of those who did the throwing, and he thoroughly approved of the killing. Stephen prayed for his persecutors as he died. "If Stephen had not prayed," says St. Augustine, "the Church would never have had St. Paul."

Soon after this Saul obtained the permission of the high priests to go to Damascus, arrest all Christians there, and bring them back in chains to Jerusalem. As Saul and his party approached the city about noon, a dazzling light enveloped him and he fell to the ground. All those who were with him saw the bright light which surrounded their leader.

Then Saul heard a voice which was not heard by the others: "Saul, Saul, why dost thou persecute me?"

Saul said: "Who art thou, Lord?"

"I am Jesus whom thou persecutest."

"Lord, what wilt thou have me do?"

Christ told Saul to go into Damascus and wait. When Saul rose from the ground he found that he could not see. He was led into Damascus and was taken to the home of a Jew named Judas where he waited for three days.

Our Lord appeared to a disciple named Ananias who lived in Damascus. He told Ananias to go to Saul. Ananias trembled at the thought because he knew why Saul had come to Damascus. But our Lord overruled the fears of Ananias and gave him his instructions. Ananias went to Saul, and said: "Brother Saul, regain thy sight." Immediately Saul's sight returned. Ananias told Saul that God had singled him out for special work and told him to go and be baptized. Saul did so, taking the name Paul. Then to the complete astonishment of everyone, he preached in the synagogue that Jesus is the Son of God.

Paul's first preachings were not well received. The Jews looked upon him as a traitor, and the Christians were suspicious of the man who had been their bitter enemy. Partly because of this treatment, but mostly to draw closer to God, Paul retired into the desert of Arabia to pray and do penance.

After his sojourn in the desert Paul returned to Damascus to preach in the synagogue. Fury against him was so great that he had to flee the city, being let down outside the city wall in a basket. He went to Jerusalem but the resentment against him was so strong that he left there, too. Next he went to his native city of Tarsus and then to Antioch, in Syria, where he made many converts.

Until this time, the new Christian Church had seemed to be entirely a Jewish affair. Jews had been its first converts, and Jews had been its fiercest persecutors. People in other parts of the Roman Empire looked upon Christianity as a sect that was growing up among the Jews. But when Paul went to Antioch, most of his converts were Gentiles. The Church had broken the bands that confined it to a small group of Jewish people. The Church had begun the growth that would eventually take it into every part of the world.

The famous "disagreement between saints" concerned the treatment of Gentile converts, with Paul on the side of the Gentiles. Peter was inclined to be conservative in his attitude toward Jewish customs. He did not wish to scandalize the Jewish converts and so he would not eat with certain Christians who did not conform to old Jewish rules regarding food. Paul told Peter that he was mistaken and was doing more harm than good. Paul argued that the old Mosaic law was dead and had been superseded by the law of Christ. In the end, Peter came around to Paul's point of view.

Gradually Paul was accepted by the Apostles. He proved to be a tireless laborer for the Gospel. He was a forceful and convincing speaker. It would be impossible in a short account such as this to tell the stories of his missionary journeys in detail. He traveled thousands of miles throughout Asia and Europe. Everywhere that he went he left behind him Christian congregations and priests to minister to them.

As he traveled on his missionary journeys Paul might have lived on the contributions of his converts, but he did not wish to be a burden to others. Everywhere he went he supported himself by his trade of tent making, which he had learned from his father.

As Paul traveled from one place to another he kept in touch with the congregations which he had founded, encouraging them, and giving them further instructions. He did this through his famous Epistles, fourteen of which are included in the New Testament. Ten of these were written to congregations, three were addressed to pastors, and one was largely personal. This one concerned a runaway slave whom Paul had met, converted, and sent back to his master, Philemon. Paul asked the master to receive the slave "as a brother most dear . . . welcome him as thou wouldst me. And if he did thee any injury or owes thee anything, charge it to me. . . . I am writing to thee, knowing that thou wilt do even beyond what I say."

About A.D. 56 Paul was arrested in Jerusalem. He was later transferred to a prison in Caesarea, where he was held for two years although there was no real evidence against him. As a Roman citizen, he demanded that his case be heard by the emperor, so it was decided that he should be sent to Rome. The ship was wrecked in a storm, but the passengers managed to reach the island of Malta. After a delay of three months, Paul went to Rome where he was kept in prison for some time and then dismissed. His last great missionary journey took him to Spain. When he returned to Rome, he was arrested and was beheaded during the persecution of Nero. It is commonly said that he died on the same day as St. Peter, but this is not certain. He was executed on the Ostian Way near the place where the basilica of St. Paul Outside the Wall stands today.

Shortly before he died, Paul wrote: "I am even now ready to be sacrificed, and the time of my dissolution is at hand. I have fought a good fight; I have finished my course; I have kept the faith. As for the rest, there is laid up for me a crown of justice which the Lord, the just judge, will render to me in that day; and not only to me, but to them also that love his coming."

OTHER SAINTS OF THE SAME NAME:

St. Paul the Hermit, died 342. First hermit, spent 90 years in the desert.
Feast, January 15.

St. Paul of the Cross, 1694–1783. Founder of the Congregation of the
Passion. Feast, April 28.

Manager of the Household

ST. MARTHA, first century
Feast: July 29

EQUIVALENTS: **Marta, Martel, Martella, Marthine, Matty**

The few facts that we know about St. Martha are told in Holy Scripture. Martha was apparently the eldest of the trio that consisted of herself, Mary, and Lazarus. Many commentators on the Bible believe that the Mary of this trio was Mary Magdalene, but this is not certain. The three were members of a well-to-do and devout Jewish family. Their parents were evidently dead, for no mention is made of them when such mention would be expected.

Martha was the efficient manager of the household which doubtless included servants. But when there were special guests, as when Jesus was present, Martha, as hostess, kept her finger on all arrangements; she entrusted no important detail to the sole discretion of others.

We know from the Gospels that Jesus loved this family and that He was always welcome at their home. They lived so near the city of Jerusalem that their home was a convenient resting place for Jesus when He visited the Holy City. In the ample accommodations afforded by a wealthy Jewish family there would be space for several, even all, of Christ's Apostles, and the Jews were traditionally a hospitable people.

On one memorable occasion it happened that when Jesus and some of His followers "were on their journey, that he entered a certain village; and a woman named Martha welcomed him into her house." It is significant that it was Martha who welcomed Him and that she welcomed Him into her house. St. Luke continues the story: "And she had a sister Mary, who also seated herself at the Lord's feet, and listened to his word." While Mary sat at our Lord's feet and drank in His words, "Martha was busy about much serving." She, perhaps more than the others, recognized the dignity of her Guest, and she would not leave the management of the hospitality to servants, however efficient they might be. Things had to be done right, and Martha intended to see that all things were in order.

The busy elder sister thought that the younger sister might be expected, in all justice, to do her share. So Martha complained a bit to Jesus: "Lord, is it no concern of thine that my sister has left me to serve alone? Tell her, therefore, to help me."

Jesus replied: "Martha, Martha, thou art anxious and troubled about many things; and yet only one thing is needful. Mary has chosen the best part, and it will not be taken away from her."

These words were hardly a rebuke to the faithful Martha. Rather, they showed a recognition of the facts of the situation and an understanding of the two women. But an important truth is also contained in the words of Jesus: divine contemplation is of more value to man, and of more worth before God, than any amount of activity which has mere material well-being for its object.

Martha appears in Scripture for a second time when her brother Lazarus was sick. Martha and Mary sent word to Jesus: "Lord behold, he whom thou lovest is sick." While they waited for Jesus to come, Martha and Mary watched anxiously at the bedside of their stricken brother. The hours crept by; the fever mounted. But Jesus did not come.

Jesus, far away, knew what was happening. But He had His reasons for waiting. Two days after He received the message He told the Apostles He was going to Bethany. The Apostles protested. They pointed out to Jesus that only recently the Jews of Judea had tried to kill Him. It would be better to stay out of Judea for a time.

Jesus said: "Lazarus, our friend, sleeps. But I go that I may wake him from sleep."

The Apostles took this literally and could not see why Jesus had to make the long trip just to wake Lazarus from sleep. Then Jesus spoke more plainly. "Lazarus is dead and I rejoice on your account that I was not there, that you may believe. But let us go to him."

When Martha learned that Jesus was coming, she went to meet Him. By this time Lazarus had been dead four days.

"Lord, if thou hadst been here my brother would not have died," Martha exclaimed. And then she showed her perfect faith in Jesus: "But even now I know that whatever thou shalt ask of God, God will give it to thee."

Jesus said: "Thy brother shall rise again."

"I know," said Martha, "that he will rise at the resurrection on the last day."

Then to Martha Jesus made this important statement: "I am the resurrection and the life; he who believes in me, even if he die, shall live on, and whosoever lives and believes in me shall never die." He ended with a question: "Dost thou believe this?"

"Yes, Lord," she said. "I believe that thou art the Christ, the Son of God, who has come into the world."

This was a simple, beautiful act of faith. St. Peter and St. Thomas did no better than Martha on this score.

Martha returned to Mary and said: "The Master is here and calls for thee." Mary hurried to Jesus and used the same words that Martha had used: "If thou hadst been here my brother would not have died."

At the tomb Jesus gave instructions to roll away the stone. Martha warned Him of the probable condition of the corpse because Lazarus had been dead four days. Nevertheless, the stone was rolled back. At the command of Jesus, Lazarus came forth.

Martha appears a third time in Scripture. A banquet was held for Jesus in Bethany. Martha, Mary, and Lazarus were all there. On this occasion Mary poured a pound of fragrant and costly ointment over the feet of Jesus. This "extravagance" drew the reproach of Judas, but Jesus defended the action, saying that Mary had anointed Him in preparation for His burial. At this banquet, Martha, as usual, was serving.

The Gospels tell us no more about Martha, but we may be sure that she was among the faithful women who watched on Calvary and who assisted at the burial of Jesus.

OTHER SAINTS OF THE SAME NAME:

St. Martha of Persia, died about 270. Martyr. Feast, January 19.

St. Martha of Edessa, died sixth century. Mother of St. Simon Stylites the Younger. Feast, May 24.

SS. PERPETUA and FELICITY, d. 203
Feast: March 6

ST. CECILIA, d. about 230
Feast: November 22

ST. BARBARA, d. 235
Feast: December 4

ST. AGATHA, d. about 253
Feast: February 5

ST. AGNES, 291–304
Feast: January 21

ST. LUCY, 283–304
Feast: December 13

ST. DOROTHY, d. about 311
Feast: February 6

EQUIVALENTS OF:

PERPETUA: None; FELICITY: Felicita; CECILIA: Cecily, Celia, Celine, Celie, Cisily, Shiela; BARBARA: Barbe, Barcia, Babora, Bab; AGATHA: None; AGNES: Agnese, Agnesine, Agnita, Agnella, Inez, Ines, Nesta, Netta, Nita; LUCY: Luce, Lucia, Lucie, Luz, Lucile, Lucille, Lucillian, Lucetta, Lucina; DOROTHY: Dorothea, Dora, Doretta, Doria, Dorice, Doris, Donna, Dolly, Dotty

---

In the ten great persecutions of the Church in the Roman Empire, thousands of Christians were martyred for their faith. Among them were the eight girls named above. Six of the eight are named in the Canon of the Mass. Four of these six are also mentioned in the Litany of the Saints.

Despite the popularity of these girl martyrs, few details are known about most of them. The stories of the martyrs were not ordinarily written down at the time of their death but were handed down from generation to generation by word of mouth. By the time they were written down they had become embellished with many legends, and today it is impossible to distinguish fact from fancy. An exception is the case of Perpetua and Felicity and their companions. We have a detailed record of their martyrdom. More than a third of this narrative was written by Perpetua herself while she was awaiting her death; part was written by St. Saturus, a fellow prisoner and martyr; and the remainder was written by an unknown person who was an eyewitness of the martyrdom.

Five persons who were taking instructions in the Christian faith were arrested in Carthage in the year 203. They were Perpetua, a young married woman who had a baby son; Felicity, a slave girl who was expecting a baby; and three men: Saturninus, Secundulus, and Revocatus. These five were joined by Saturus, their instructor in the faith, who voluntarily shared their imprisonment. At first, they were kept under guard in a private house.

Perpetua's father was an old man and a pagan. Her mother and two brothers were either Christians or were taking instructions. Her father came to visit her and begged her in vain to renounce Christianity so she could save her life. "I grieved for my father," she said, "for he alone of all my kin would find no comfort in my suffering." The five catechumens were baptized during the period they were under arrest. At the time of her baptism Perpetua asked God for nothing but the power to endure the sufferings that were coming.

"A few days later we were lodged in prison, and I was greatly frightened because I had never known such darkness. What a day of horror! Terrible heat, owing to the crowds! Rough treatment by the soldiers! To crown all I was tormented with anxiety about my baby." Perpetua had her baby in prison with her because he had not yet been weaned. In those days, bottle feeding was unknown and a baby that could not be breast fed would die.

Perpetua had a dream in which she saw a narrow golden ladder reaching up into heaven. On the sides of the ladder were swords, lances, and hooks which would mangle anyone who made the ascent carelessly. At the foot of the ladder was a huge dragon. Saturus climbed the ladder and then called down to Perpetua: "I wait for you, but take care lest the dragon bite you." She said: "In the name of Jesus Christ, he will not hurt me." The dragon meekly put his head down, and she climbed the ladder. At the top of the ladder there was a garden where a white haired shepherd was milking sheep while thousands of people clad in white stood around him. The shepherd said, "Welcome, child," and gave her some curds of milk which she ate. Those who stood about said: "Amen."

A few days later the prisoners were taken to the market place for their trial. The procurator begged Perpetua to offer a sacrifice to the pagan gods. "Spare your father's white hairs," he said. "Spare the tender years of your child." She refused. Her father tried to plead with her but he was beaten with a rod. "This I felt as much as if I myself had been struck, so greatly did I grieve to see my father thus treated in his old age. Then the judge passed sentence on us all and condemned us to the wild beasts." They were to be put to death during the games held in honor of the festival of Geta Caesar.

When sentence was passed Perpetua's baby was taken from her. God was good to her, she reported, for God so willed it that the baby no longer needed to be nursed, "nor did the milk in my breasts pain me."

A few days later Perpetua dreamed of a brother, Dinocrates, who had died at the age of seven. He looked hot and thirsty and was trying to drink from a fountain that was too high for him to reach. She awoke and prayed for him every day. On the day before she was to go to her death she had another dream. The fountain was lower now and overflowing with water. Dinocrates played happily and went to drink from the fountain. "And so I awoke and I knew he suffered no longer."

She had another dream in which she had to fight an ugly Egyptian. A man of huge stature, in beautiful clothes, told her that if she defeated the Egyptian she would get the bough with golden apples that he held in his hand. She defeated him and received the bough.

"And so I awoke. And I saw that I should not fight with beasts but with the Devil; but I knew victory would be mine. I have written this up to the day before the games. Of what was done in the games themselves, let him write who will."

Felicity was worried that she might not be able to suffer martyrdom with the others, for it was unlawful to execute a pregnant woman. Her fellow prisoners joined her in prayer, and two days before the games she gave birth to a girl who was adopted by a Christian. Her labor was difficult and one of the guards said to her: "You suffer now, but what about when you are thrown to the beasts?" Felicity answered: "Now I suffer what I suffer, but then Another will be in me who will suffer for me, because I am to suffer for Him."

The day before the games the prisoners were given the customary last meal, which was eaten in public. To those who crowded around, they spoke of God's judgments and of the joy of their own suffering. Many were converted.

On the day of the games the prisoners marched into the amphitheater. The three men came first (Secundulus had died in prison), followed by Felicity, "from the midwife to the gladiator, to be washed after childbirth in a second baptism." Last of all came Perpetua, singing a psalm of triumph.

Saturninus and Revocatus were attacked first by a leopard and then by a bear, but the animals did not kill them. Saturus was exposed to a wild boar, but the boar turned on the keeper, wounding him so severely that he died within a few days. Then Saturus was tied up before the bear, but the bear refused to come out of his den. Next a leopard was turned loose. The leopard sprang upon him and in a moment he was covered with blood. The mob jeered and cried out: "He is well baptized!" Saturus dipped a ring in his blood and gave it to the jailer, Pudens, saying: "Farewell! Remember the faith and me. And let not these things disturb but strengthen you." And so

Saturus died, going to await Perpetua, as in the dream. Pudens later became a martyr.

The two women were thrown to a savage cow which tossed them both. Perpetua pinned up her disheveled hair lest she seem to be mourning. Then she helped Felicity to her feet. Perpetua seemed to emerge from a state of ecstasy and asked when they were to be thrown to the cow. When she was told that this had already happened she could scarcely believe it. She turned to her brother and another catechumen and said: "Stand fast in the faith, and love one another. And do not let our sufferings be a stumbling block to you."

The four prisoners were taken to the center of the arena and struck with swords. Saturninus, Revocatus, and Felicity died without a stir. But Perpetua's executioner was a novice who failed to kill her with the first blow, so that she shrieked with pain. His second blow found her throat.

That is the story of the martyrdom of St. Perpetua, St. Felicity, and their companions as told in the ancient document. The stories of the other martyrs listed at the beginning of this sketch must be briefer, because the known facts are meager.

Cecilia was a member of a noble family in Rome. She became a Christian through the teachings of her childhood nurse. She married a young Roman named Valerian, but, by mutual agreement, she kept the vow of virginity which God had inspired her to make. Because of Cecilia's example, Valerian came into the Church and was followed by his brother. The two brothers were arrested and put to death for their Christianity. Cecilia recovered their bodies and gave them a decent burial. This was considered a "treasonable" act, and she, too, was put to death on November 22, about the year 230.

Pope St. Paschal (817–824) built the Church of St. Cecilia in Rome. At that time, St. Cecilia appeared to him in a dream and told him where her body could be found. He had her remains transported to the church, and they are in the restored church today. Below the table part of the altar is a statue carved by Stefano Maderno, in 1594. It bears this inscription: "Behold the body of the most holy virgin

Cecilia, whom I myself saw lying incorrupt in her tomb. I have in this marble expressed for thee the same saint in the very same posture of body."

It is not known whether Cecilia was a musician, but we are told that there was always "a hymn of love for Jesus Christ, her true spouse, in her heart." She has been named the patron of musicians.

Barbara was a member of a noble family in Heliopolis, in northern Egypt. We are told that she was denounced by her own father when she became a Christian, was arrested and put to death in the year 235. She is invoked against final impenitence and sudden death. She has procured the last sacraments for her clients, even when miraculous intervention was required.

Both Catania and Palermo in Sicily claim the honor of being Agatha's birthplace. In the region around Mt. Etna she is invoked against eruptions of the volcano, and in other places she is invoked against lightning. It is believed that she was put to death in the persecution of Decius, 250–253.

Agnes is one of the best known of all saints even though the known facts about her are meager. When she was only thirteen years old she attracted the eye of Eutropius, son of a Roman governor. She refused to marry him because she had dedicated her virginity to God. Eutropius, therefore, denounced her as a Christian, and she was summoned before the governor. The governor tried soft words and flattery at first and then dire threats. When nothing would induce her to marry or to compromise her faith, she was put to death. St. Agnes is remembered for her purity, her love of Jesus, and her courage when threatened with violent death. She is usually represented holding a palm branch, symbol of her martyrdom, and with a lamb, representing purity, at her feet. The Church gives her a complete Mass on January 21 — an honor not accorded many saints.

Lucy met her martyrdom in Syracuse, on the island of Sicily, the same city in which she had been born. She is the patron of Syracuse. The Church has honored Lucy in a special way, for along with Agatha, Agnes, Cecilia, Perpetua, and Felicity, she is mentioned in the Canon of the Mass. She is also mentioned in the Litany of the Saints, along with Agatha, Agnes, and Cecilia.

Dorothy was a Christian girl whose home was in Caesarea in Asia Minor. She was condemned to death during the persecution under Diocletian. During the last hours of her life she brought back to Christ two young women who had apostatized. A religious community founded in Italy bears her name; its members are known as the Sisters of St. Dorothy, or Dorothean Sisters. The body of the saint is venerated in the Church of St. Dorothy in Rome.

OTHER SAINTS NAMED AGNES:

St. Agnes of Poitiers, d. 588. Abbess. Feast, May 13.
St. Agnes of Assisi, d. 1253. Sister of St. Clare. Feast, November 16.
St. Agnes of Montepulciano, d. 1317. Dominican nun. Feast, April 30.

OTHER SAINTS NAMED DOROTHY:

St. Dorothea of Venice, d. first century. Martyr. Feast, September 3.
St. Dorothy of Alexandria, d. about 320. Martyr. Feast, February 6.

OTHER SAINTS NAMED LUCY:

St. Lucilla, d. about 260. Martyr. Feast, October 31.
St. Lucy of Scotland, d. 1090. Daughter of a Scottish king. Feast, September 19.
St. Lucy the Chaste, d. 1420. Dominican Tertiary. Feast, December 3.

God's Soldier

ST. MARTIN OF TOURS, 316–397
Feast: November 11

EQUIVALENTS: Marius, Marten, Marti, Martil, Martino, Martinus, Marvin, Mertin. FEMININE: Martina, Martene

---

St. Martin of Tours is often called the "soldier saint" and has been named Patron of Soldiers. Yet he did not make a career of being a soldier; he served in the army only for a rather short period in his youth. We usually associate obedience with a soldier, however, and Martin's career was marked by perfect obedience to the will of God. Therefore he might well be called God's Soldier.

When Martin was born, the Christians of the Roman Empire were enjoying a period of peace. The tenth, and last, of the great persecutions had ended three years earlier. The Church was coming out of the catacombs. Now it faced a tremendous job of building and of converting the pagans. Martin was to play a big part in this work.

Martin was not born a Christian. He was born to a pagan family in what is now Hungary. When he was very young his father, a tribune in the Roman army, was transferred to Pavia in northern Italy. Here, Martin became interested in the Christian religion. When he was ten years old, he became a catechumen — which was the name given to a person taking instructions.

When Martin was fifteen he joined the Roman army at the command of his father. He became a cavalryman and was stationed in Gaul, which is now France.

One cold day in 335 when Martin was coming through the gates of Amiens with his fellow legionnaires, he saw a beggar sitting by the side of the road. The man was poorly clad and shaking with the cold as he held out his hands for alms. Nobody paid any attention to the miserable creature. Martin had no money with him so he drew out his sword, cut his cloak into two pieces, and gave one piece to the beggar.

That night in a dream Martin saw Jesus Christ wrapped in the half of the cloak he had given away. He heard our Lord say to the angels around Him: "The catechumen Martin covered me with his garment."

Martin's earliest biographer tells us that after this dream Martin "flew to be baptized."

Martin served his required five years in the army, and then he felt that God was calling him to another kind of life. He asked to be discharged from the army. His commanding officer was angry because he was expecting an attack by the Germans. He accused Martin of cowardice. Stung by the accusation, Martin asked to be assigned to the place of greatest danger in the forthcoming battle, and he promised to hold the position unarmed. Unexpectedly, German envoys came seeking peace, and there was no battle. Those who knew Martin attributed the bloodless victory to his prayers. He received his discharge.

For the next thirty years or so, Martin spent most of his time as a hermit. He founded a hermitage about four miles from Poitiers, in Gaul. This developed into a great monastery. He made a trip across the Alps to visit his parents in Hungary. He converted his mother but only enraged his father. On this trip he was captured by robbers and succeeded in converting one of them. When heretics gained control of Poitiers, he spent ten years in Italy. Then he returned to Poitiers. He became a priest so he could minister to his fellow hermits.

In those days it was the custom for the clergy and people of a diocese to select their own bishop. When the Bishop of Tours died, the priests and people said they wished Martin for their bishop. The idea frightened Martin. He had not wanted even to be a priest. He declined the invitation and said that he would continue to be a hermit.

The people of Tours were not to be denied. They asked him to make a sick call, a request he could hardly refuse. Then they went out to meet him and tell him that they demanded him for their bishop. Martin decided that this must be God's will, and so he submitted.

Martin refused the comfortable house which the people had provided their bishop and lived in a cell adjoining his church. Here he had so many visitors that he did not have enough time to pray. He withdrew to a cave in a secluded cliff about a half-hour's walk from the church. Other monks came to join him and occupied similar cliffs. This was the origin of the great monastery of Marmoutiers.

But Martin could no longer live a hermit's life. He was a bishop now, a bishop in a Church just emerging from three centuries of persecution. There was much work to be done, and Martin threw himself into it. This was not the lifework he would have chosen, but it was God's will, and he determined to do his best.

On the cliff near his cave Martin started a school. He taught some of the courses himself, and his monks taught others. Here, boys and young men were trained in their religion and in other subjects. Some of the students went on to become priests, priests that were so greatly needed by the newly liberated Church.

Martin himself traveled to every part of his diocese, strengthening the faith of those who were born Catholics, bringing the word of God to the pagans. Everywhere, he tore down pagan temples and erected Christian chapels. Then he left a priest or a monk to build the new parish.

At Amboise Martin found a tall stone tower which the pagans venerated as being sacred to their gods. Martin left a priest there and told him to have the tower destroyed. When Martin returned some time later, he found the tower still standing. The priest told him that no workman would lay his hands on it. Martin turned to God. He prayed all night long. Then a terrible storm arose and demolished the tower without destroying anything else. As usual, a Catholic chapel was built on the site.

Once as Martin was pulling down a temple a man attacked him, sword in hand. The bishop bared his breast to him. The pagan lost his balance, fell backward, and was so terrified he begged for forgiveness. Marvelous tales are told of miracles wrought through Martin, even of dead people being restored to life.

After twenty-six years as bishop, Martin was stricken while visiting Cannes. He felt that his death was approaching. He insisted upon lying on the floor as usual and he insisted that the floor be covered with ashes. His followers wept and begged him not to leave them. Martin prayed: "O Lord, if I can be of any further use to your people, I do not refuse the work. Thy will be done."

These words are the key to the saint's life. He never refused any work that God wished him to do. As a soldier he had learned obedience, and during his whole life he had been obedient to the will of God.

OTHER SAINTS OF THE SAME NAME:

St. Martin I, died 655. Pope who died in exile. Feast, November 12.
Bl. Martin de Porres, 1579–1630. Dominican lay brother, apostle of interracial understanding. Feast, November 3.

Model Wife and Mother

ST. MONICA, 332–387
Feast: May 4

EQUIVALENTS: Mona, Monique

Monica is known to us principally because she gave us the great saint, Augustine. She not only gave bodily life to the great theologian and doctor of the Church, but she was also the principal means by which God brought about his birth to spiritual life.

Monica prayed for many years for her erring son, seemingly with no results. One day she pleaded with a bishop to speak to her son. The bishop told her that Augustine was not ready to listen. She tormented the bishop until one day he told her to go in peace and to continue as she was doing. "The child of such prayers and tears can never be lost," he told her. And his prophecy came true.

Not much is known of Monica aside from what St. Augustine tells us in his *Confessions*. We know that she was born of Christian parents at Tagaste, a small town in northern Africa. Her mother died when she was small and she was brought up by a good and rather strict governess. She grew into a happy, sprightly little creature who was a great joy and comfort to her father.

One anecdote comes to us from her childhood. Her father often sent her to the basement to draw wine for his guests. The child yielded to temptation and sipped the wine before she brought it up the stairs. The sips became longer and soon she was drinking a cupful at a time. One day a maid saw her drinking the wine and called her a "wine bibber." Monica was overwhelmed by shame and never yielded to this temptation again.

41

Her father arranged for her to marry a wealthy pagan named Patricius, a man much older than she. Since she was a good Catholic, the thought of marrying a pagan must have been displeasing to her, but she obeyed the wishes of her father. Once married, she was a dutiful and devoted wife, a task that was not easy under the circumstances.

Patricius was a pleasant man to meet and affectionate in disposition. Since he was not a Christian, however, he did not consider himself bound by Christian rules of behavior, and he was dissolute in his habits. He also had a violent temper. Matters were made worse by the fact that Monica had to live with her mother-in-law, a cantankerous woman who did not take kindly to Monica's Christianity.

Monica endured the situation with patience and forbearance. When her husband flew into a rage, she never answered back. In time, the mother-in-law came to admire Monica's serenity and decided that her religion was the reason for it. The mother-in-law became a Catholic and was followed into the Church by several other members of the household. Some years later Patricius also became a Catholic. He died after leading a good Christian life for a year. Monica's sorrow at his death was mixed with joy for he had died at peace with God.

Patricius and Monica had three children of whom the eldest was Augustine. We know little about the other two children, Navigus and Perpetua, except that they led good Christian lives and caused their mother no worry. Monica instructed Augustine in the Christian religion and taught him how to pray. Once he became dangerously ill and asked to be baptized. His mother got everything ready for baptism, but he suddenly became better and it was put off. Infant baptism was not the general practice at that time. Many persons put off baptism so that they could avoid staining their baptismal innocence. This was a mistaken and dangerous custom which St. Augustine later condemned in his own writings. As a result of this custom, Augustine grew to adulthood without the saving grace of a Christian baptism. But Monica cannot be condemned for this; she was doing what she thought was right.

Augustine received his initial schooling at Tagaste and then went to Carthage which was a noted educational center. In Carthage he fell in with dissolute young men and soon became a leader among them. He was always a leader, whether in study, in fun, or in vice. Soon he took a mistress and became a Manichean. The Manichees taught that the body is wholly evil and that sins of the flesh cannot be avoided. This was a comforting idea to people like Augustine: if sins of the flesh cannot be avoided, why try to avoid them?

Monica was grief stricken when she learned of the life her son was leading. She wept and prayed and offered sacrifices. For a time, she forbade him to come into her house because he tried to teach heresy at her very table.

In 377 Monica had a dream in which an angel told her to wipe away her tears, adding: "Your son is with you."

After this, Monica again allowed Augustine to visit her. She told him about her dream.

"Good," said Augustine with a laugh, "that means you will come over with me to the Manichees."

"No," said the mother, "the angel did not say I would be with you. He said that you would be with me."

Augustine was greatly pleased that his mother had been so quick to see the flaw in his argument.

Augustine decided to go to Rome to become a teacher. Monica decided to go with him, so she could keep an eye on him and work for his conversion. But Augustine did not wish to have his mother with him. While they were waiting for the ship, which was delayed, Augustine suggested that she go somewhere to rest or to pray. Monica would not move.

When the ship finally came in, Augustine said: "I have changed my mind. I am not going to Rome after all. I'll just get on this ship long enough to say good-by to my friend and then I'll get off."

"In that case," said Monica, "I *will* go to the chapel and pray."

When Monica returned from the chapel, the ship had gone and Augustine had gone with it.

In Rome, Augustine found that teaching conditions were not very satisfactory and so he moved on to Milan where he became a teacher of rhetoric. Milan had a Bishop Ambrose (St. Ambrose) who was famous for his eloquence. Augustine went to hear Ambrose, thinking he might learn something new in the way of technique. He was impressed with Ambrose and went back again and again to hear him. Then he paid personal calls on Ambrose. Augustine was learning more than rhetoric.

Monica had grieved when Augustine fled from her. She went to Rome and found that he was no longer there. She finally tracked him down in Milan. She learned to her dismay that he was again living with a mistress, but she was happy to hear from his own lips that he was no longer a Manichee. He had lost his belief in that heresy but he had not become a Catholic. Perhaps he was reluctant to give up his way of life. He tells us himself that he prayed: "Give me chastity, but not yet awhile." Monica prayed a different kind of prayer and she prayed almost without ceasing.

At last, in August, 386, Augustine announced that he had completely accepted the Catholic faith. He was baptized by Ambrose the following Easter. This was the greatest moment of Monica's life. It was the moment she had lived and prayed and sacrificed to see. Now that the moment had arrived, it seemed that she had no more to live for. She died a few weeks later, at Ostia, while she and Augustine were waiting for a ship that would take them back to Africa. Augustine broke down completely and shed bitter tears for the mother who had shed so many tears for him. He wept not only because of his loss but because of his own unworthy conduct toward this saintly mother.

Successive generations have prayed to St. Monica as a special patroness of married women and as a model for all mothers.

Apostle of Ireland

ST. PATRICK, 387(?)–465(?)
Feast: March 17

EQUIVALENTS: Paton, Payton, Patrig, Patrizio, Peyton.   FEMININE:
Patricia, Patrice

"I am Patrick, a sinner, most unlearned, the least of all the faithful,
and utterly despised by many. My father was Calpornius, a deacon,
son of Potitus, a priest of the village of Bannavem Taburniae; he
had a country seat nearby, and there I was taken captive."

Thus St. Patrick begins his *Confession*, which he wrote toward the
end of his long life. This is one of two documents written by Patrick
that have come down to us. For authentic information about Patrick
we must turn to these two documents. The early biographies are
confusing, contradictory, and filled with legends. Unfortunately,
Patrick himself does not give us many details. He mentions no dates
and he mentions very few names. Where was the village of Bannavem
Taburniae? No one knows. Most authorities think it was somewhere
on the island of Britain, but some think it was in Gaul (France). It
must have been near the sea, because the raiders who captured him
came and went by ship.

"I was then about sixteen years of age," Patrick continues. "I did
not know the true God. I was taken into captivity to Ireland with
many thousands of people — and deservedly so, because we turned
away from God and did not keep His commandments, and did not
obey our priests. . . ."

That is all Patrick tells us about his boyhood, and that is just about
all we know. We see that his father was a deacon and his grandfather

45

a priest; there was no strict law of celibacy for priests in Britain in those days. The two men were probably government officials also. Christianity had become the official religion of the Roman Empire, and clergymen often held government posts.

A picture emerges of the young Patrick living very comfortably in the family home. Perhaps the family had two homes, since he mentions a "country seat." He seems to have been willful and somewhat spoiled. He did not take his religion seriously despite the fact that his father and grandfather were members of the clergy, and he probably did not take his schoolwork seriously either.

Then suddenly this spoiled, carefree boy was snatched from his home and carried off to Ireland, at the outermost limits of the then known world. Even the Romans had not conquered Ireland, and they had conquered most of the western world that was known at that time. Patrick was sold to a chieftain who gave him the job of tending sheep. This boy who had known a comfortable home, loving relatives, and jolly companions now spent lonely hours in the fields and forests of an alien land, and he often had only the ground for his bed.

In his solitude, Patrick turned to God. He tells us: "The love of God and his fear came to me more and more, and my faith was strengthened. And my spirit was moved so that in a single day I would say as many as a hundred prayers, and almost as many in the night, and this even when I was staying in the woods and on the mountain; and I used to get up for prayer before daylight, through snow, through frost, through rain, and I felt no harm, and there was no sloth in me — as I now see, because the spirit within me was then fervent."

After Patrick had been in Ireland six years a voice said to him in his sleep: "It is well that you fast. Soon you will go to your own country." Soon after, a voice said: "See, your ship is ready."

Patrick interpreted these words as a command to leave his master and go to the sea coast. This was a difficult, dangerous trip of 200 miles for the young refugee. At the coast he found a ship ready to sail, but the captain at first refused to take him on board. Then after Patrick said some prayers the captain changed his mind. After a journey of three days the ship reached a coast that had been desolated by raiders. There were no people, no crops, no livestock. After twenty-eight days Patrick and the crew members were at the point of starvation. The sailors asked Patrick to pray to his God for help. He did so. "And with the help of God, so it came to pass: suddenly a herd of pigs appeared on the road before our eyes and they killed many of them; and there they stopped for two nights and fully recovered their strength. . . . And from that day they had plenty of food."

Eventually, Patrick was able to return to his family, and he was joyously received by them. They had given him up as dead and here he was, safe and sound. He was a quiet serious man, far different from the carefree lad who had been snatched from them. They begged him to take his place in the community and never leave them again. But he had more dreams in which he heard the people of Ireland calling to him: "We beseech thee, holy youth, come and walk among us once more."

Until this time Patrick had apparently never thought of becoming a missionary, but he considered the dreams a direct call from God. From this time on he directed all his energies toward preparing for a return to Ireland.

Patrick had apparently neglected his education during the first sixteen years of his life, and then he had been a captive in Ireland for the next six years. When, as a young man in his middle or late twenties, he decided to acquire the education required of a missionary, he had a lot of "catching up" to do. In his own opinion, he never completely caught up.

No one today can say with accuracy where Patrick was educated and by whom he was ordained and later consecrated. It seems certain that much of his education was obtained in France, some of it at Auxerre, under Bishop St. Germanus. He also spent some time in monasteries learning the monastic way of life; he was later to found a number of monasteries in Ireland. Some highly respected biographers say that Patrick spent twenty years preparing for his mission to Ireland. Others say the time must have been much shorter. Patrick himself is silent on the subject.

Patrick seems to have made friends while attending school, but he also seems to have been the object of amused condescension. His fellow students had years of schooling behind them while he was just beginning his education. Some of his fellow students no doubt thought it presumptuous that this "rustic" should aspire to be a missionary.

Even at the end of his life Patrick had what almost amounted to an inferiority complex about his lack of education. In the very first sentence of his *Confession*, as we have seen, he calls himself "most unlearned." He also says: ". . . I long had in mind to write, but hesitated until now; I was afraid of exposing myself to the talk of men, because I have not studied like the others. . . ." A little farther on, he says: ". . . I blush and fear exceedingly to reveal my lack of education; for I am unable to tell my story to those versed in the art of concise writing. . . ."

Patrick was made a deacon and then ordained a priest. When it was planned to make him a bishop, considerable opposition arose. A friend of his student days to whom Patrick had confided a sin he had committed at the age of fifteen made the confidence public and said it disqualified Patrick for the office of bishop. This betrayal by a trusted friend pained the sensitive Patrick even in his old age. He mentions it in the *Confession* which he wrote at the age of seventy-five or seventy-six.

Despite the opposition, Patrick was eventually consecrated bishop. Later, when other bishops were consecrated in Ireland, Patrick was the chief bishop with the powers that an archbishop would have today.

If Patrick is exasperatingly silent about his education, he is even more so about his work in Ireland, a mission which lasted at least twenty-eight years and which may have lasted forty years.

"Now it would be tedious to give a detailed account of all my labors or even a part of them. . . . I do not wish to bore my readers."

During his six years of captivity, Patrick had learned something of the political organization of Ireland. There was a High King for all of Ireland, five lesser kings over the districts into which Ireland was divided, and a large number of petty kings or chieftains. Patrick knew that it was to these kings and chieftains he must appeal first. If he could convert them, the conversion of the people would follow. He also needed the help of the kings in establishing churches, schools, and monasteries.

Patrick was never able to bring about the conversion of the High King, but the King's wife and daughters came into the Church. He was able to convert most of the lesser kings, and the mass conversion of their people usually followed.

Patrick and his priests moved north, south, west, and east — into every part of the island. Patrick's sermons were forceful, beautiful, and simple — easily understood by the earnest, unlettered people to whom he spoke. Soon he had so many converts that he did not have enough priests for them. This meant that he had to train and ordain priests and later to consecrate bishops. He had to build churches, too, and he often worked on them with his own hands. A retinue followed wherever he went. It consisted of members of his household, artisans needed in building and decorating churches, students, and men who were studying to be priests or bishops. Where Patrick was, there was a village, a construction camp, a seminary, and a primary school. Patrick introduced the Latin language and the Latin alphabet into Ireland and taught them everywhere he went, thus ending the island's isolation from the rest of Europe.

As might be expected, Patrick encountered considerable opposition, especially from the druid priests who did not wish to lose their hold on the people. These priests appealed to the kings not to give up the religion of their fathers. They performed feats of magic to show how powerful they were. They made several attempts on Patrick's life. Once, a druid's shaft intended for Patrick pierced the heart of his charioteer. Despite the opposition, Patrick's work went on.

In addition to his hard work, Patrick prayed earnestly and performed severe penances. He taught by example as well as by word.

He lived simply, austerely. His personal needs were few, and he never accepted a gift from any of his grateful converts.

The results of Patrick's work are almost unbelievable. One biographer says that he consecrated 350 bishops during his apostolate in Ireland. The number of people baptized cannot even be estimated. Patrick speaks of the "so many thousands" whom he baptized and confirmed. His work can be summed up by saying that he found Ireland a pagan land and left it a Christian land.

When he was about seventy Patrick left the active work to others while he prayed, meditated, drew up a rule for the government of the Church in Ireland, and wrote his *Confession*. He was about seventy-eight when he died. Almost everyone agrees that he died on March 17, but the year of his death is not certain and neither is the place of his burial. Because his burial place is unknown, Patrick has no great monument to mark his grave. But none is needed. All Ireland is his monument.

OTHER SAINTS OF THE SAME NAME:

St. Patricia, date uncertain. Martyr. Feast, March 13.
St. Patrick, fifth century. Abbot of Nevers, France. Feast, August 24.

ST. MICHAEL THE ARCHANGEL

Feasts: May 8 and September 29

EQUIVALENTS: Miles, Myles, Micha, Michal, Michaud, Michel, Michele, Mickel, Miguel, Mikel, Misha, Mitchell. **FEMININE:** Michaela, Michelle, Michon

---

St. Michael, with St. Gabriel and St. Raphael, is one of the three archangels mentioned in Holy Scripture. Michael and the loyal angels thrust out of heaven Satan and his cohorts who refused to serve the Almighty because they aspired to be like God. In contrast, Michael recognized that however magnificent he might be, he owed all that he was to God, and, as a creature of God, he especially owed Him worship.

Michael was venerated by the Jews under the Old Law as the protector of the chosen people, and he performed many services for them. He has continued to be venerated under the New Law. St. Michael's was one of the three "voices" which directed St. Joan of Arc in the liberation of France. He is the patron of knights and warriors, which is interpreted to mean all defenders of law and order.

On May 8, 492, Michael appeared on Mount Gargano in southern Italy. The cave where he appeared became a celebrated shrine. Another apparition prompted the famous shrine Mont-Saint-Michel which stands high on a barren rock overlooking the sea in northern France.

ST. GEORGE, d. 303

Feast: April 23

EQUIVALENTS: Georg, Giorgio, Geort, Jorge, Joris, Jurgen. FEMININE:
Georganna, Georgetta, Georgette, Georgina, Georgine

In legend, George slew a fire-breathing dragon which until then
had annihilated all opposition. In actual fact, all we know about
George is that he suffered martyrdom at Lydia in Palestine shortly
before the time of the Emperor Constantine.

Despite the lack of information about him, George has always
been one of the most popular of saints. Kings and emperors in the
East delighted to honor him. Five churches were dedicated to him
in the one city of Constantinople. St. George is the national patron
of England and appears on the British flag, on the military banners,
and on official documents. In Canada, he shares with St. Anne the
title of chief patron. Christopher Columbus' native city of Genoa
claims him as patron.

ST. HELENA, d. about 329

Feast: August 18

EQUIVALENTS: Aileen, Celine, Eileen, Elaine, Elena, Eleanor, Ella,
Ellen, Eveline, Evelyn, Helen, Helene, Honora, Ilsa, Ilse, Lena,
Leonora, Leonore, Leona, Leora, Nell, Nora, Norah, Pamela

The date of Helena's birth is not certain, nor is the place. She married
a Roman soldier, Constantius Chlorus, and had one son, Constantine.
When Constantius rose to a high government post, he found it

useful politically to repudiate Helena and to take the stepdaughter of the emperor as his wife. Helena bore the repudiation with dignity and devoted herself to the worthy upbringing of her son.

Constantine became emperor after a victory which he attributed to the God of the Christians. He brought an end to three centuries of persecution. He brought his mother to Rome and showered her with honors. She was now sixty years old, and at some time in the intervening years she had become a Christian. She was the first Christian to receive such great acclaim in Rome. Helena took advantage of her position to build churches and to help the poor.

Helena made a pilgrimage to Palestine in 326. She directed excavations on the supposed sight of the Holy Sepulcher, where in the course of the following year the Holy Cross was found. The empress, then over seventy-five years of age, venerated the relics of the Saviour and built various monuments to commemorate their recovery.

POPE ST. LEO I, d. 461

Feast: April 11

EQUIVALENTS: Lee, Leon, Lionel. FEMININE: Leona, Leonilla, Leonita

---

Only three popes have been popularly acclaimed as "Great," and Leo was the first of the three. He became pope in 440, in the declining days of the Roman Empire of the West. The emperor no longer lived at Rome but at Ravenna, so Leo became the protector of the city. When Attila approached with his Huns, Leo went out to meet him and persuaded him to spare the city. Three years later when the Vandal king Genseric sacked the city Leo persuaded him to spare the people of Rome and to spare certain churches.

Worse than the physical dangers to the city of Rome were the spiritual dangers to the Church that came from the heretical teachings of Nestorius and Eutyches. Leo successfully combated these heresies.

This pontiff left 173 letters and 96 sermons, but they tell us little about himself.

ST. GENEVIEVE, 420–500
Feast: January 3

EQUIVALENTS: Geneva, Genever, Guinevere, Gwen, Jenifer, Winifred

---

Genevieve lived during the dying days of the Western Roman Empire and the establishing of the Kingdom of the Franks. From this kingdom evolved the modern country of France.

When barely seven, Genevieve promised St. Germain, Bishop of Auxerre, that she would embrace the religious life. When fifteen she made her vow of virginity before the Bishop of Paris. She lived in Paris in partial seclusion and became known for her great sanctity. In 451 when Attila and his Huns swept toward Paris she persuaded the people not to flee the city. She told them that instead they should pray and do penance. They did so, and Paris was spared.

Later, when the Franks were besieging Paris, Genevieve secured food for the people and kept them from starving. When the Franks eventually captured the city they treated Genevieve with great respect. King Clovis, who later became a Catholic, had great admiration for her.

Genevieve died and was buried in Paris. Many miracles took place at her tomb. She is venerated as the patron of Paris.

ST. EUGENIUS, d. 505

Feast: July 13

EQUIVALENTS: Eugene, Eugenio, Gene. FEMININE: Eugenia, Eugenie

---

After the Vandals conquered northern Africa their king Genseric, an Arian heretic, declared war against the Catholic Church. The policy was continued under his successor, Huneric. An arrangement was eventually made between Huneric and the emperor in Constantinople whereby the Catholics of Carthage were allowed to elect a bishop. Thus Eugenius, in 481, became the first bishop that Carthage had had in almost thirty years.

Eugenius worked marvels. Soon many of the Vandals were coming into the Catholic Church. This enraged Huneric, and he began the persecution once more. Eugenius was exiled to the desert country of Tripolis and was placed in charge of an inhuman Arian.

Huneric died and was succeeded by Gontamund who recalled Eugenius to Carthage. In 496 Gontamund died and was succeeded by Thrasimund who vacillated between support of the Church and persecution of it. In one of his fits of persecution he ordered Eugenius to be beheaded. Eugenius, with his head on the block, made his profession of faith. Then the king changed his mind and ordered Eugenius exiled to an Arian section of France. There Eugenius died on July 13, 505.

SAINTS OF THE
MIDDLE AGES

There is a long gap in this book between the death of St. Eugenius in 505 and the birth of St. Adelaide in 931 — more than four centuries. This is not the result of any planning. It just happens that the prominent saints of this period did not bear names that are popular today: Benedict, Boniface, Cyril, Methodius, Bruno, etc.

These centuries were a period of rebuilding for the Church and for European civilization. The Church was just beginning to make great progress under the protection of the Roman Empire of the West when that empire collapsed. The former empire was overrun by Germanic peoples who knew little about the Catholic faith and who had little respect for Roman law and order. The monks and missionaries faced a huge task. Their work was hard, unspectacular, unsung — but successful. By the year 1000 almost everyone in Western Europe was a Catholic.

When we emerge from this period with St. Adelaide we find ourselves in a Europe where almost everyone from king down to humblest peasant was united in the Catholic faith. There was also an attempt to unite Europe politically under the Holy Roman Empire. There was much that was good in Western Europe, but also much that was evil. There was still greed, and thirst for power, and intrigue. The Moslems threatened Christian Europe from without and heresies threatened it from within. Un-Christian living among the influential — including some bishops, cardinals, and popes — proved a scandal.

This was the age of powerful kings and nobles. We find saints among their ranks: Adelaide, Edward, Elizabeth, and Louis. We also find saints among those who battled kings for the rights of the Church, Hugh and Richard. Bridget of Sweden carried God's messages to powerful rulers.

Raymond of Penafort and Francis of Assisi both recognized the Moslems as creatures of God and worked for their conversion. Anthony of Padua combated heretics. Albert the Great demonstrated anew that great learning and great sanctity can go together. Louis typified the Crusaders — Christian warriors trying to rescue the Holy Land from the Moslems. Francis, Clare, Anthony, and Elizabeth imitated the poverty of Christ and thus offered an antidote to luxurious pagan living.

The nations of modern Europe were beginning to emerge during this period. God used Joan of Arc to save France, and He used Nicholas von Flüe to save Switzerland. Both saints showed that love of country can be beautiful, disinterested, and holy.

In the Middle Ages there were some martyrs, but they did not predominate. Men and women at this time were called upon to live and work for Christ rather than to die for Him.

ST. ADELAIDE, 931–999

Feast: December 16

EQUIVALENTS: Adele, Adelheid, Alice, Alicia, Alix

Before Adelaide was nineteen years old she had been a princess, a queen, a wife, a mother, and a widow. When she was nineteen she was made a prisoner and was kept in what was practically solitary confinement. These first nineteen years were to be typical of Adelaide's life. At times she had great prestige and power and at times she knew great adversity. From a material point of view her life was a series of ups and downs.

Adelaide's father was King Ralph II of Burgundy, in what is now France, so Adelaide was born a princess. Royalty always married royalty, so when Adelaide was sixteen years old she married King Lothaire of Lombardy, in northern Italy. The marriage was blessed with one child, a daughter named Emma.

Lothaire was king in name only. The real power was held by Berengarius, the Marquis of Ivrea, who longed to have the title as well as the power of the king. Lothaire died three years after his marriage, and there was a strong suspicion that he had been poisoned by Berengarius, who now succeeded him. Berengarius tried to arrange a marriage between his son and the widowed Adelaide, but she refused even to consider the idea. He then had her imprisoned in a castle on Lake Garda. That is why we find her a prisoner at the age of nineteen after having been a princess, a queen, a wife, a mother, and a widow.

Adelaide had many devoted friends. One of her friends dug a tunnel to the section of the castle where she was held, and by this means she escaped imprisonment. For a time she hid in the forest. Then the Duke of Conossa took her to the relative safety of his castle.

The nobles of Italy wished to be free from the unjust rule of Berengarius. They joined Pope Agapetus II in inviting Otto, the German king, to invade Italy and to re-establish justice. Otto went to Conossa where he met the popular ex-queen of the land he had been asked to liberate. The young widow and the considerably older Otto were married on Christmas Day, 951. The marriage made the conquest of Lombardy an easy matter, for the people loved Adelaide.

After gaining control of Lombardy, Otto generously offered to restore Berengarius to the throne provided he would promise to rule justly and hold all his lands as a fief, or dependency, from Otto. Berengarius readily promised, and just as readily broke the promise. Pope John XII begged Otto to take the situation in hand once more.

Otto sent his son to take control of Lombardy. His son died before the work was completed, so Otto took personal charge of the campaign. Berengarius was taken prisoner and sent to Germany, where he died.

Adelaide's marriage to Otto lasted twenty-one years, till the latter's death in 973. The couple had five children. Adelaide was as popular among the German people as she had been among the Italians of Lombardy.

Otto was really more of an emperor than a king, because he ruled a vast part of Europe and had kings who were subject to him. In 962, the Pope recognized both Otto's great power and his devotion to the Church by crowning him emperor of the Holy Roman Empire. This meant that Adelaide was now the empress. No other woman in the Western world held such a lofty position. She was thirty-one years old.

Whatever Adelaide had of riches or power she used in the services of God. Her generosity to the poor was so great that some people thought it excessive. She and her husband supported many missionaries both inside and outside their realm. They established monasteries which became great centers of Christian learning. They were especially zealous in trying to convert the Slavs in the northeastern section of the empire.

Adelaide became a widow for the second time when she was forty-two. Her nineteen year old son became Otto II. He ruled well as long as he kept his mother as a counselor. After the death of his first wife he married a Grecian princess named Theophana. The new queen induced Otto to banish his mother from the court. Instead of grieving over her misfortune Adelaide made use of her extra time by saying more prayers and performing more exercises which brought her closer to God. She offered many prayers and sacrifices for her erring son. After a time, Otto came to his mother and begged forgiveness. Adelaide returned to court and under her wise counsels Otto reformed many abuses in his government.

Otto II died after a reign of only nine years. His son, Otto III, was only three years old, and so Theophana became regent. Theophana had burned with resentment ever since Adelaide returned to court, and now she had her opportunity for revenge. She went out of her way to heap dishonor upon Adelaide and to make life uncomfortable for her. Adelaide suffered the ill-treatment and neglect with patience, and she prayed for Theophana.

Theophana died suddenly and Adelaide became regent for her grandson. This was more power than she had ever held in her life. When she had been queen and empress earlier her two husbands held the actual power. Now the power of the vast empire was in her hands. She did not welcome this. She was advancing in years, and the power was a burden. Honor and position meant nothing to her. Nevertheless, she applied herself with assiduous care to the affairs of government. She showed no ill-will toward those courtiers who, in Theophana's time, had treated her with contempt and caused her so much suffering.

Although obliged to give much time and attention to public affairs, Adelaide did not neglect her spiritual life. At regular intervals she retired to her oratory to seek light from heaven. Whenever she saw an injustice for which she could find no remedy, she did penance for the wrongdoer and begged God to set him right.

The last effort of Adelaide's life was an act of charity. When she was sixty-eight years old she undertook a difficult journey to Burgundy, the home of her childhood. Her purpose was to bring about a reconciliation between King Ralph, her nephew, and his rebellious subjects. She died on the way, at Salces in Alsace, on December 16, 999.

St. Adelaide was a worthy mother, a devoted wife, a charitable and beloved queen, a zealous empress, and a just and able regent.

OTHER SAINTS OF THE SAME NAME:

St. Adelaide (or Alice), died 1015. Daughter of the Count of Guelders. Abbess of two convents in Germany. Feast, February 5.

St. Adelaide (or Alix) of Schaerbeck, died 1250. Cistercian nun, remarkable for the intense sufferings she bore patiently in the spirit of penance. Feast, June 11.

ST. EDWARD THE CONFESSOR, 1003–1066

Feast: October 13

EQUIVALENTS: Edsel, Edson, Eduard, Edvard, Ned. FEMININE: Edwarda, Edwardina, Edwardine, Edwina

---

Edward was the son of Ethelred II, sometimes called Ethelred the Unready, last of the Anglo-Saxon kings of England. His mother was Emma, daughter of Richard, Duke of Normandy. Thus, Edward was half Anglo-Saxon and half Norman-French. By training and environment he was more Norman than Anglo-Saxon.

In 1013 the invading Danes made themselves masters of England and Ethelred fled across the English Channel with his family. Within a short time, he returned to England to try to regain the throne. Ten-year-old Edward remained at the court of his uncle, the Duke of Normandy. In 1016 Ethelred died, and Canute, the Dane, became undisputed King of England. A short time later Edward's mother, Emma, married Canute and once more became England's Queen.

Thus, Edward grew up in exile and virtually an orphan. Because he was the son of the last legitimate king, Canute did not want him in England. He was not allowed to visit his native country, even to see his own mother.

The long years of exile gave Edward an opportunity to secure a good education, to observe life at the Norman court, and to advance in his spiritual life. He prayed much, assisted at Mass frequently, and enjoyed conversations with religious minded people. Much of what he saw at the Norman court displeased him, but he admired the efficiency and wisdom with which the Normans ruled. Edward's principal recreations during these years were hawking and hunting.

King Canute died in 1035 and his two sons, one of whom was Edward's half brother, fought over the throne. The two sons both died and neither left an heir. In 1042, therefore, Edward was called to the throne of England. His saintly character was well known, and he was welcomed by the Danes as well as by the Anglo-Saxons. His coronation took place at Easter the following year. Edward was now forty years old. He was physically strong and robust, had a ruddy face, and his hair and beard were prematurely white. He was a quiet man of distinguished appearance, and he was even more distinguished for his humility and prudence.

Edward ruled wisely and well. He knew that all authority comes from God and must be exercised in accordance with the laws of God. He recognized the fact that government exists not for the glory of the ruler but for the good of the people. "Good King Edward's laws" were considered so just and fair that later generations of Englishmen clamored for them when they felt they were being oppressed.

Edward repealed the heavy tax that the people had been paying into the king's treasury, and said he would live on the income from his estates. From his private income he also supported numerous charities. His reign of twenty-three years was a peaceful one. He undertook no wars except to repel an invasion by the Welsh and to assist the legitimate King of Scotland against the usurper Macbeth.

Thirty of Edward's first forty years had been spent in Normandy, and he had come to admire the Norman way of doing things. He brought in a number of Normans and appointed them to high positions. He did this only because he wished to give the English the best possible government, not because he wished to impose foreign rule upon the country. Some people resented this move, however. Earl Godwin, a powerful noble, became a leader and spokesman of the "England for the English" movement, and he caused Edward much trouble. Despite this opposition, or perhaps because of it, Edward married the earl's daughter, Edith. Edward had early in life made a vow of celibacy. He made this known to Edith, and she accepted the situation. The two agreed to pattern their wedded life after that of the Blessed Virgin and St. Joseph.

Edward had made still another promise to God. While in Normandy he had made a vow to go on a pilgrimage to St. Peter's tomb in Rome if the family misfortunes came to an end. After he came to the throne he made this promise known to the council of nobles. The nobles begged him not to go. They said that the country needed him. The king appealed to the pope who agreed to cancel the vow provided that the money collected for the pilgrimage be given to the poor and provided that the king restore the Church of St. Peter in London. Edward not only fulfilled these conditions but he went farther; near the church he erected an abbey for the Benedictine monks. This was the beginning of the famous Westminster Abbey.

Westminster Abbey was to be dedicated on the Feast of the Holy Innocents, December 28, 1065. King Edward was ill on that day, so the queen represented him at the ceremonies. He died January 5, 1066. The next day he was buried in the newly dedicated Westminster Abbey.

The year in which Edward died, 1066, is a well-remembered date in history. It is the year that Duke William of Normandy defeated the Anglo-Saxons in the Battle of Hastings and made himself King of England. William said that Edward had named him as his successor, and this is probably true. Edward had no children and William was his cousin. Nevertheless, Edward would probably have deplored the way in which William became king. He had said that no kingdom in this world was worth any man's life.

Fifty-six years after his death, Edward's body was found to be incorrupt and the limbs still flexible. Six blind men who prayed at his tomb had their sight restored immediately. These miracles and many others, all duly authenticated, led to the canonization of Edward by Pope Alexander III, in 1161. The title of Confessor was conferred upon him in the Bull of Canonization. This title meant that he had given heroic testimony to the Christian faith. Two years later, on October 13, 1163, the saint's body was transferred to a shrine in the Abbey. The ceremonies were conducted by Thomas à Becket, who would himself become a famous saint, in the presence of King Henry II. St. Edward's tomb is still pointed out to everyone who visits Westminster Abbey. It is one of the few shrines that was not profaned during the Protestant Revolt. The day that St. Edward's remains were moved to their present resting place, October 13, is observed as his feast.

ANOTHER SAINT OF THE SAME NAME:

St. Edward the Martyr, died 878. Also a King of England. Feast, March 18.

ST. HUGH OF LINCOLN, 1140–1200
Feast: November 17

ST. RICHARD OF CHICHESTER, 1197–1253
Feast: April 3

EQUIVALENTS OF HUGH: **Hugo, Hugues, Hutchin**
EQUIVALENTS OF RICHARD: **Ricardo, Rich, Rykart**

Hugh of Lincoln was born in France and became a member of a religious community when he was fifteen. Richard of Chichester was born in England and was a layman until he was forty-four. But the similarities between the two men are more notable than their differences. They lived about the same time — Richard was three years old when Hugh died. Both were bishops of dioceses in England. Both faced the opposition of English kings. Both have been canonized.

Hugh was the youngest of three sons of a knight named William. The family home was the castle of Avalon in eastern France. When William's wife died, he joined the Canons Regular of St. Augustine and took with him the eight-year-old Hugh. "I needed no persuasion," said Hugh, "to renounce pleasure of which I knew nothing, and to follow him as a fellow soldier in the spiritual army."

Hugh attended classes with the boys who were being educated by the Canons. When he was fifteen he became a member of the community. His first task was to care for his father, now old and frail, and he was with his father when the latter died. When Hugh was nineteen he was made a deacon.

The young deacon was sent on a visit to the famous Carthusian monastery, the Grand Chartreuse. He was attracted to the austere Carthusian life and with some difficulty secured permission to become a Carthusian. He entered the Grande Chartreuse when he was twenty-three. He lived in his own little cottage and had his own little garden. In common with the other monks he fasted and abstained from flesh meat, wore a hair shirt, and practiced complete obedience. With his brethren he chanted the Office morning and evening and at midnight. Silence was observed at all times except from noon until vespers on Sundays and great feasts. Everything in his life tended to dispose his soul to recollection. This was the kind of life Hugh desired, and he was happy.

Hugh was ordained a priest and at thirty-three was made procurator of the monastery. He supervised the lay brothers, welcomed visitors, and distributed alms to the poor. He performed these active duties well, but he longed to return to the solitude of the monastery.

King Henry II of England, in penance for his part in the murder of Thomas à Becket, had vowed to establish two Carthusian monasteries in his country. The first, started at Witham in 1178, was not successful. The serfs, who made a living from the soil, did not wish to give up their land to the foreigners. The first prior broke down from the strain, and the second died. One of the king's advisers then prompted him to ask for Hugh to be the new prior, and the king did so.

Hugh did not wish to accept the post, saying that he could not govern his own soul and so could not govern others. The prior of the Grand Chartreuse also opposed the move because he did not wish to lose Hugh. The Bishop of Grenoble, who was himself a Carthusian, overruled both. He commanded Hugh to accept the post, saying: "The only Son of the Eternal Father, quitting . . . ineffable tranquillity . . . clothed himself in our human nature for the salvation of the world. You too must make the sacrifice of your quiet cell, and of the companionship of the brothers you love."

When Hugh left the Grande Chartreuse he took at least one lay brother with him, an old monk named Aynard. It was a long journey by mule and ship to a foreign land and an unfriendly people. At Witham he called together the serfs who would be forced to move and promised them either complete freedom or a transfer to other lands. He also told them that they would be paid for the huts they would have to give up. After this, the serfs felt more friendly toward the Carthusians.

King Henry agreed to all this but then failed to keep his promises. This conduct so angered Aynard that he told the king what he thought of him and said that the Carthusians should leave England. The king, on the verge of one of his violent explosions of temper, turned to Hugh and said: "Will you leave also?"

In a gentle voice, Hugh said: "No." He said he knew the king had many things on his mind but that he was confident the king would keep his pledged word.

The king was so happy with this that he at once repaid the serfs for their losses. Soon afterward he sent Hugh a costly present, a Bible which he had coaxed from another monastery, St. Swithin's. Hugh was embarrassed by this gift, and he returned it.

For six years Hugh governed the Witham Charterhouse. Then in 1186, Henry announced that he had appointed Hugh to be Bishop of Lincoln. Hugh had no intention of accepting the post, saying that the king had no right to make such an appointment. But the appointment was confirmed by the proper ecclesiastical authorities, and once more Hugh was forced to accept a post he did not wish. His last hope of returning to the Grande Chartreuse had gone. Only for a short period each year was he able to return to the solitude of the monastery he loved.

Lincoln had been without a bishop for many years, so Hugh faced the problem of restoring and rebuilding. His duties were not only ecclesiastical; they included the administration of the Church courts, which were very important at that time. He was also obliged to maintain a running fight with the civil power, headed by three temperamental kings. When Henry II died, he was succeeded first by his oldest son Richard the Lion-hearted, and then by his younger son John. Hugh came into conflict with all three. He resisted the royal demands on the Church for money, for armed men, and for clergy to serve as ambassadors at their own expense. Hugh seldom resorted to his authority, preferring to use tact and persuasion. But his authority was very effective when he used it, as King Richard found out. Richard published a decree confiscating all the possessions of the diocese of Lincoln. To his great consternation, he could not find anyone to carry out his decree; the bishop had announced that all who took Church property would be excommunicated.

The bishop showed deep sympathy for the sick. He regularly visited the leper hospital in his diocese and did not shrink from the touch of those suffering the dread disease. He was especially attentive to the burial of the dead at a time when corpses were often neglected. Once he risked being late for an appointment with King Richard, in order to conduct a funeral for an abandoned corpse that had been found in the street.

At a time when Jew-baiting was rampant in England, Hugh took a strong stand in defense of the Jews. He once threw himself unarmed into a crowd of anti-Semitic demonstrators and was almost killed. It is not surprising that the Jews wept in the streets of Lincoln when Hugh's funeral procession passed.

In 1200 Hugh went to France on an errand for King John. He visited his old home, the Castle of Avalon, and his beloved monastery, the Grande Chartreuse. He was ill when he returned to England. He died in November, 1200, wearing his Carthusian habit and lying on a cross of ashes on the floor. At his direction, Compline was being recited in his room. The chanters had reached the words *Nunc dimittis* (Now Thou dost dismiss Thy servant) when he breathed his last.

Twenty years after his death Hugh was canonized by Pope Honorius III.

Richard was the younger of two sons born to the middle class owner of the Manor of Wyche, about four miles from Worcester in England. The father died when Richard was young and the management of the estate fell to the older brother. He proved to be a poor manager and before long the estate was in deplorable condition. Richard was invited to take over, and he restored the family fortunes through his hard work and wise management. After that, he returned the management to his brother and spent a number of years studying at Oxford and on the continent. He became a professor of law at Oxford and then Chancellor of the University. St. Edmund, Archbishop of Canterbury, made Richard his legal adviser and then chancellor of the Archdiocese.

Edmund had stoutly defended the rights of the Church against the encroachments of King Henry III and had aroused the king's anger. In 1240 Edmund decided that he should leave the country. He took up residence in a Cistercian abbey in Burgundy, now a part of France. Richard accompanied the archbishop into exile. Within a year Edmund died.

After Edmund's death Richard retired to a Dominican monastery in Orleans, studied theology, and was ordained a priest. He returned to England, hoping to be assigned a parish somewhere in the archdiocese of Canterbury. But Archbishop Boniface, who had succeeded Edmund as archbishop of Canterbury, ordered him to resume his post as chancellor.

In 1244 the Bishop of Chichester died. The canons of the cathedral, in order to please Henry III who was bent on controlling the Church and its revenues, recommended a court favorite for the see. But Archbishop Boniface and his suffragan bishops named Richard de Wyche to the post. The enraged king then seized all the property that belonged to the diocese. Richard and the king laid their cases before Pope Innocent IV who was then in Lyons. The pope decided in favor of Richard and consecrated him. But the king kept the property, and Richard did not have even a home of his own. The Bishop of Chichester lived like a beggar, dependent on the hospitality of such priests as dared to befriend him. After two years the king, threatened with excommunication, returned the property, with the revenues greatly reduced, to the diocese.

In person Richard visited the sick, buried the dead, and relieved the needs of the poor. When his steward complained that his gifts were greater than his income he said: "Sell the gold and silver plate and my horse to make up the difference." He refused to curtail his charity even after suffering a great loss from a fire. He ordered that the alms should be more abundant than usual. "Perhaps God has sent this loss to punish us for our covetousness," he said.

Richard was a true shepherd to his people. People liked the eloquence of his sermons, and they were attracted by an example that was more eloquent than words. He received penitent sinners with great kindness but was stern with those whose bad example had led others astray.

The pope asked Richard to arouse the enthusiasm of the English people for another Crusade. He preached the Crusade first in his own diocese and then in the archdiocese of Canterbury. While engaged in this work he fell ill and was taken to a hospital in Dover. He foretold his own death, which took place April 3, 1253.

Richard's body was taken to Chichester and interred in his cathedral before the altar which he had consecrated to the memory of his friend, St. Edmund. Immediately, miracles began to take place at the tomb. Nine years after his death Richard was canonized by Pope Urban IV. Richard's tomb was a favorite place of pilgrimage until it was destroyed in the time of Henry VIII.

OTHER SAINTS NAMED HUGH:

St. Hugh of Cluny, 1024–1109. Adviser to popes and sovereigns. Feast, April 29.
St. Hugh of Grenoble, 1053–1131. Austere Bishop of Grenoble. Feast, April 1.
St. Hugh of Montaigu, died about 1136. Abbot and later Bishop of St. Germain in Auxerre. Feast, August 10.

OTHER SAINTS NAMED RICHARD:

St. Richard, died about 772. King of West Saxons. Feast, February 7.
St. Richard of Andria, twelfth century. Native of England who became Bishop of Andria in southern Italy. Feast, June 9.

ST. RAYMOND OF PENAFORT,
1175–1275
Feast: January 23

EQUIVALENTS: **Raimundo, Ramon, Raymund.** FEMININE: **Ramona**

When King James of Aragon went to visit the island of Majorca, newly liberated from the Mohammedans, he took along a Dominican friar, Raymond of Penafort. Raymond, then ninety years old, was the king's confessor and also his adviser on matters of state. Raymond was happy to go along because he was interested in the progress of the Church on the island.

When the party reached Majorca, according to an old story, Raymond found that the king had a mistress in his retinue. The priest protested, and the king promised to dismiss the creature. She was not dismissed, and Raymond protested again. When the king still delayed Raymond asked permission to leave the island and return to Barcelona. The king not only refused but said he would put to death any seaman who attempted to take Raymond off the island.

The aged friar said to his Dominican companion: "God will show us a way." He walked to the coast, spread his cloak on the water, tied one corner to a staff for a sail, made the sign of the cross, and then knelt on the cloak which bore him up. He invited his companion to follow, but the other friar's faith was not strong enough for the test. Raymond pushed off on this strange craft and sailed swiftly across 180 miles of Mediterranean Sea to Barcelona. There was great

73

astonishment in the port when Raymond came sailing in. He gathered up his cloak which was perfectly dry, threw it about his shoulder, and walked to his monastery.

It is not possible to guarantee the accuracy of this story, but it has been widely believed, and a chapel and tower were erected in Barcelona to mark the spot where Raymond landed. Whether or not the story is true, it illustrates several important points about Raymond of Penafort: (1) He lived in Spain at a time when the Christians and Mohammedans were struggling for mastery; (2) Raymond was the trusted adviser of the king of Aragon as well as other kings and princes; (3) He put his duty toward God above all else; (4) He had unlimited confidence in the providence of God; (5) His willingness to make the difficult trip at the age of ninety shows the zeal of a true missionary.

Raymond had other outstanding qualities that are not illustrated by this story: humility, learning, wisdom, and charity.

Raymond was born into a devout and noble family at the castle of Penafort near Barcelona in Aragon. Aragon was one of the Christian kingdoms on the Spanish peninsula. Raymond's parents sent him to the Cathedral school in Barcelona. He made such progress in his studies that he was invited to become a member of the faculty when he was twenty. He was devoted to the intellectual progress of his students but he was even more concerned that they acquire a love of virtue. The students with whom he worked were among the well-to-do, but he never forgot the poor of Barcelona. He sought out the most needy and helped them to the limit of his resources.

After he taught at Barcelona for fifteen years, Raymond decided to become a student once more. In 1210 he went to the University of Bologna, in Italy. After six years, he received a doctor's degree and then became a member of the faculty. The Senate of Bologna voted him a sum of money each year for his services. He accepted the money and gave it to the poor.

Berengarius, Bishop of Barcelona, visited Bologna in 1219. On all sides the bishop heard about the brilliant doctor, Raymond of Penafort. He also heard about the remarkable work of the newly founded Order of Preachers. The bishop sought out Raymond and persuaded him to return to Barcelona to become a Canon of the Cathedral. He also sought out the founder of the Order of Preachers, Dominic Guzman (St. Dominic), who happened to be in Bologna at that time. Dominic agreed to send a group of friars to Barcelona.

Raymond already had the education necessary for a priest, and so he was ordained by the bishop. Three years after his return to Aragon, he entered the Order of Preachers, or the Dominicans as they are commonly called today. He was forty-seven years old. The founder had died just eight months before.

When he received his habit Raymond asked his superior to impose a severe penance upon him so he might atone for the sins of his youth. To his surprise the provincial ordered him to write a collection of cases of conscience for the guidance of confessors and moralists. The assignment was a tribute to Raymond's success as a confessor, and was the first work of its kind.

Spain had been completely overrun by the Mohammedan Moors in the eighth century. By Raymond's time Aragon, Castile, and a few other kingdoms had freed themselves, but most of the Spanish peninsula was still in Moorish hands. During the centuries of Mohammedan rule many Christians had become lax in their faith. Raymond and his Dominican brethren preached missions throughout those parts of Spain that were held by Christian princes. The results were remarkable. People were awakened to a new religious fervor. Two centuries later, the Spanish people were to bring their faith to an immense section of the Western Hemisphere.

Raymond was not content with strengthening the faith of the baptized Catholics; he also wished to convert the Moors. He persuaded the kings of Castile and Aragon to establish colleges where priests could learn the Arabic languages and thus be able to preach to the Moors. He also induced his superiors to include the Hebrew and Arabic languages in several Dominican houses. Later, he himself was to work among the Moors.

It is commonly said that Raymond was associated with St. Peter Nolasco in the foundation of the Mercedarians, or the Order of Our

Lady of Mercy for the Ransoming of Captives. This, however, is a subject of controversy. The purpose of the order was to ransom Christians who had been captured by the Mohammedans, a work in which Raymond was very much interested.

Pope Gregory IX called Raymond to Rome in 1230 and took him for his confessor. The pope gave Raymond the task of codifying all the scattered decrees of popes and councils. This took three years of hard work. When it was completed the pope declared that this work alone was to be considered authoritative.

The pope appointed Raymond Bishop of Tarragona, in Aragon, but Raymond begged to be allowed to return to the seclusion of a Dominican monastery. The pope reluctantly consented. Raymond returned to his native country and a life largely given to contemplation, preaching, and hearing confessions. He was instrumental in making a great number of conversions. The king and the Holy See frequently called on him for special missions.

In 1238 Raymond was thunderstruck to learn that he had been elected Master General of the Dominicans. He wept and entreated but in the end accepted the office as an act of obedience.

While he was General, Raymond made the visitation of his order on foot. He instilled in his spiritual children a love of regularity, solitude, studiousness, and the work of the ministry. His most notable work was in clarifying the constitutions of the order and adding notes on doubtful passages.

At a general chapter of the order, held in Paris in 1239, Raymond secured the adoption of a rule which would permit a superior to resign if he had a good reason. The very next year Raymond took advantage of the rule and resigned. The reason he gave was his age: he was now sixty-five years old. The Dominicans soon found that they did not care for the new rule, and it was changed, but Raymond was already out of office by this time.

Raymond had said that he was too old to be General, but he had thirty-four years of work ahead of him. He threw himself with renewed energy into converting the Mohammedans. In 1236 when he was eighty-one years old, he wrote to his General that 10,000 former Mohammedans had been baptized. In order to help in the work of converting the Moors, Raymond requested his fellow Dominican, St. Thomas Aquinas, to write the now celebrated work, *Summa Contra Gentiles*.

When Raymond was ninety years old he accompanied King James to Majorca and it is then that the incident described at the beginning of this sketch is supposed to have taken place.

This energetic, zealous missionary priest lived to be almost a hundred years old. During his last illness he was visited by King Alphonsus of Castile who brought his family to receive a blessing. The penitent King James of Aragon also came, accompanied by his court. Raymond received the last sacraments and died on the morning of January 6, 1275. The kings of Aragon and Castile, together with their households, came to his funeral. Many miracles took place at his tomb. Raymond of Penafort was canonized by Pope Clement VIII in 1601.

ANOTHER SAINT OF THE SAME NAME:

St. **Raymond Nonnatus**, died 1240. Contemporary of Raymond of Penafort and a member of the Mercedarian Order which, it is said, Penafort helped found. Feast, August 31.

ST. FRANCIS OF ASSISI, 1182–1226
Feast: October 4

EQUIVALENTS: Fran, Frank, Franz, Franc, Francesco, Francois, Franchon, Franco, Franklin, Pancho.   FEMININE: Frances, Francesca, France, Francella, Francette, Francine, Franchon, Fran, Franny

---

In the picturesque town of Assisi, in the mountain country about a hundred miles northeast of Rome, a son was born in 1182 to a rich merchant, Pietro Bernardone. The boy was baptized John but was called Francisco, which means "Frenchman." This may have been due to the fact that Pietro carried on much trade with France and had a great admiration for that country. As a young man, Francis was something of a playboy and a favorite with the young people of Assisi. He dressed in expensive clothes and spent money lavishly. He was the leader in every sport. He wrote light gay songs for every occasion and was always in demand as a singer. When Francis was twenty, war broke out between Assisi and Perugia. Francis was captured and held prisoner for a year. While in prison he devoted himself to keeping up the spirits of his fellow prisoners. He was even kind to the one whose carelessness or treachery had been the cause of their capture and to whom the others would not speak.

After being released from prison, Francis was attacked by a severe illness followed by a long convalescence. Imprisonment, illness, and convalescence gave Francis time to think and gave God's grace an opportunity to work.

One night after his health had returned Francis had a dream in which he saw a magnificent palace equipped with all sorts of weapons,

78

each marked with a cross. A voice told him that all this belonged to him. Francis took this to mean that he should become a soldier. The next day he rode off to join the army. On the way, he stayed overnight at Spoleto and had another dream. "Return to Umbria," Francis was told. "Your soldiers will be your brethren, and your weapons will be mortification and penance."

Francis returned to Assisi. His companions noticed that he was more quiet and thoughtful than before. "You must be in love," they told him.

"Yes," Francis answered, "I am going to take a wife more beautiful and worthy than any you know."

He was speaking of Lady Poverty, but his companions did not know this at the time.

Francis did not know what God wanted him to do, but he understood that a person who wished to be a warrior for Christ must first win a victory over himself. He devoted much of his time to prayer and to mortification. While riding out of Assisi one day he saw in the road before him a leper so loathsome that he was struck with horror. Conquering his repugnance, he got off his horse, gave the man an alms, and embraced him. After that he spent much time in the hospitals serving the sick and helping them with gifts of money and clothes.

One day, Francis was praying in San Damiano Church, which was in a run-down condition. A voice from the Crucifix said: "Francis, go and repair my church which you see is falling to ruin." Francis took the command literally. He took bolts of costly cloth from his father's shop, loaded them on a horse, and sold them in a neighboring town. He also sold the horse. Then he took the money to the priest at St. Damiano's. The priest, knowing Pietro, refused to have anything to do with the money. Francis left it on a window sill. The father came in great indignation to St. Damiano's and took the money, but he could not find Francis.

Francis had retired to a cave outside Assisi to pray. After a month-long retreat he appeared in Assisi, thin and emaciated, his clothes in tatters. Some of the townspeople threw things at him and said he was mad. His father beat him unmercifully and locked him up. After a time his mother released him, and he returned to the cave. Soon after that, his father asked him to renounce his inheritance, and he did so gladly. He even returned to his father the clothes that he was wearing and put on a suit borrowed from a laborer.

On the property of the Benedictine monks near Assisi there was a little chapel dedicated to Our Lady Queen of the Angels and commonly called Portiuncula, which means "tiny." Francis was attracted to the chapel because it was secluded and because it was dedicated to our Lady. With the permission of the monks, he repaired it and built a hut nearby. Later, when other holy men came to join Francis, the Benedictines offered to give them the chapel and surrounding land. Francis would not accept the ownership; he and his followers were to own nothing. Every year he sent a basket of fish to the monks as a token rental payment. (The city of Los Angeles traces its name directly to Francis' chapel. The original name of the city is *El Pueblo de Nuestra Senora la Reina de los Angeles de Porciuncula*.)

When Francis' little band had grown to twelve, he drew up a rule for them and then made a pilgrimage to Rome to seek the approbation of Pope Innocent III. At first, the pope did not give his approval but changed his mind when in a dream he saw Francis propping up the Lateran Church which seemed ready to fall. He sent for Francis, gave oral approval to the new order, made Francis a deacon, and conferred tonsure on those of his followers who had not yet received it. All were commissioned to preach penance anywhere Francis should direct. With typical humility Francis called his order the Friars Minor.

After the order had secured the pope's approval, 127 persons joined almost immediately. The growth after that seemed miraculous. Houses sprang up all over southern Europe. In 1219, after ten years of existence, a General Chapter of Franciscans was held at the Portiuncula. It was attended by 5000 monks!

From all his Friars Francis exacted poverty, labor, mortification, and prayers for the good of their own souls, for the Church, and for the whole world. For their daily bread they worked at their trades and in the fields. When they could not find work they begged from door to door but they were not allowed to accept money. They were always at the service of anyone who needed them, especially the lepers.

Many people who could not join a religious congregation desired to become followers of Francis, so he founded the Third Order. (The Poor Clares constituted the Second Order; see St. Clare.) The members of the Third Order lived in the world, attended to their regular duties, and devoted themselves to the love of God and to the relief of the poor. Among prominent members of the Third Order we find King Louis IX of France, Elizabeth of Hungary, the poet Dante, and Christopher Columbus.

Francis and his Friars wished to become foreign missionaries, and they especially desired to convert the Mohammedans. When five of the Friars were martyred by the Moors in Morocco in 1220, Francis rejoiced. The story of his own visit to the Mohammedan Sultan at Damietta in Egypt reads like a fairy tale. The Sultan was defending his land against the Crusaders and he had put a price on the head of any Christian. He was so charmed by the humility and the simplicity of Francis, however, that the latter was allowed to preach for a week in his camp. At the end of the time, the Sultan sent him back to the Christian camp with a military escort.

Francis was truly a minstrel of Christ — God's troubadour. He sang the praises of God at every opportunity. He wrote a remarkable Te Deum called A Hymn in Praise of God. His devotion to Mary, to whom he dedicated every Saturday, is shown in a beautiful poem called A Salutation of Mary. In Praise of Lady Poverty expresses his love of Lady Poverty who attended our Lord from the crib to the tomb. His Canticle of the Sun calls on all creation to praise God.

During his last years Francis left the direction of his order to others and spent his time alone with God, mostly at Mount Alverno. He fasted and contemplated the Passion of Christ. He wept constantly and yet there was joy in his heart. He rejoiced so much in the Lord that his weak body was able to endure unbelievable hardships. To his spiritual sons Francis has left this legacy: missionary zeal, the spirit of joy, the spirit of poverty, and devotion to the Crucified Christ.

On September 15, 1224, while engaged in contemplation, Francis received the stigmata, the five wounds of Christ. These wounds increased his suffering, but also his gratitude to God and his joy.

Francis foretold the time of his own death which took place at the Portiuncula on October 4, 1226. The funeral procession extended the mile long distance from the Portiuncula to the church of San Giorgio in Assisi where the body was temporarily interred. Later, the body was moved to a great new basilica in Assisi.

Francis was canonized less than two years after his death. He has always been a favorite saint among Catholics and he is also immensely popular among non-Catholics. He well deserves the title "Everybody's Saint Francis."

OTHER SAINTS OF THE SAME NAME:

St. Francis Xavier, 1506–1552. Missionary to India and Japan. Feast, December 3.

St. Francis Borgia, 1510–1572. Third Superior General of the Society of Jesus. Feast, October 10.

St. Francis de Sales, 1566–1622. Bishop of Geneva, patron of writers. Feast, January 29.

ST. CLARE OF ASSISI, 1193–1253

Feast: August 12

EQUIVALENTS: Clara, Claire, Clarice, Clarita, Clarissa, Clareta, Clarinda, Clarine, Claribel, Claribelle, Chiara

---

Clare, daughter of a noble family of Assisi, was eighteen years old when she heard Francis of Assisi preach. This was in 1212, just two years after Francis' Friars Minor had been approved by the pope. Clare was impressed by the joyous spirit of Francis and by his love of holy poverty. She told Francis that she was sure God was calling her to the Franciscan way of life. But there was a problem, she said. Her family wished her to get married and would never consent to her becoming a religious.

Francis recognized in Clare a soul capable of doing great things for God. He thought the matter over carefully, and we may be sure that he consulted the bishop, because he never took any important action without the bishop's approval. Francis decided that the family had no right to interfere with Clare's religious vocation. But since the family would oppose Clare's action, with force if necessary, it would be better for the girl to make her profession secretly. Palm Sunday was the day that was decided upon.

On Palm Sunday, 1212, Clare accompanied her family to Mass as usual. Her mind was in a turmoil. This was *the* great day of her life. She was in love with Jesus Christ, and this was to be her "wedding" day. It was also the last time she would be at church with her family, although her family did not realize this. Clare could not help being a little sad at leaving her family, and she was no doubt apprehensive about what the family would do when they found out, but above all she had a feeling of great joy. Clare was so overcome by her conflicting emotions that she could not leave her place when it was time to walk up and receive the blessed palms.

The bishop, who knew of Clare's plans, saw that she was quite overcome. To the great surprise of everyone in the church, he came down to the place where she knelt and gave her a palm.

There seems to be something symbolic in this incident. The palm has been regarded as a symbol of victory, and Clare was winning a victory over the world (her family), the flesh, and the devil. The palm can also be regarded as her "bridal bouquet" for her "wedding" to Jesus Christ.

That evening Clare secretly left home, accompanied by a sympathetic relative, and went to the Portiuncula where Francis lived with his little community. Francis and his brethren met her with lighted candles in their hands. The little procession entered the chapel of Our Lady of the Angels, and Clare made her profession: "I want only Jesus Christ, and to live by the Gospel owning nothing, and in chastity." Francis cut off her luxuriant golden hair; she exchanged her rich clothing for a garment of sackcloth bound at the waist with a cord. Her head was covered with a white veil to signify chastity, over which was a black one signifying penance. When the simple ceremony was over, Francis and his brethren accompanied Clare to the Benedictine convent of St. Paul, where Clare was to receive her first religious training.

Very soon, Clare's father found her, and the family joined in demanding that she return home at once. Having failed to persuade her to leave the convent, they resorted to force. Then Clare removed her veil showing them her shorn head, a symbol of her dedication to Christ. Then the family left her, convinced of her sincerity and baffled by her determination.

Soon Francis transferred Clare to another Benedictine convent, St. Angelo, near Assisi. Here she was joined by her sister, Agnes. Again the family protested, but Agnes was just as determined as Clare. Although Agnes was only fifteen, Francis gave her the habit. Francis drew up for the two sisters a simple rule which placed great emphasis on poverty. They called themselves the Poor Ladies. By 1215 the Poor Ladies were recognized as a community, and they were established in a convent near the church of San Damiano. Francis appointed Clare the superior of the community. Other women, some of whom had been ladies of wealth and rank, joined the community. Clare's mother followed her two daughters to the convent after the death of her husband, and she took a vow to obey Clare as superior. In time her third daughter, Beatrice, joined the group as did several other relatives.

Within a few years other convents of Poor Ladies were founded in several places in Italy, France, and Germany. Within Clare's lifetime convents were established in many parts of Europe. Clare remained superior only of her own community in Assisi, but she corresponded with the other houses and offered them advice. Some of her letters are still in existence. They show that Clare was an able person possessed of common sense, sound judgment, and insight into character. Above all, they show her deep spirituality.

Today, the nuns are known as the Poor Clares in honor of their founder. They are also known as the Second Order of St. Francis.

Clare set the example of a life devoted to prayer, mortification, and such extreme poverty as had been, until then, unknown among women. Her ideal was the poverty practiced by Francis. The Poor Ladies would own nothing either individually or in common. They would depend entirely on alms. When Clare received her inheritance she gave it to the poor, reserving nothing for the community. Pope Gregory IX wished to dispense the vow of strict poverty, but Clare replied: "I need to be absolved from my sins, but I do not wish to be absolved from the obligation of following Jesus Christ." A later pope, Innocent IV, ruled that communities of the Poor Ladies could own property in common, but he said he did not wish to force the rule on any community unwilling to accept it. Clare was unwilling, and her community in Assisi continued in the tradition of St. Francis.

Clare not only loved poverty, but she practiced obedience with all the ardor of her soul. To Francis she said: "Send me where you choose. My will is no longer my own, since I have consecrated it to God."

Although Clare was the superior, she sought to be the last of all, the servant of all. She shared in all the work of the house. She was especially attentive to the sick. She was the first to rise in the morning, and she rang the bell for the others.

The motto of the convent was "In and for God." Clare's special devotions were to the Babe of Bethlehem, the Passion of Our Lord, and the Blessed Sacrament. Penances were performed in a spirit of joy, being offered for the love of Jesus Christ, and for the souls for whom He died. Francis had never ceased to inculcate the idea of joy among his sons, and the same spirit of joy was cultivated by Clare.

Francis died in 1226 at the Portiuncula. His death was a great loss to Clare. During his last illness Clare had hoped that he might recover sufficiently to pay the convent a last visit. When Francis realized that he would never again visit anyone he sent a message assuring Clare that she and the nuns would see him again and that they would be consoled. The promise was fulfilled when the funeral procession stopped at San Damiano and the body of Francis was taken to the chapel. The stigmata of Francis, so carefully concealed during his life, were shown after his death. Clare tried to remove one of the flesh-like "nails" from his hand; the "nail" moved, but it would not come out. With a piece of linen Clare dried the blood that oozed from the wounded hand, and she kept the stained cloth as a relic.

About 1240 Emperor Frederick II, who was at war with the pope, sent an army of Saracens to the vicinity of Assisi, which was papal territory. Some of these non-Christian soldiers pounded on the portal of the convent, which was outside the walls of Assisi. The nuns were terrified. Clare was ill, but, supported by two companions, she took into her hands the pyx containing the Blessed Sacrament, and went to the door of the convent. There she begged the Lord of Hosts to protect the nuns. From the pyx came the assurance heard by Clare and those about her: "I will always protect them." Immediately the soldiers scattered, leaving the nuns in peace.

Clare then prayed that Assisi be spared. Our Lord told her that although the city would suffer attack, it would not fall.

Some time later Assisi was again attacked by the emperor's troops. The city's defenses were very weak and it seemed destined to fall in a short time. After the Poor Ladies spent the day and night in prayer and penance, dissension broke out among the besieging troops and they were forced to withdraw from the area.

Clare governed her community for forty-two years. She was in poor health for many years. She died in the convent of San Damiano on August 11, 1253, while the Passion of Our Lord was being read at her request. Pope Innocent IV, who was in Perugia, came for the funeral. The funeral sermon was preached by the Cardinal of Ostia, who, as Pope Alexander IV, canonized Clare two years later. Today, Clare's body, still intact, reposes in a glass case in a church dedicated to her honor in Assisi. She is a treasured saint of Assisi, ranking in the general estimation second only to the great St. Francis.

On Christmas eve, the year before she died, Clare was too ill to attend midnight Mass, a mile and a half away. But through a miracle she was able to see the Mass in all its details. This incident was the basis for naming St. Clare the patroness of television in our own day.

OTHER SAINTS OF THE SAME NAME:

Bl. Clare of Rimini, d. 1344. A devotee of pleasure in early life, later a model of penance. Feast, February 10.

Bl. Clare Isabella Fornari, 1697–1744. A Poor Clare who had the stigmata. Feast, December 9.

ST. ANTHONY OF PADUA, 1195–1231

Feast: June 13

EQUIVALENTS: Anton, Antoine, Antonio, Antony. FEMININE:
Antonia, Antonina, Antonita, Antionetta, Antionette, Antonetta

---

The saint we know as Anthony of Padua was not baptized Anthony
and he was not a native of Padua or even of Italy. He was baptized
Ferdinand and was born near Lisbon, Portugal. His father was a
knight of King Alphonso II, and he held an important post in the
treasury department of the Portuguese government. Ferdinand was
sent to the Cathedral school where his uncle was a Canon. At fifteen,
he joined the Canons Regular of St. Augustine at Lisbon. Two years
later he was transferred to the Canons' monastery at Coimbra. Here,
he spent the next eight years and was ordained a priest.

One day some visitors came to Coimbra. Ferdinand was the guest
master, and it was his duty to show the visitors around. They changed
the course of his life. The guests were five members of the Friars
Minor (Franciscans), the community that had been recently established by Francis of Assisi. They were on their way to Morocco to
work among the Mohammedans. Not many weeks later, the remains
of the five friars were brought back to Portugal. They had become the
first Franciscan martyrs. Largely because of this incident, Ferdinand
became fired with the desire to become a Franciscan and a martyr.

It was unusual for a priest to obtain permission to leave an old,
well-established religious order so as to join a new religious group
of undetermined status. Ferdinand's prior was convinced of the
young priest's sincerity, however, and granted the necessary permis-

sion. Ferdinand was admitted to the small Franciscan monastery at Coimbra. It was named in honor of St. Anthony of the Desert, patriarch of monks. The new recruit received the habit and the name of Anthony in 1221, at the age of twenty-six.

After some time spent in prayer and penance, Anthony received permission to cross the Mediterranean and to preach to the Moors. Soon after he arrived in Africa he became very ill. He was put on a ship that was to take him back to Portugal. The ship was blown off its course and went to Sicily instead. Anthony learned that Francis had called a General Chapter of the Friars Minor to be held in Assisi. Despite the fact that he was very weak from his illness, Anthony went to Assisi. He was charmed by Francis whom he then met for the first time.

At the close of the chapter, most of the 5000 monks went back to their regular stations. Nobody seemed to know what to do with the weak, emaciated Anthony. At length he was assigned to the hermitage of Mount-Paola. Here he said Mass for the lay brothers and did various kinds of menial work. He offered all to God in a spirit of penance.

One day the monks were invited to an ordination ceremony at nearby Forli. An immense crowd gathered, but the priest who was to preach the sermon failed to appear. The Franciscan Provincial commanded Anthony to preach. Anthony protested that he was not prepared, but his protests fell on deaf ears. He preached the sermon, and his theme was obedience. Anthony held his hearers spellbound, and preaching was to be his work for the rest of his life.

The Church needed good preachers because of the heresies of the Catharists, the Waldenses, and the Albigensians. Many of the heretics remained in the Church, claiming to be Catholics and basing their claims on Scripture. Anthony's knowledge of Scripture, his burning zeal, his pleasing manner, and his excellent voice fitted him to be a champion of the Church, especially when the teaching of the Bible was in question. So effective was he in this kind of work that he became known as the "Hammer of the Heretics."

Father Anthony became exceedingly popular. When the crowds

that turned out to hear him became so great that the churches could not hold them, he set up a platform in front of the church. When that was not sufficient he took to the public square. When even that was not enough he preached in an open meadow. After he finished preaching he spent hours in the confessional. Countless sinners were converted to a better life, and numerous heretics were brought back to the Church by his prayer, penance, and preaching.

Anthony's exhausting program of preaching lasted for ten years. During that time he preached in every section of France and Italy. His last Lent was spent preaching in Padua. So many people poured into Padua to hear him that the town could neither feed nor house them. Worn out by his labors and poor health, Anthony retired, with two lay brothers, to a country place near Padua. The sick friar built a shelter for himself and started to write out some sermons which an archbishop wanted. The work was never completed. When Anthony knew the end was near, he asked his companions to take him back to the monastery. They departed with him in an open cart. He died before they reached Padua, on June 13, 1231.

Some well-authenticated miracles were attributed to Anthony during his lifetime. Many, many more occurred at his tomb. Forty-six of these were accepted in the process of his canonization, which took place the year after his death. Thirty-two years later, his remains were transferred to a Franciscan church in Padua. St. Anthony's flesh had disappeared except for his tongue, which remained as in life. This relic is preserved in the church at Padua.

On January 16, 1946, Pope Pius XII declared Anthony a Doctor of the Church. No one knows just how or when St. Anthony became known as the Finder of Lost Objects. But everyone who has called on him agrees that he is very good at it.

OTHER SAINTS OF THE SAME NAME:

St. Anthony of the Desert, died 356. A great ascetic. Feast, January 17.
St. Antonius of Florence, died 1446. Bishop of Florence. Feast, May 10.
St. Antonio Maria Claret, died 1870. Founder of the Missionary Sons of the Immaculate Heart of Mary and Archbishop of Santiago, Cuba. Feast, October 24.

ST. ALBERT THE GREAT, 1200–1280
Feast: November 15

EQUIVALENTS: Adelbert, Alberto, Albertino, Albertus. FEMININE: Alberta, Albertina, Albertine, Albrette

---

Albert of Bollstadt, known even in his own time as "the Great," is a medieval saint whose life has a modern appeal. We are living in the Age of Science, and Albert is the only canonized saint who can truly be called a scientist. He was many other things, too, but it is his work in science that makes him unique.

Albert was born in the castle of Nauingen on the Danube River, in what is now Germany. The date of his birth is not certain; it may have been as early as 1193 or as late as 1206. His father was Count of Bollstadt. Blue eyed, light-haired, sturdily built Albert had an inquiring mind. He was interested in everything on the family estate, the wild and domestic animals, the birds, the insects, the plants, the stones, and the minerals.

When Albert was about seventeen he was sent to the University of Padua. Here he met the future St. Dominic, founder of the Order of Preachers. Despite the opposition of his father, Albert joined the Order. He turned his back on wealth and on the life of a noble to serve God as a Dominican friar. After leaving Padua he taught philosophy and theology in several Dominican houses. In 1240 he was sent to the University of Paris where he took a master's and then a doctor's degree in theology. In 1248 Albert was sent to Cologne where he established a new university for the Order.

Albert was primarily a philosopher and a theologian, but he had a great interest in everything that God created. He read all the books he could find about the natural sciences, but he did not accept everything he read. He made his own observations and experiments. In his writings, he corrected many errors which had been handed down from generation to generation. For centuries, for example, people had believed that eagles wrap their eggs in fox skins and leave them in the sun to hatch. Albert was able to correct this by a personal observation of the habits of eagles. In such ways, he added to the sum total of human knowledge and prepared the way for modern science with its motto of: "Observe. Investigate. Experiment."

In the field of geography, Albert traced the chief mountain ranges of Europe, explained the influence of latitude on climate, gave a physical description of the earth, and told why he believed the earth to be spherical in shape. He also wrote treatises on biology, botany, physics, chemistry, astronomy, and mineralogy. In all, his writings comprise thirty-eight volumes, which include biblical and theological treatises and sermons.

This is not to say that Albert's scientific writings were always accurate. In some cases he did not have the opportunity of making a personal investigation and had to accept the faulty findings of others. At times he did not have all the knowledge he needed to make a proper evaluation of his findings. But he was far ahead of his time, and scientists who followed him owe him a great debt.

Albert's greatest scholarly contribution was in rewriting the works of Aristotle so as to make them acceptable to Christian critics and in applying Aristotle's methods and principles to the study of theology. This was the foundation of scholastic philosophy, which was brought to perfection by Albert's pupil, St. Thomas Aquinas.

Thomas was a young Dominican studying at the University of Paris when Albert first met him in 1244. Later, Thomas studied under Albert at Cologne. One of the glories of Albert is the part he played in the intellectual and spiritual development of Thomas. When Thomas died in 1274, Albert was so grieved that he said: "The light of the Church has gone out." Thomas was the most famous in a large number of noted scholars who were students of Albert the Great.

Albert loved learning, but he was not permitted to live solely the life of a scholar. In 1254 he was elected Provincial Superior of the Dominicans in Germany. In 1256 his superiors sent him to Rome to represent the Dominicans in a famous controversy concerning mendicant orders. In 1260, much against his wishes, he was named Bishop of Ratisbon, now Regensburg, in Germany. He traveled all over his diocese on foot, in all kinds of weather, and earned the nickname of "the bishop with the boots." After two years of this, he was permitted to resign and return to his teaching at Cologne. The next year he was called from his work to preach a Crusade to the German people. His superiors appointed him prior first in Wurzburg, then in Strassburg, and afterward in Cologne. He took an active and important part in the Council of Lyons in 1274.

In 1277, word reached Albert that the Bishop of Paris was urging the condemnation of several theses that had been advanced by the recently deceased Thomas Aquinas. Albert was old and in poor health, but he walked all the way from Cologne to Paris to defend the theses. He presented his case well but could not avert the local condemnation of certain points. He then walked back to Cologne. (The theses are not condemned today anywhere.)

This was his last long walk. In 1279 he seemed to have suffered a stroke, for his physical powers and most of his mental powers left him. However, he retained the power to pray until his death, which took place in his cell on November 15, 1280.

The scientist Albert well realized the limitations of the material world and the limitations of man's power to observe and reason. He knew that faith alone gives certainty and that faith is a gift from God. Natural science, he knew, can deal only with what is clear in outline; it has nothing to do with the world of love and pity. For this reason, Albert had a very great devotion to our Lady, who is a veritable fountain of love and pity.

In 1931, Pope Pius XI proclaimed Albert a Saint and Doctor of the Church. In 1941, Pope Pius XII named him patron of those who devote themselves to the natural sciences.

OTHER SAINTS OF THE SAME NAME:

St. Albert of Montecorvino, died 1127. Bishop of Montecorvino. Feast,
April 5.

St. Albert of Louvain, 1166–1192. Bishop of Rheims, martyr. Feast,
November 21.

Bl. Albert of Bergamo, died 1279. Peasant farmer remarkable for patience
and charity. Feast, May 11.

ST. ELIZABETH OF HUNGARY, 1207–1231

Feast: November 19

EQUIVALENTS: Bella, Bess, Beth, Babette, Betta, Betsy, Betty, Belle, Elisa, Elna, Elsa, Helsa, Isabeau, Isabel, Isabella, Lee, Libby, Lisa, Lizette

---

When Princess Elizabeth of Hungary was still an infant, her marriage was arranged for her. This was a common custom in those days, especially in royal families. It was decided that she should marry Ludwig, eldest son and heir of Herman, Landgrave of Thuringia. Herman was a powerful German prince and it was thought that the marriage would be an advantage both to Hungary and to Thuringia.

Elizabeth was four years old when she was sent off to live at the Thuringian court. This was also a fairly common custom. In all probability Elizabeth would some day be the wife of the landgrave, so it was thought that she should become accustomed to the people, the language, and the customs of her adopted land. When Elizabeth left Hungary she was accompanied by a large military escort, a retinue of servants, and thirteen wagon loads of gifts. The gifts included a large sum of money, gold and silver plate, quantities of jewelry, richly embroidered linen, beautiful furs, and costly clothes and bed hangings. Queen Gertrude, Elizabeth's mother, sent word to Herman that he should not despise "these small offerings" and that she would send more later if God spared her life. Elizabeth, herself, as she rode forth to meet her adopted family, was dressed in silken clothes interwoven with gold and silver.

Elizabeth's new home was the great Wartburg castle perched on a high and rugged hill overlooking the leafy Thuringian forest. Ludwig and Elizabeth were reared as brother and sister and always called each other Brother and Sister even after they were married. There was another boy, Heinrich, about a year younger than Ludwig; a third boy, Conrad; and a girl, Alice, about Elizabeth's age.

Life in the castle was not completely happy for Elizabeth. Ludwig's mother, Sophia, did not entirely approve of her. At times, in fact, Sophia seemed to have a positive dislike for Elizabeth. The girl was of a very religious nature, and Sophia, who was considered a model of correctness and propriety, may have thought that she went too far with her religious practices. Sophia was probably annoyed by Elizabeth's openhanded generosity to the poor. Perhaps Sophia also resented the fact that Ludwig was so fond of Elizabeth and that she had such a great influence upon him. The second son, Heinrich, entirely agreed with his mother.

Elizabeth was nine and Ludwig was fourteen when Herman died. In the meantime, Queen Gertrude had died without sending the additional dowry. Sophia and many courtiers and officials — especially Heinrich — descended upon Ludwig and demanded that he send Elizabeth back to her father before it was too late. The boy answered: "Nothing on earth will ever persuade me to part from my dear sister Elizabeth." This silenced the opposition, but it only increased the resentment toward Elizabeth.

When Ludwig was seventeen, he became landgrave in his father's place. Three years later, he and Elizabeth were married. Six happy years followed during which a son and two daughters were born to the young couple. Ludwig put no obstacle in the way of his wife's charity, her mortified life, or her long prayers. "My lady," said one of her ladies-in-waiting, "would get up at night to pray, and my lord would implore her to spare herself and come back to rest, all the while holding her hand in his. . . ." Elizabeth told her maids to wake her gently when Ludwig was asleep so she could get up and pray without disturbing him. But sometimes he only pretended to be sleeping.

Every day Elizabeth went to the door of the castle and gave out food to the poor and needy. Some could not climb the steep grade to the castle, so Elizabeth carried food down to them. One day, according to a beautiful legend, Elizabeth was coming down the path carrying a basket under her mantle, when she met her husband coming up. He asked her what she had. She drew aside the cloak, and he saw only red and white roses. This was in February. Ludwig took one of the roses for himself and told Elizabeth to proceed with a work that was pleasing to God. Even if he had found loaves of bread in the basket, Ludwig would not have objected.

Elizabeth founded two hospitals, one for lepers. She often fed the patients herself, made their beds, and attended all their wants. Later, she founded poor houses and other institutions.

Elizabeth lived at the same time as St. Francis of Assisi, and she was similar to him in her love of poverty, her generosity to the poor, and her charity toward the sick, especially the lepers. When some Franciscans came to Thuringia and Elizabeth learned that Francis had started a Third Order for lay people, she was quick to join. Later, she came into possession of Francis' original habit — a torn and patched garment. This was one of her greatest treasures. She asked Pope Honorius III to appoint a priest for her spiritual director. He named Conrad of Marburg, although Conrad was not a Franciscan. Elizabeth vowed him obedience with one reservation: her duty to her husband was not to be affected. She took the vow with her husband's permission.

Conrad was strict with Elizabeth — too strict, most biographers agree. But she had taken a vow of obedience to him and she never questioned his orders.

In feudal times the nobles often took a large share of the crops that had been raised by the peasants, leaving the peasants too little for their own needs. Conrad told Elizabeth that he would not permit her to eat any food which she suspected might have been obtained unjustly. Ludwig himself was an honest and upright man, but he could not always be sure what his officials had done. Often Elizabeth could eat only one dish at a table laden with food. At other times she could take only bread and water. Such actions reflected upon the nobles and their officials and did not increase Elizabeth's popularity at the court.

There was a severe famine in 1224–1226. Elizabeth did not believe that the people of the castle had a right to an abundance of food while the peasants were starving. She redoubled her generosity during this period. Relatives and "friends" protested that she was ruining Ludwig and his family, but Ludwig gave Elizabeth his complete approval.

In 1228 Ludwig and his knights joined the Sixth Crusade under the Emperor Frederick II. Elizabeth, who was expecting her third child, begged Ludwig not to go "if it is not contrary to God's will." But he looked on the Crusade as the fulfillment of a vow. She accompanied him to the Thuringian border, convinced in her heart that she would never see him again.

At Otranto, in southern Italy, Ludwig was stricken with fever and died. He was fully prepared and resigned. His followers put his body in a temporary grave before going on to the Holy Land. Elizabeth heard the word of her husband's death soon after the birth of her second daughter. "The world is dead to me, and all that was joyous in the world," she exclaimed.

Elizabeth's son, Herman, was then only five or six and not old enough to rule in his own right. Ludwig's brother Heinrich, who had never liked Elizabeth, became regent. All the pent-up resentments of the years were now released. Elizabeth was forced to leave the castle in the middle of winter with her three children, including the baby in her arms. Her rich former friends were afraid to give her shelter, and the only place she could find to stay was a shed behind an inn, a shed that was used to store tools and keep pigs. The wealthy princess had become the poorest of paupers. She would not have cared for her own sake, but she was worried about the health of her children.

Eventually Elizabeth was furnished shelter and protection by her aunt, the Abbess of Kitsingen on the Main, and by her uncle, the Bishop of Bamberg. The bishop had what he thought was an excellent plan for Elizabeth: she was still in her early twenties and very attractive; she should marry Emperor Frederick II. It seems certain that he must have secured the emperor's approval of the idea before he broached it to Elizabeth. Elizabeth, however, had made a promise that she would never marry again.

When the Crusaders came back from the Holy Land they disinterred the remains of Ludwig and brought them back to Thuringia. Nothing was left but his bones. The bones had turned white, and the people took this as a sign of his purity. This, and the fact that he had died on a Crusade, plus the fact that he had always backed Elizabeth in her charities, caused the people to refer to him, without official warrant, as St. Ludwig. A wave of popular enthusiasm for Ludwig swept the land as his bones were buried in Bamberg Cathedral.

Kneeling beside Ludwig's coffin, Elizabeth prayed: "You know, O Lord, that I loved him more than anything in this world, because he loved You, and because he was my husband. You know that all my life I would have been glad to live with him in want and wretchedness, to beg my bread from door to door, only to have the happiness of being with him. But it has pleased You to take him to Yourself; I am perfectly resigned to Your holy will. And if by saying one Our Father, I could recall him to life against Your will I would not say it. Only this I ask: grant unto him eternal rest and to me grace to serve You faithfully until my last breath."

Heinrich saw that Elizabeth had a powerful friend in the bishop of Bamberg, and possibly in the emperor. He also saw that the people loved her. He decided it would be best to make peace with her. He assigned her the castle of Marburg and the town of Eisenach. She desired nothing for herself, but now she had funds for helping the lepers and the poor. She had already become a member of the Third Order; she wore the habit from then on.

Her spiritual director, Conrad, seems to have been away when Elizabeth was undergoing her persecution at the hands of Heinrich. He was back when the reconciliation took place. In some respects Conrad acted as a prudent restraint upon Elizabeth. He would not

allow her to beg from door to door, or to give away all her possessions, or to risk infection from the lepers. In other respects he was
very harsh. He deprived her of the company of the two women who
had been her dearest companions for years and substituted two
"harsh females" who reported to him on all her actions. He punished
her with slaps in the face and blows of a "long thick rod."

Elizabeth was afraid of Conrad, and she said: "If I am so afraid of
a mortal man, how awe-inspiring must be the Lord and Judge of
the world!"

One day Conrad, who was ailing, said to Elizabeth: "Who will be
your spiritual director after I die?"

Her reply startled him: "I shall die before you; in fact my death
is quite near."

She died twelve days later, at the age of twenty-four.

Even before Elizabeth was buried, miracles occurred in profusion.
Among those miraculously cured were the lame, the blind, idiots,
paralytics, and lepers. Elizabeth was a medieval St. Thérèse of
Lisieux; she let fall a "shower of roses." She was canonized four
years after her death.

When the saint's body was removed from its temporary resting
place it was found to be incorrupt. Bishops, nobles, and royalty
took part in the ceremonies. Among them was Heinrich who had
persecuted Elizabeth while she was still alive. Emperor Frederick II
placed a crown on Elizabeth's beautiful head, saying: "Since in life
I was denied the privilege of crowning you as my empress, I now
crown you a saint."

Although more than seven centuries have passed since her death
Elizabeth is still intensely popular in the area around Wartburg and
throughout Western Germany. She is referred to as "dear St.
Elizabeth."

OTHER SAINTS OF THE SAME NAME:

St. Elizabeth, Queen of Portugal, 1271–1336. A great grandniece of Elizabeth of Hungary. Feast, July 8.

St. Elizabeth Bichier des Ages, 1773–1838. Cofoundress of the Daughters
of the Cross. Feast, August 26.

ST. LOUIS, 1214–1270
Feast: August 25

EQUIVALENTS: Lewis, Luigi, Luis, Ludwig, Clovis

"I love you as much as a mother can love her child," Queen Blanche of France said to her son Louis, "but I would rather see you dead at my feet than have you commit one mortal sin."

Under his mother's capable direction young Louis was receiving an excellent education in art, languages, literature, music, philosophy, history, military science, and the art of governing. But, above all, the Queen impressed upon Louis the importance of living not for time alone but for eternity. He learned the lesson well, for he is a canonized saint. With his disposition and his mother's training he no doubt would have been a saint under any circumstances. It so happened that he was born into the royal family and became King of France when he was twelve years old.

Louis was born on April 25, 1214, in Poissy, France. His parents were King Louis VIII and Blanche of Castille. As a boy, Louis was inclined to be irritable and quick tempered, faults for which he was chastised by the tutors and masters who were under his mother's direction. As an adult he was able to keep his temper under strict control. He was tall and slim with bright blue eyes and light hair. Usually he had a serious expression but his face was so transformed when he smiled that his charm was almost irresistible.

Because Louis was so young when his father died, his mother acted as regent. Later, when he assumed complete power, he constantly turned to his mother as a counselor. Rebellious nobles were causing much trouble when Louis became king. Queen Blanche saw that it was necessary to put down these revolts if the country was to have peace. The young king accompanied his armies to the battlefields. Louis was a good soldier and an excellent military strategist, but it pained him to have to fight other Christians. During his long reign he found it necessary to go to battle on several occasions, but often he was able to avoid war by means of diplomacy, at which he was very adept. His reputation for diplomacy and honesty was so great that he was called upon several times to arbitrate disputes between other powers.

In spite of the exacting duties of his office Louis found time to assist at Mass and to recite the Divine Office every day. He confessed frequently. When a courtier suggested that he devoted too much time to prayer, he replied: "If I spent the same time in hunting or at a tournament or in playing games, no one would think it too much." He wore a hair shirt, scourged himself frequently, seldom partook of delicacies, and drank little wine. He was very generous to the poor, and he built homes for the disabled and the afflicted. He started a number of religious institutions. If there was one sin he hated more than any other it was that of swearing. "I had willingly," he once remarked, "be branded by a hot iron if by that covenant all evil swearing might be banished from my realm."

For all his penances, which were performed strictly in secret, King Louis could be the genial host. When there was an important feast or when new knights were created he celebrated the occasion with magnificence. Once when a friar started to talk about a grave religious topic at the table Louis changed the subject, saying: "All things have their time."

An incident of a different kind occurred when the future St. Thomas Aquinas and his prior came to dinner. Thomas Aquinas did not want to go to the dinner. He was writing a theological essay, and he did not care for social affairs anyway. His prior told him that no one refused an invitation from a king, so he went. While the king and the others chatted during dinner, Thomas' mind was still with his essay. Suddenly, in the middle of the meal, Thomas banged his fist on the table and cried: "Here is a decisive point against the Manichean heresy!" The horrified prior pulled Thomas' sleeve and reminded him where he was. The king, far from being offended, called for a secretary to take down the "decisive point" lest it be lost.

When he was nineteen Louis married Margaret of Provence. The marriage was blessed with five sons and six daughters. The descendants of Louis and Margaret were to be kings of France for another five hundred years, till the monarchy ended. Louis was strict with his children. He expected prompt obedience when he spoke and the respect due him as king and father. He hoped that some of his children would enter the religious life, but such was not God's will. His daughter Isabella became Queen of Navarre. Once he sent her two exquisite ivory boxes as a present. In one of the boxes was a chain about a yard long with sharp metal points attached. He suggested that she scourge herself occasionally in expiation of her own sins and those of her father. The other box contained a broad horsehair belt which he recommended she wear next to her skin for penance.

The king kept the honor of God, the welfare of the Church, and the good of his subjects ever before his mind. He saw that justice was done his subjects regardless of rank. All his subjects, high and low, were welcome to come to him and present their pleas. He had a keen sense of justice. In his instructions to Philip, his heir, he wrote: "If you come to be king, do that which befits a king . . . deviate in nothing from justice, whatever befalls you. If a poor man goes to law with one that is rich, support the poor man rather than the rich man until you know the truth, and when the truth is known, do that which is just." He also wrote: "Take heed lest your love for any person should cause you to deviate from justice."

Although Louis was opposed to war with other Christians he felt strongly that the Christians of Europe should try to rescue the Holy Land from the Moslems. In 1099 the Crusaders had set up Jerusalem as a Christian kingdom, and four other small Christian states were established in the vicinity. After many years Jerusalem had again fallen to the Moslems and the other Christian states were in grave danger. In 1248 Louis left France at the head of a large army whose purpose was to recapture Jerusalem. The odds against the expedition were too great. Louis was able to visit such Holy Places as were still in Christian hands, but he accomplished nothing in a military way. In 1252, his mother, who ruled France as regent during his absence, urged him to return to France. He stayed on eighteen months longer, hoping against hope that he might be able to liberate Jerusalem. In 1254 he received word that his mother had died. He was stricken with grief but he thanked God for having spared her to him, and to France, for so long. For the rest of his life he had a Mass offered daily in his presence for the repose of her soul.

After Louis returned from the Holy Land his penances and mortifications became even more severe than they had been before. Domestic affairs occupied his attention for the next sixteen years, but he never gave up his hope of making another Crusade.

In 1270, at the call of the pope, he and three of his sons, together with a large number of nobles and knights, engaged in the Eighth, and last, Crusade. They landed in Tunis in North Africa. Here many members of the expedition, including Louis himself, were stricken by the plague. Louis prayed earnestly and with resignation during his sufferings. He received the last sacraments and entrusted France to his eldest son, Philip, whom he had trained for the job. Shortly before the end he asked to be laid on a bed of ashes on the ground. With his hands folded peacefully upon his breast, he died, August 25, 1270. He was canonized twenty-five years later.

OTHER SAINTS OF THE SAME NAME:

St. Louis of Cordova, died 855. Killed by Moors. Feast, April 30.

St. Louis of Anjou, died 1297. Bishop of Toulouse. Nephew of St. Elizabeth of Hungary and great-nephew of St. Louis of France. Feast, August 19.

St. Louis Bertrand, died 1589, Dominican apostle of northern South America. Feast, October 9,

ST. BRIDGET OF SWEDEN, 1303–1373
Feast: October 8

EQUIVALENTS: **Bride, Brigid, Brigetta, Birgitta**

On the Sunday before Ash Wednesday in 1314, ten-year-old Bridget was deeply affected by a sermon on the Passion of Christ. The next night Bridget was looking at a crucifix on the wall of her room. Everything else seemed to vanish and the crucifix became vivid and luminous.

"Look upon me, my daughter," said our Lord from the cross.

"Oh Lord," said Bridget, "who has done this to you?"

"Those who despise me, and spurn my love for them."

The incident made an impression on Bridget's mind that was never erased. From that time, the sufferings of the Crucified Christ became the center of her spiritual life. From that time, too, Bridget was to have mystical experiences. She has been called God's Ambassador because she carried God's message to nobles, to bishops, to kings, and to popes.

Bridget of Sweden was born in the castle of Finsta near Uppsala. She was the youngest of the seven children of Sir Birger Persson, governor of the province of Upland, and of his wife, the Lady Ingeborg. When Bridget was 11, her mother died, and the girl went to live with her Aunt Karin. Here she was educated as a daughter of the nobility. When she was about 14, her father arranged a marriage with a young nobleman, Ulf Gudmarsson. Bridget wept because she did not wish to marry, but she carried out her father's wishes.

The wedding took place in the chapel of the castle of Ulfasa, Bridget's future home.

The couple grew in their love and appreciation of each other. Eight children were born to them, two of whom died in childhood. In 1328 Bridget's father died. Her share of the estate made her one of the richest women in Sweden.

About 1335 Bridget was summoned to the court of the young King of Sweden, Magnus II. She was to be a teacher to the young queen and a sort of motherly adviser to the king. She became the godmother of their first child, Erik. For a time the king and queen seemed to appreciate Bridget's efforts and to be guided by her counsel. But the queen was weak and luxury-loving, while the king was unsteady. He sometimes went to extremes in pious practices, and then to extremes in vice. Some of Bridget's children were also causing her anguish. Her eldest and youngest daughters made unfortunate marriages. The behavior of her flighty son Karl also caused her many tears. During this time, Bridget was receiving the personal revelations which were to make her famous. The revelations ranged from seemingly minor matters to the Hundred Years' War between France and England. Most people in the court of the king did not take these revelations seriously. "What was the Lady Bridget dreaming about last night?" became a standard joke.

In 1339 Bridget and Ulf made a pilgrimage to the shrine of St. Olaf in Norway. She returned to Sweden and made a further vain attempt to curb the excesses of the king and queen. Then, in 1341, she and Ulf made a pilgrimage to the tomb of St. James in Spain. During the return trip Ulf became dangerously ill at Arras in Flanders and received the last sacraments. Bridget prayed; Ulf must not die now! While she watched at Ulf's bedside, St. Dionysius appeared and told her that Ulf would have to return to Sweden, that she would eventually go to Rome and Jerusalem, and, he added: "By thee God will be made known to the world."

When Ulf was able to travel they returned to Sweden. Ulf died at the guest house of the Cistercian monastery at Alvastra. Bridget and their eight-year-old son Bengt were with him when he died.

After the death of her husband Bridget divided her possessions among her children and the poor. Karl, as the eldest son, became master of the family castle at Ulfasa, and the other children were well provided for. Bridget was free from earthly ties and able to follow Christ in poverty.

One day while Bridget prayed alone in the chapel at Ulfasa, her soul was uplifted and she was given a moving prayer in honor of the wounds of Christ. This prayer was repeated daily for the remainder of her life. It was in keeping with her never-ceasing devotion to the sacred passion.

From 1345 to 1349 Bridget lived in the guest house of the Cistercian monastery. It was against the rules for her to be there, but certain supernatural events convinced the monks that her presence was the will of God. In Alvastra, as elsewhere, Bridget visited the sick and often discovered the spiritual malady that underlay the physical one. She was the instrument of numerous cures of body and soul.

While in Alvastra Bridget received so many visions and revelations that she became alarmed, fearing that she was deluded by the devil or by her own imagination. But a thrice repeated vision told her to submit her revelations to a certain priest of experience and learning, and he said they were of God. The subprior of the monastery, Petrus Olai, became her unwilling secretary for the revelations. She needed one, because often in ecstasy she was not able to write; she could only dictate.

God gave Bridget practically the whole of Christendom as her field of labor. He was to use her as an instrument in the spiritual rebirth of Sweden, in ending the devastating war between France and England, and in securing the return of the pope to his see city of Rome. (Because of chaotic conditions in Rome, the popes had deserted the city and had been residing at Avignon, in France.)

At God's command, Bridget went to the royal court and reprimanded King Magnus for his sins. She also included the queen, the nobles, and the bishops in her denunciation. For a time Magnus mended his ways. He liberally endowed a monastery which Bridget wished to found at Vadstena. After some years this monastery was established and it housed 60 nuns and 25 monks who lived in completely separate buildings. This was the beginning of the Order of the Holy Savior, or Bridgettines as they are commonly called. There are no men in the order today. In the fifteenth century the monastery at Vadstena was Sweden's greatest center of learning.

As a result of a vision Bridget wrote a very strong letter to Pope Clement VI telling him to return to Rome, to try to bring about peace between France and England, and to tell the ruler of the latter country that disaster awaited unless he abandoned the war. The pope declined to leave Avignon, but he sent an emissary to the King of England. The king refused to abandon the war. Later, England was struck by the Black Death and suffered a great defeat when Joan of Arc led the French forces to victory.

In 1349 our Lord told Bridget to go to Rome and stay there until she should see both the pope and the emperor in the Eternal City. The conditions which she found in Rome were unbelievable. Control of the city was divided between the Orsini and Colonna families who were bitter enemies. Churches were neglected; some were in ruins. Streets were dirty. Crime and disorder were everywhere.

For 20 years Bridget remained in Rome. She became known throughout the city for her charity. She cared for the poor and the sick; she rescued the abandoned. Despite her charity, she was once threatened by an angry mob because of her supposed preference for the Orsini family. On one occasion she ran out of funds and had to beg. Through all this she never slackened her efforts to bring the pope to the city.

The young emperor came to Rome as a pilgrim in 1355. Twelve years later Pope Urban V paid a visit to the city. She submitted to him the rule for her proposed monastery, and he approved it. The Emperor Charles IV visited Rome a second time in 1368. Bridget had seen the pope and the emperor in Rome. Was her mission then fulfilled?

Pope Urban V wished to return to Avignon. Bridget told him

that death awaited him if he went there. He went nevertheless and died three months later. Bridget hoped that the new pope would come to Rome. She sent four letters, each stronger than the preceding, but the pope did not come.

At length Bridget received her long-awaited message: "Go to Jerusalem." Her sons Karl and Birger and her daughter Catherine decided to accompany her. At Naples, they awaited a ship. A number of miraculous cures were attributed to Bridget's intercession while she was in Naples. Karl was attracted to beautiful, thrice married Giavonna, Queen of Naples. Although neither was free to marry, they determined upon a sinful union. Bridget stormed heaven for the soul of her son. He became seriously ill. He died after two weeks of suffering during which he repented and received the last sacraments. Later Bridget was told that Karl had been saved.

Bridget had been warned that her visit to the Holy Land must be limited to Jerusalem, Bethlehem, and Jordan. There would be time for no more. Reverently she walked the ways that our Lord had trod. Here she received revelations concerning the birth of our Lord, His crucifixion and death.

Bridget was back in Rome in 1373 and spent her last Lent there. She died July 23, 1373, apparently in an ecstasy during the celebration of Mass. Two of her children, Birger and Catherine, were with her. Wearing the gray habit of a Franciscan tertiary, she was buried on July 27 in the convent of the Poor Clares, San Lorenzo in Panisperna. Before the year ended her bones were disinterred to be taken back to Sweden. At every stop the remains were received with reverence by clergy and people who regarded Bridget as a saint.

Bridget did not see the pope permanently established in Rome. She did not see the end of the Hundred Years' War. She did not see the completion of her monastery at Vadstena. Was her life's work, then, a failure? She received assurance from heaven that it was not. All these things would come about after her death.

The revelations of St. Bridget cover a period of many years. The Church has declared that Catholics may read them with spiritual profit, but they have merely the status of private revelations. Bridget was canonized 18 years after her death, not because of the revelations but because she had led a holy life and had practiced charity in a high degree.

ANOTHER SAINT OF THE SAME NAME:

St. Brigid of Kildare, died 525. One of the patrons of Ireland where she founded several convents. Feast, February 1.

ST. JOAN OF ARC, 1412–1431
Feast: May 30

EQUIVALENTS: Jane, Janet, Janice, Jean, Jeanne, Jeanette, Jenny, Jessica, Jenifer, Joanna, Johanna, Juana, Juanita, Nita

---

"Joan! Joan!"

Thirteen-year-old Joan, who had been standing quietly in the garden, was startled. She had not thought that anyone was around and the voice was different from any she had ever heard. It seemed to be coming from the direction of the church nearby, and she turned in that direction. She beheld a male figure unearthly in its radiance.

"Joan!" the figure repeated.

Terrified, she sank to the earth. Yet she realized that there was no reason for terror. The voice was of such beauty and gentleness that she knew it must belong to an angel. The vision told Joan that she should be a good girl, go often to church, and be prepared for God's commands.

This happened on a hot summer day in the year 1425. The place was the village of Domremy on the Meuse River in the Lorraine section of France. Domremy was in the small part of France which had not yet been conquered by the English and their allies, the Burgundians.

The vision returned to Joan at frequent intervals. By the third time she knew him to be the Archangel Michael, although he never identified himself. He spoke to her of "the great pity" that was over France and told her that she would be the means by which

God would save her country. This would seem to be an astounding piece of information. A peasant girl — only thirteen years old when the visions began — would be the savior of France! But Joan appears to have accepted the news as calmly as did Mary at the Annunciation. If this was God's will, who was she to question it? At this point she apparently took a vow that she would remain a virgin until her mission had been accomplished.

St. Michael told Joan that St. Catherine of Alexandria and St. Margaret of Antioch would come to her and guide and comfort her. They did so at intervals for the remaining seven years of her life.

The mission that was about to be entrusted to Joan was hopeless by human standards. The King of England had long claimed to be the rightful King of France, and the English had invaded France in 1337 to begin the Hundred Years' War. They had gradually extended their control over most of the country. To make matters worse, Burgundy had allied itself with England. The man who was the heir to the throne of France, the Dauphin, had never been crowned. Perhaps the authorities had felt that coronation ceremonies would seem a hollow mockery under the circumstances.

At first, Joan did not tell her family or anyone else about her "Voices" as she called them, but she continued to receive their instructions. Under their guidance she prepared for her mission by prayer and meditation. When at last, in 1428, Joan knew it was time to go to war, she told her father her intentions. He was violently opposed and even threatened her life if she tried such a thing. Joan was reluctant to disobey her father but she knew that she could not disobey a command from heaven. Her mission, given her by the Voices, was twofold: she was (1) to relieve the seige of Orleans, the last French stronghold, and (2) to see that the Dauphin was crowned King of France.

She went first to Robert de Baudricourt, local commander of the French forces. At the first meeting Baudricourt dismissed her and said that her father should give her a good hiding. When she told him the results of a battle which had just taken place some distance away, and when the news of the battle was later confirmed, Baudricourt was shaken in his skepticism. He not only gave her permission to pass his post but he also assigned her four soldiers as her escort.

The Dauphin was at Chinon at the time and much of the route lay in enemy territory. Joan disguised herself as a boy and set off with the four soldiers. It was necessary to travel under cover of darkness and to hide during the day. Bertrand de Poulengy, one of Joan's soldier companions during these days, marveled at Joan's goodness and likened her to a saint. The little party reached Chinon on March 6, 1429, after a journey of eleven days. The Dauphin deliberately kept Joan waiting for two more days, during which time she was carefully watched.

The Dauphin did not believe in Joan's mission. He consented to receive her only to amuse his friends at court. Before she was admitted to the court the Dauphin exchanged places and garments with a courtier. Joan was brought in and presented to the courtier. She was not deceived. She glanced casually at the supposed Dauphin and then walked directly to the real one whom she had never seen. The members of the court were spellbound. Joan convinced the Dauphin of the reality of her mission when she took him aside and told him something known only to himself. She then asked the Dauphin for soldiers whom she could lead in relieving the siege of Orleans. But many advisers of the Dauphin had misgivings about Joan. She was examined for three weeks before a board of theologians. The council could find nothing to disapprove in Joan and advised the Dauphin to make use of her services.

Less than a month later, after assisting at Mass and receiving Holy Communion, Joan left Chinon with her army. She was clad in armor and rode a horse. She had no sword but carried a banner containing the words "Jesus" and "Mary," together with a representation of two angels presenting the Fleur-de-lis (emblem of France) to God the Father.

Joan and her army entered Orleans without opposition on the night of April 29. The soldiers in the city were inspired by her presence and fought as they had never fought before. By May 8 the English forts which surrounded Orleans had been captured. The unbelievable had happened; the siege had been raised! In one of the battles Joan was struck by an arrow just below her collarbone. She pulled the arrow out and, although suffering great pain, continued to lead her soldiers on to victory.

The French scored more victories, and it was possible on July 17, 1429, to have the Dauphin crowned in the cathedral at Rheims. When the coronation ceremony was over, Joan knelt before the newly crowned Charles VII and said: "My mission has been fulfilled." She had done everything her Voices had told her to do and she expected to return home. But neither the king nor the army was willing to give up her services.

After Joan had completed the mission given to her, she met little more military success. In an unsuccessful attack on Paris, Joan was wounded and had to be carried from the field. Her Voices gave her no positive instructions but they told her that she would be captured before St. John's Day, which is June 24. She was captured by the Burgundians on May 23, 1430, at the gates of Compiegne. For six months she was a prisoner of the Duke of Burgundy. Not once during that time did King Charles VII try to ransom her. But the English desired Joan if the French did not. On November 1, she was sold to them for a very large sum.

The English could not put Joan to death for defeating them on the battlefield, but they could condemn her for witchcraft and heresy. The English believed, rightly, that Joan could not have won such amazing victories without supernatural help, but to them, this could only mean that the help had come from the devil. If we put ourselves in the place of the English, we can follow their reasoning. They thought their cause was just, and so any supernatural help for the enemy must necessarily be from the devil.

On February 21, 1431, Joan appeared for the first time before a tribunal presided over by Peter Cauchon, Bishop of Beauvais. The trial was held in the city of Rouen. The judges were churchmen of various ranks, all selected by Cauchon. The bishop was under strong pressure from the English to bring forth a verdict of guilty, and he himself was strongly convinced that Joan was in league with the devil. Therefore, it was impossible for Joan to have a fair trial.

During the protracted and grueling trial, the court came back repeatedly to one point: was Joan ready to admit that her visions and her voices were the work of the devil? She was not. She was told that she was defying the Church when she failed to "co-operate" with the bishop and his court. She replied that she owed allegiance in matters of faith to the Catholic Church, but this court was not the Church. Once she begged: "Let all that I have said and done be sent to Rome, to our Holy Father, the Pope." Once, when she was ill and exhausted, she said to the judges: "I leave it all to our Lord."

The result of the trial was that Joan was condemned as a witch and a heretic. She was handed over to the secular government for her punishment, burning at the stake.

During the twelve months of Joan's imprisonment and trial, she had not been permitted to receive the sacraments. Then, after she had been condemned as a heretic, she was allowed to receive the sacraments of penance and Holy Communion! On the day of her execution she received these sacraments with the utmost fervor and gratitude. Then, accompanied by soldiers, she was taken to the market place of Rouen to be burned. This was Wednesday, May 31, 1431. Joan was not yet twenty years old.

At the stake Joan asked the bystanders to forgive her any harm she may have done them and she forgave all who had injured her. She prayed aloud, making acts of faith and love, invoking the Blessed Trinity and the Blessed Virgin Mary. As the faggots were lighted she kept her eyes resolutely on a cross held up by a Dominican friar. The flames enveloped her and the last word she was heard to utter was "Jesus."

There was a scream from someone in the crowd, and many present shared in the sentiment: "We are lost. We have burned a saint!"

Twenty-five years after her death, Joan's mother and brothers, seconded by the king of France, appealed to the pope for a new trial. The original trial was reviewed, and Joan was pronounced innocent. Joan of Arc was beatified in 1909 and canonized in 1920. She is not listed as a martyr because she did not die for her faith. She is revered as a girl who practiced heroic virtue.

OTHER SAINTS OF THE SAME NAME:

St. Jeanne de Valois, 1464–1505. Daughter of King Louis XI of France, foundress of the Franciscan Order of the Annunciation at Bourges. Feast, February 4.

St. Jane de Chantal, 1572–1641. Widow, foundress (under the direction of St. Francis de Sales) of the Visitation nuns. Feast, August 21.

ST. NICHOLAS VON FLÜE, 1417–1487
Feast: March 22

EQUIVALENTS: Claus, Colin, Klas, Klaus, Niel, Niles

All saints are similar in their great love of God, but they differ widely in the missions which God entrusted to them. St. Nicholas von Flüe had a mission that was unique: he was the Savior of Switzerland. Without Nicholas, it seems certain that there would be no Switzerland today, at least no Switzerland as we know it.

Nicholas was born March 21, 1417, near beautiful Lake Lucerne in Unterwalden. Unterwalden was one of three forest cantons that had formed a league for mutual defense. The other two were Uri and Schweiz. The league soon grew into the Swiss Confederation.

Nicholas' parents were Henry and Emma von Flüe. Henry was a well-to-do peasant in a canton where all the people were peasants. He was influential and respected. Both Nicholas' parents were devout in the practice of their religion.

Young Nicholas, like most boys of his time, did not learn to read or write. But he learned to love God, and he learned to think, and he learned to take a great interest in the government of his canton. These forest cantons were direct democracies. Every male citizen took part in the assembly which decided important matters and which chose the officials for the coming year. From the age of fourteen Nicholas attended the assembly and voted. He soon acquired a reputation for integrity and shrewd intelligence.

Despite his love of peace, Nicholas fought in two wars. Both were against Austria, which was a constant threat to Swiss liberty. He distinguished himself on the field and rose to be captain. Often it was his influence that spared churches, convents, women, children, and prisoners. Once he saved a monastery in which the Austrians had barricaded themselves. On this occasion, Nicholas prayed before a crucifix and then begged the Swiss not to storm the monastery. "If we wait three days, the Austrians will evacuate their position," he promised. The Swiss waited, and the prophecy was fulfilled.

Between the wars and after the wars, Nicholas worked on the family farm. When he was thirty years old he married Dorothy Wiss, the sixteen-year-old daughter of a neighboring farmer. The couple lived in a house not far from his father's. During the next twenty years, ten children were born to them, five boys and five girls.

During these years, too, Nicholas was elected to a succession of political offices. He could have been made landamann, highest office in the canton, but he would not accept the post.

Nicholas was a cheerful, hard-working man, friendly to all. He must have taken part in the games and dances or he would not have been as popular as he was.

But there was another side of his character. From early youth he practiced severe mortifications and spent long hours in prayer. As a boy, he fasted every Friday; later he increased this to four days a week. On these days he ate nothing but a piece of bread or a few dried pears. His wife and children knew that he often rose while they were asleep and prayed before a crucifix in the living room. Sometimes he would keep a vigil in the woods, or by the river, or in the village church. With little food and little rest he was able to perform his arduous duties as farmer, soldier, and public official.

The last public office held by Nicholas was that of judge. A case came before the court involving a poor man who had borrowed money from a wealthy neighbor and had pledged his garden as security. By hard labor and sacrifice the poor man was able to save enough money to pay the debt. The creditor, however, wished to own the garden and pretended he had bought it. Nicholas, who was one of the judges, left his seat in order to plead the cause of the poor man. The other judges would not listen to reason, for they were big property owners and favored the rich. After the unjust verdict, Nicholas expressed his opinion in no uncertain terms before the other judges. Then he retired from public life.

Two difficult years followed. During this time Nicholas felt that God was calling him to give up everything he held dear on earth and become a hermit. He argued with himself: Could God be calling him away from his family? He discussed the matter with his confessor and with the parish priest. Both agreed that the call was from God. But how could he leave his dear ones? On the other hand, how could he resist a call from God?

He knew that the family would be well provided for if he left. The older boys were fully grown and able to run the farm. His own father, Henry von Flüe, still lived and could advise the young people. But what about his wife, Dorothy, who had just borne his tenth child? He must have her consent if he was to become a hermit.

Dorothy had observed her husband's anguish and was not surprised when he spoke his mind to her. She agreed to his leaving her and the children, the youngest of whom was four months old. She knew that this was the will of God, and that she must not oppose it. So Nicholas departed from his home and his loved ones on October 16, 1467.

God had not revealed to Nicholas where he should go, so he assumed that he should go far from home. He decided to join other hermits who lived in Alsace. On the way there, as he slept behind a hedge, a brilliant light flashed upon him. The light pierced his body, causing him extreme pain, and leaving him with the conviction that he must be a hermit in his homeland. The place where he should live was made known to him; it was about a fifteen minute walk from his home. This experience left Nicholas unable to eat or drink for the rest of his life, except for taking Holy Communion.

Retracing his steps, Nicholas reached his farm after dark. He did not make his presence known but slept in the barn behind his home and slipped away before daybreak.

At the place that had been indicated to him he threw up a shelter of boughs. This was his first hermitage. On Sundays and holydays Nicholas assisted at Mass in the parish church. Going and returning he passed his own house, but he never went in or even looked that way.

Nicholas wore a habit of rough brown material, and he went barefoot at all seasons. He slept two or three hours a night on a log and spent the rest of the night in prayer. He was cheerful and friendly, as he had been in his days as a farmer. He has been described as a tall, slim, wiry person; he had bright eyes, a well-shaped nose, excellent teeth. His hair was thin and he had a short beard.

At first the people of Unterwalden were shocked by Nicholas' action. How did he dare go off and leave his wife and children? It was not long before the hostility changed to veneration. The people noticed that Nicholas went without food and drink, and they took this as a sign of God's approval. Nicholas himself would never admit that he did not eat or drink, always giving evasive answers when questioned about it. But the people of the district kept watch for forty days to see if Nicholas was receiving any food and they found that he was not.

The neighbors built a small but substantial hermitage for "Brother Claus" as they called him. In a few years they added a chapel which joined his cell in such a way that he could look into the sanctuary through a narrow opening and assist at Mass without leaving the cell. During the last ten years of his life Mass was celebrated daily in the chapel. People came to assist at Mass and remained afterward to hear Nicholas speak to them from his window. The crowds became so large that the authorities had to make regulations to control them. Nicholas gave excellent advice, some of it based on knowledge not given by the visitors. He told a jealous wife, for example, that she was wrong in suspecting that her husband was involved in an affair with a neighbor. Among those profiting by his advice were his own wife and children, who came to him regularly.

The Swiss Confederation won a great victory over Charles the Bold, Duke of Burgundy. This victory almost ended the Confederation. For some time there had been friction between the forest cantons and the urban cantons. During the war the urban cantons of Lucerne and Zurich had made alliances outside the Confederation. Now they were demanding the lion's share of the booty captured from the Burgundians, and they wished to have their allies, Freiburg and Soleure, admitted to the Confederation. The forest cantons flatly refused to admit the proposed new members because they would increase the power of the urban cantons. Representatives from the various cantons met in a conference which began at Stans on December 18, 1481. The representatives could not agree, and it looked as if a civil war might result. If the cantons became divided against each other it was probable that all of them would be swallowed up by powerful neighbors. The very existence of Switzerland was at stake.

In a last desperate effort to preserve peace and unity, the parish priest of Stans, Heini Amgrund, hurried to Nicholas' hermitage and spent the night consulting with the hermit. When the priest arrived back in Stans in the morning he found the members of the conference dispersing in anger. He begged them to reassemble and to hear the advice of Nicholas. The delegates knew that Nicholas was a saintly man who had the good of Switzerland at heart, and they agreed to reassemble.

Nicholas proposed that Frieburg and Soleure be admitted to the Confederation, but that all the cantons be free to rule as they pleased in local matters. This plan would strengthen the Confederation by adding two cantons and it would also protect the forest cantons from domination by the urban cantons. Nicholas also proposed that no canton should be allowed to make alliances outside the Confederation. This plan was hailed by the delegates and adopted as the Agreement of Stans.

Civil war had been avoided, and the bonds between the cantons had been so strengthened that they have lasted through the centuries. In the century after Nicholas, the Protestant Revolt divided the people as far as religion is concerned, but the unity of the country survived this blow. Three languages — German, French, and

Italian — are spoken in the little country, but this has proved no barrier to unity. Switzerland stands as an example to the world that people of different religions and different languages can work together in peace and harmony and without sacrificing liberty and democracy.

Nicholas had been told in a vision that he would die on his seventieth birthday. A few days before this birthday he contracted his first and last illness. His last sufferings were short, but they were intense. He suffered agonizing torments of the body, and his condition was such that he could not lie down but must always be moving. He also suffered a great darkness of the soul. He was able, however, to speak to visitors and to receive the last sacraments. He died, as had been foretold, on his seventieth birthday — March 21, 1487.

Immediately after his death Nicholas was venerated as a saint in his canton. He was not canonized until 1947. The canonization came at an appropriate time. By that time Switzerland had remained neutral and had preserved its independence during two World Wars that had spread devastation among its more powerful neighbors. Thanks to the work of Nicholas, the Swiss people had been spared the horrors of the two greatest wars in history. No wonder that Nicholas von Flüe has been named chief patron of Switzerland.

OTHER SAINTS OF THE SAME NAME:

St. Nicholas Bara (or Myra), fourth century. Bishop. "Santa Claus." Feast, December 6.

St. Nicholas Tolentino, 1245–1305. Augustinian friar noted for his successful preaching. Feast, September 10.

ST. MATILDA, 895–968

Feast: March 14

EQUIVALENTS: Mathilde, Matilde, Maud, Maude

Matilda was a member of a noble family of Saxony, a section of Germany. She married Henry the Fowler who soon became Duke of Saxony and was later raised to the German throne. Henry's reign was a successful one, and people attributed this as much to his wife's prayers as to his own talents. Five children were born to Matilda and Henry: Otto, who later became emperor and who was known as "the Great"; Henry, who became Duke of Bavaria; St. Bruno, who became Archbishop of Cologne; Gerberga, who married King Louis IV of France; and Hedwig, who became the mother of Hugh Capet. Henry died after twenty-three years of marriage.

Henry had wished his eldest son Otto to succeed him. Matilda, however, favored Henry, and she induced a few nobles to vote for him. If this was a fault in Matilda, she paid dearly for it. Otto was chosen king and was crowned. Henry started a rebellion and was defeated. Otto then made Henry Duke of Bavaria. Then both brothers turned on their mother and accused her of wasting the crown money on her charities. They even set spies to watch her movements and her donations. She bore this with patience saying that she was glad to see her sons united even though it was against her, "provided they can do it without sin."

Matilda resigned her inheritance and took refuge in a convent where she redoubled her fervor and austerity. Then Otto called her back to court and restored her possessions. She used them to build hospitals, monasteries, and churches and to help the poor.

As she lay dying, her grandson, Archbishop of Mainz, came to minister to her. She died as she lay on a haircloth stretched out on the bare earth.

ST. HENRY THE EMPEROR, 972–1024
Feast: March 14

EQUIVALENTS: Enrico, Hal, Harry, Hawkins, Heinrich, Hendrick, Henning. FEMININE: Etta, Harriet, Hatty, Henrietta, Henriette

---

Henry was the grandson of St. Matilda (above), the son of Duke Henry of Bavaria, and the nephew of Emperor Otto the Great. He was reared in the abbey of Hildesheim and was greatly influenced by St. Wolfgang, Bishop of Ratisbon. He married Kunegunde, daughter of the Count of Luxemburg. After Otto's death, he was chosen emperor and was crowned in the cathedral of Mainz on June 16, 1007. His territory included most of Germany, Austria, Switzerland, the Low Countries, and the northern part of Italy. As emperor, he had to go to war often to defend his possessions. He appeared in Italy a number of times, sometimes to defend the pope.

Henry is regarded as one of the most Christian princes who has ever reigned in the West. He worked hard for the glory of God and the good of the Church. He established many churches and monasteries, and sent missionaries to the heathens. He gave St. Stephen assistance in making Hungary a Christian nation. Henry himself was known for his great virtue, especially for his humility and forgiveness.

ST. STEPHEN, 977–1038

Feast: September 2

EQUIVALENTS: Steven, Etienne. FEMININE: Etiennete, Stephana, Stephanie

---

Geysa, Duke of Hungary, and his wife, Sareloth, became converts to the Catholic faith while most of their subjects were still pagan. They hoped to bring their people to a knowledge of Christ. When they had a son, they named him Stephen after the first martyr. The boy was baptized by St. Adalbert, Bishop of Prague, who later helped him in his work. When Stephen was twenty his father died and he became duke. In the year 1000 he was crowned first king of Hungary. The pope sent a special crown for the occasion and this "Crown of St. Stephen" was used ever after at the coronation of the king of Hungary.

Stephen carried out the work of his parents. He invited missionaries to his country and often accompanied them on their journeys. He rooted out idolatry and made Hungary a Christian nation. He publicly placed his realm under the protection of the Blessed Virgin Mary.

ST. GREGORY VII, POPE, 1020–1085

Feast: May 25

EQUIVALENTS: Gregoire, Gregor, Gregorio

The saint we know as St. Gregory VII was baptized Hildebrand. He was born in the little village of Rocaco in northern Italy. Hildebrand would have preferred to spend his life in a monastery, but his talents were so great that he was called to Rome to serve one pope after another. Then in 1073 Hildebrand was himself elected pope and took the name Gregory VII.

The task which lay before the new pope was appalling. There was widespread corruption not only among rulers of the state but in the Church as well. Bishoprics and abbeys were sold by kings to the highest bidders or bestowed on court favorites. In many districts priests lived openly as married men. The system of lay investiture, whereby kings and nobles bestowed the crozier and ring upon newly consecrated bishops, was a great evil. This made it appear that the bishops were subservient to laymen even in matters of religion. Gregory's life was devoted to fighting these evils and to purifying the Church. He met great opposition from rulers, from priests, from bishops, and even from some cardinals. Many bishops had to be deposed before the struggle was over.

Emperor Henry IV, angered by Gregory's strictures against lay investiture and by other matters, fought Gregory. He even sent word to the cardinals that they must elect another pope, one of whom Henry would approve. Gregory then excommunicated Henry. The German nobles announced that Henry would lose his crown if he remained excommunicated. In order to save his crown, Henry crossed the Alps in severe winter weather and went to the castle of Canossa where Gregory was staying. Henry was refused admittance at first and remained at the castle gate, in the garb of a penitent, for three days. The pope probably suspected Henry of bad faith but he admitted the emperor, heard him accuse himself, and absolved him.

Later, Henry marched against Rome and captured it after a siege of more than two years. The pope retired into the Castle Sant' Angelo and remained there until rescued by an army of Normans. The behavior of the Normans aroused the ire of the Roman people, and Gregory shared the unpopularity of the Normans because he had summoned them. As a result he retired first to Monte Casino and then to Salerno, where he died. On his deathbed he said: "I have loved righteousness and hated iniquity. That is why I die in exile."

ST. GILBERT OF SEMPRINGHAM, d. 1189
Feast: February 16

EQUIVALENTS: Gilberto, Gisbert, Gibson

Gilbert was the pastor of a church at Sempringham and one at Terrington, in Lincolnshire, England. Under his guidance and example, many of his parishioners led lives of sanctity. He drew up a rule for seven young women who lived in strict enclosure in a house adjoining St. Andrew's Church at Sempringham. As the foundation grew, Gilbert added lay sisters and then lay brothers to work the land. Then he added the canons regular, as chaplains. This was the origin of the order that became known as the Gilbertines. It was primarily a women's order, but at its head was a canon, the master general. Eventually, Gilbert himself became master general. He resigned when he lost his sight. The order grew until it had twenty-six houses. It was dissolved at the time of Henry VIII.

Gilbert led a very austere life. He ate so little that those around him wondered how he stayed alive. He always had on his table a plate which he called "the plate of the Lord Jesus." Into this he put all the best food that was served at his table, and he saved it for the poor. He wore a hair shirt. He took his rest sitting up. He spent most of every night in prayer. When Thomas à Becket, Archbishop of Canterbury, was exiled, Gilbert was accused of sending him aid. This was not true, but Gilbert did not deny the charge because he did not want to be classed as an enemy of the archbishop. He faced a sentence of exile but was saved by the intervention of King Henry II. When he was nearly ninety Gilbert had another cross to bear; he was slandered by some of the lay brothers of his order.

He died at the age of 106 and was canonized twelve years later.

ST. DANIEL OF MOROCCO, d. 1227
Feast: October 10

EQUIVALENTS: Danil, Dannel.   FEMININE: Daniela, Danette, Danita

---

Five Franciscans were martyred in Morocco in 1220, as related in this book under St. Francis and under St. Anthony. Seven years later six other friars of the same order secured permission to go to Morocco to preach Christ to the Mohammedans. Their names were Samuel, Angelo, Leo, Domnus, Nicholas, and Hugolino. On their way through Spain they were joined by Brother Daniel who became the superior of the band. They went to Ceuta, in Morocco, and on Saturday, October 2, 1227, made their confessions, washed one another's feet, and spent the night in prayer. On Sunday morning they began to preach in the streets.

Their preaching lasted only a few days. They were arrested and imprisoned. When they refused to deny Christ and to acknowledge the rule of Mohammed, they were condemned to death. They were beheaded on October 13. Their bodies were mangled by the infuriated people but rescued by the local Christians. All seven have been recognized as saints.

SAINTS OF
MODERN TIMES

During the lifetime of St. Thomas More, forces were set in motion which distinguish our modern world from the world of the Middle Ages: the increased use of printing brought about a wider and quicker diffusion of knowledge; Columbus, Vasco da Gama, Magellan, and other navigators and explorers brought Europeans knowledge of new lands and new routes to old lands; Martin Luther broke with the Catholic Church, and the religious unity of Western Europe was shattered. The world we are living in today has been shaped largely by these forces.

Soon after Martin Luther's break, King Henry VIII declared himself head of the Church in England. To many Englishmen, this break did not seem so drastic. The Roman martyrs had faced a clearcut choice: renounce Christ or die. The choice did not seem so clear cut to many of the English of the sixteenth century. After all, the Church of England was still the Catholic Church to all outward appearances. It is to the credit of Thomas More that he saw the issue for what it was and gave his life rather than compromise. Hundreds of others followed his example. Among these were the two Howards: Philip and William.

The Protestant Revolt was followed a century or two later by a revolt against all religion. Men were so impressed by their great discoveries in science that they felt they no longer needed God. Many became freethinkers, agnostics, and atheists. Many who remained Catholics in name were lukewarm in their faith. The situation in modern times has become so bad that our Lord and His Blessed Mother have appeared on earth to plead with us to amend our lives. Through Margaret Mary Alacoque, our Lord pleaded with us to offer reparation to His Sacred Heart which bears so much love for us. Julie Billiart is one who answered this plea by offering her years of suffering to the Sacred Heart in reparation. The Blessed Mother has also appeared again and again, asking for prayers and penance. Two of the persons to whom she has appeared in modern times have been canonized: Catherine Labouré and Bernadette Soubirous.

The Church has faced three great tasks in modern times: (1) reinforcing the faith of those who have remained in the Church; (2) winning converts and reconverting those who have fallen away; (3) combating heresy, irreligion, indifferentism, materialism, and other false ideas. God has raised up many saints to assist in this work. Robert Bellarmine preached and wrote in defense of the Church. Angela Merici and Julie Billiart founded communities of nuns to teach Christian doctrine. Vincent de Paul brought the word of Christ to the poor and neglected while also caring for their material needs. John Bosco worked among homeless boys who were in danger of losing their faith. Isaac Jogues and Charles Garnier preached the truths of the Catholic religion to the North American Indians and gave their lives for the cause. Mother Cabrini, first United States citizen to be canonized, traveled thousands of miles over three continents to establish schools, orphanages, and hospitals.

The Church has needed active saints and it has needed saints who would remain hidden from the world and who would help by their prayers and sacrifices. Thérèse of Lisieux was denied her ambition to be a missionary but she aided the missionaries during her lifetime by her prayers, and today she is aiding them in heaven. Other saints who lived in relative obscurity were Rose of Lima, Gerard Majella, and little Maria Goretti who gave her life in defense of the Christian virtue of purity.

All of us owe a great debt to the saints — both the canonized and the un-canonized. They brought down great showers of graces upon the world while they were alive and they are sending down even greater showers today.

ST. ANGELA MERICI, 1474–1540
Feast: May 31

EQUIVALENTS: Ancela, Angele, Angelica, Angelique, Angelita, Angeline, Aniela, Anjela

---

Angela Merici lived in exciting and troubled times. She was born into a Europe that was almost entirely Catholic, at least in name. But in many places the faith had been weakened by the worldliness and the pagan spirit of the Renaissance. Angela lived in the time of Martin Luther and Henry VIII, and before she died the Protestant revolt had shattered the religious unity of Europe. She lived in the time of Emperor Charles V and his enemy, Francis I of France. Europe was torn internally by wars and threatened externally by the Mohammedan Turks.

It was a time when the Church seemed to be in great danger, but God raised up great saints to meet the challenge. Among these were Ignatius of Loyola, Francis Xaxier, Thomas More, John Fisher, Philip Neri, Andrew Avellino, Francis Borgia — and, of course, Angela Merici.

Angela was born on March 21, 1474, at the little town of Desenzano on the shore of Lake Garda, in northern Italy. Her parents, both fervent Catholics, died when she was about ten years old. Angela, an older sister, and a brother went to live with a well-to-do uncle at Salo. Angela and her sister were very devoted to each other, and the death of the sister came as a great shock to Angela when she was thirteen. Angela was worried because her sister had died without receiving the last sacraments. She was consoled by a vision in which she saw her sister radiantly happy in the company of the Blessed Virgin and the other saints. In gratitude, Angela consecrated herself more completely to God and joined the Third Order of St. Francis. She tried to live a life of complete poverty as St. Francis did. She wished to possess nothing of her own, not even a bed. She lived almost entirely on bread, water, and a few vegetables.

When Angela was about twenty, she left Salo and returned to her home at Desenzano. On the way, she had another vision in which she saw a ladder of light extending from earth to heaven. A group of maidens were ascending the ladder, accompanied by a multitude of angels. This vision is believed to have marked for Angela the beginning of her vocation. The maidens ascending the ladder into heaven no doubt represented the future members of her Institute.

Angela was appalled by the ignorance of the poorer children in her home town. The children lacked even the most elementary religious knowledge and there was no one to teach them. Angela felt that she was called upon to do something about this situation. She gathered the neighborhood children about her and taught them Christian doctrine, reading, and writing. She organized a group of her friends to help her. Later, Angela accepted an invitation to go to the larger city of Brescia where she continued the work on a larger scale.

Angela visited many shrines in Italy, but the great ambition of her life was to visit the Holy Land. She was happy in 1524 when she was able to join a pilgrimage to the Holy Land. The travelers stopped at Canea on the island of Crete. Here Angela suddenly became blind. She insisted on continuing the pilgrimage and visited the holy places with great devotion, "seeing" through the eyes of the others. She was happy to bear her cross along the way made holy by the cross of her Redeemer. On the return voyage the pilgrims again visited Crete. Angela suddenly recovered her sight at the very place where she had lost it.

The year 1525 was a Holy Year, and Angela went to Rome to gain the special indulgences. She had an interview with Pope Clement VII who wished her to stay in Rome and do her work there. But Angela preferred to return to Brescia where she had established herself in two small rooms attached to the church of St. Afra, and the pope respected her wishes.

She was not able to stay in Brescia long because the city was being attacked by the troops of Charles V, and it was essential for non-combatants to leave. Angela went to Cremona until peace was restored. Her return to Brescia was greeted with joy by the citizens who regarded her as a saint. Shortly after this Angela fell into an ecstasy while assisting at Mass and was seen by many people to be raised up from the floor.

In Brescia Angela prayed, fasted, and suffered. She instructed the ignorant, comforted the sorrowful, and visited the sick. Thus her life passed until she was sixty years old. And still Angela felt that God wanted more of her, that she had not yet begun the most important work of her life. Her spiritual director assured her that this was the case.

What work was required of Angela? She was convinced that she should prepare an organization of women to carry on the work she had started. This organization was needed to save Christian families from the worldly and pagan ideas of the Renaissance and from the heresy which was rampant throughout Europe.

Angela's idea was something new in the life of the Church. Until then, all religious communities of women had been cloistered. The members lived a life of prayer and penance, secluded from the world. But Angela proposed to found a community whose members would go out into the world to teach and to perform acts of charity. They would work for their own sanctification, and they would spend much time in prayer and in doing penance, but they would not be secluded from the world. They would try to change the world by their work as well as by their prayers. There is nothing unusual about this idea today, but it was considered a radical step when Angela proposed it.

On November 25, 1535, Angela launched her Institute. Twenty-eight devoted young followers, both virgins and widows, assisted at Mass, received Holy Communion, and then formed themselves into a permanent association. They became known as the Ursulines because Angela had chosen as their patron St. Ursula, who, by word and example, had encouraged her companions to die in defense of their virginity and their faith. Within a year, fifty-four recruits joined the original band.

At first the Ursulines were not really a religious order. They had no regular habit, although a black dress was recommended. They took no vows, and they did not lead a community life. They met for classes and for prayers, carried out the duties that were assigned to them, and lived holy lives in their own homes. The idea of a teaching order of women was so new that it took time to develop.

Angela's original program for the sisters included all the work she had been doing. Her sisters were to teach catechism, work in the hospitals, visit the sick and the poor, and care for small children. But the primary purpose of the Institute was the Christian education of girls, especially girls of the poorer classes. This remains the principal purpose of the Ursulines today.

At the first election Angela was unanimously chosen superior, a post she continued to fill for the remaining five years of her life. These were years of intense labor and of even more intense spiritual life. Her energy was about spent, but she remained active to the end.

During her last illness Angela gathered her company about her and told them to practice charity, humility, and obedience. Many citizens of Brescia came to seek advice. When she was at the point of exhaustion she said to one: "Whatever you would wish at your dying hour to have done in health, that do now while you may."

Toward the close of the day, realizing that her hour had come, Angela asked to be clothed in the habit of the Franciscan Tertiaries and placed on a straw mat on the floor. Here she died while repeating the words of our Lord: "Into thy hands, I commend my spirit." It was January 27, 1540, about six o'clock in the evening. Angela was beatified in 1768 and canonized in 1807.

The Ursuline Order proudly looks to St. Angela Merici as its foundress, but all noncloistered orders, and especially the teaching orders, can look to her as their originator.

Angela's labor and self-sacrifice were inspired by her ardent love of God. When she saw a situation which she knew was not pleasing to God she couldn't rest till she had done something about it. She lived long before the term Catholic Action had been defined, but what an ardent disciple of Catholic Action she would be if she were alive today!

OTHER SAINTS OF THE SAME NAME:

St. Angela of Prague, died about 1230. Daughter of a king of Bohemia and the author of several devotional works. Feast, July 6.

Bl. Angela of Foligno, died 1309. Converted from a life of sin, she did severe penance, and became a mystic. Feast, January 4.

ST. THOMAS MORE, 1478–1535

Feast: July 9

EQUIVALENTS: Thoma, Tomas, Tomaz. FEMININE: Thomasine

Thomas More was equipped to rise far in the world. He was well born, well educated, good looking, witty, and possessed of good common sense. He was not wealthy, and a lack of wealth combined with such a store of talents often fills a man with great ambition. But Thomas More was not ambitious in a worldly way. His thoughts were on spiritual matters. He wore a hair shirt under his clothes from the time he was about eighteen. Great renown came to Thomas More, but not because he sought it.

More was born in London in 1478 and spent most of his life in that city. He was the son of Sir John More, a lawyer and distinguished jurist. Thomas received an excellent education which included the study of law. He lived three years in a Carthusian monastery while studying law and shared the austere life of the monks. In 1504 he became a member of Parliament. The next year he married Jane Colt. In a few years Jane died, leaving him with three daughters and a son. In order to keep his family together, Thomas married a widow, Alice Middleton. He was devoted to his children and supervised their education. His daughters were as well educated as his son, which was unusual in those days.

In 1510 More became Under-Sheriff, a position of honor and responsibility. In 1518 he became a member of the king's Council on which he served for eleven years. During this time he ably discharged several duties. He was Under-Treasurer, Speaker in Parliament, Chancellor of the Duchy of Lancaster, and High Steward of two universities: Oxford and Cambridge. A number of diplomatic missions were also entrusted to him. It was while he was on a mission to Holland that he wrote his famous book *Utopia*.

King Henry VIII had married Catherine of Aragon, daughter of Ferdinand and Isabella. Never a model of marital fidelity, Henry had fallen under the spell of Anne Boleyn, who desired to be queen. In order to rid himself of Catherine, Henry developed "conscientious scruples" about his marriage to her. Catherine had been the widow of his elder brother. The marriage had never been consummated, and Pope Julius II had given a special dispensation for the marriage of Henry and Catherine. Now Henry said that the dispensation had been an error. Catherine said that the marriage was perfectly valid and appealed to Pope Clement VII.

Cardinal Wolsey was at that time the highest-ranking member of the hierarchy in England and also the chancellor. Enraged at the delay in securing the annulment, Henry discharged Wolsey from his office. Thomas More was made chancellor; he was the first layman to hold that post. Wolsey's lands were confiscated by the king and he was arrested for "high treason."

As chancellor, Sir Thomas refused to take any part in Henry's marriage case, and he refused even to commit himself on the subject. He was no doubt personally convinced that the marriage to Catherine was valid, but he knew that this was a matter for the Church to decide. He confined himself largely to the judicial functions of his office and made a lasting reputation for himself for justice tempered with mercy. Years later when a group of Elizabethan playwrights, of whom William Shakespeare was probably one, wrote the play *Sir Thomas More*, he appeared as the good judge and friend of the poor.

As the marriage case dragged on, Henry became more and more angry with the pope. The clergy were forced to acknowledge the king to be "their singular, only and supreme Lord, and so far as the law of Christ allows even Supreme Head." The saving words "so far as the law of Christ allows" were inserted at the insistence of Archbishop William Warham of Canterbury. Later, Henry denounced the priests as "but half our subjects — yea, and scarce our subjects." A subservient Parliament passed successive bills to hamper the work of the Church. In May, 1532, at the order of Parliament, most members of the clergy renounced their oath of allegiance to the pope. The next day, Thomas More resigned his office.

In 1533, Henry went through the form of a marriage with Anne Boleyn. This was approved by Archbishop Cranmer, a tool of Henry. Thomas More incurred the wrath of Anne when he failed to attend her coronation. In 1534, came the announcement that Rome had rejected Henry's plea for an annulment; his marriage with Catherine was valid. A week later, in defiance of the pope, Parliament passed the Law of Succession. This provided that the king's subjects must take an oath saying that the king's marriage to Anne was valid and their offspring would be the heirs to the throne. In the oath the subjects also repudiated "any foreign authority, prince or potentate." To oppose this Act was high treason.

On April 13, More was requested to take the oath, and he refused. A short time later, he was requested again and once more he refused. He was then imprisoned in the Tower of London. At first he was made fairly comfortable in his prison. He wrote *Dialogue of Comfort* in which he defended the right of free conscience, and he wrote *Treatise on the Passion* with which he prepared for his own death. He had frequent visitors, including members of his family, who begged him to take the oath and thus save himself.

More's imprisonment was entirely illegal. There was no penalty for refusing to take the oath. The only penalty was for opposing the Act of Succession, and More had been careful not to do this, even to members of his family. He did not fear death, but he feared that he was unworthy to be a martyr. He thought that it was his duty to try to preserve his life as long as possible.

In 1535 Parliament passed a new and stricter law. It became an act of treason to deny that the king was the sole head of the Church of England. The penalty for this was disemboweling. More knew that his days were numbered. About the same time, More's writing materials and his books were taken from his cell. He was allowed few visitors. His property was confiscated. His wife had to sell her clothes in order to buy necessities.

Among the first to be convicted under the new law were a group of Carthusian monks who were also imprisoned in the Tower. More's beloved daughter Margaret paid her last visit to him the day the first three monks went to their martyrdom. The authorities probably allowed this visit in the hope that Margaret would be able to talk her father out of suffering the same fate as the Carthusians. But as they looked out the window Thomas said: "Look, Meg, do you see that those blessed fathers are going forth to their deaths as happily as bridegrooms to their marriage?"

On June 19 the second group of three Carthusians was martyred. On June 22 Bishop John Fisher, the only bishop who had not yielded to Henry, was led from the Tower and beheaded on Tower Hill. Nine days later Thomas More was indicted and tried in Westminster Hall. He was weak from illness and captivity and was permitted to sit during the trial. He was found guilty of treason and condemned to death. After the sentence was passed More reminded his judges that St. Paul had persecuted St. Stephen and that the two were now happy together in heaven. He said that he would pray that he and the judges who condemned him would likewise meet in heaven.

Shortly before his death More expressed the conviction that his "crime" had been not approving the marriage to Anne rather than his refusal to acknowledge Henry as head of the Church.

King Henry ruled that Thomas More should not be disemboweled but should be beheaded. On July 6, Thomas was told that his day had come. He put on his best clothes and began to walk to Tower Hill. He talked to various people along the way. When he came to the rickety scaffolding he asked an attendant to help him up. "I can manage to get down alone," he said.

The king had sent word that More should be allowed to say only a few words from the scaffold. He feared the man's eloquence. More asked the people for their prayers. Then he said that when Henry had given him his office the king had told him to look first to God, and after God to him. More said that this was what he had done. "I die the king's good servant, but God's first."

He recited the *Miserere*. He gave a gold coin to the executioner and told him to be careful. "My neck is short, and you must think of your reputation." He put his head on the block. Then he asked the headsman to wait for a moment while he pushed aside the beard he had grown in prison. "It has committed no treason," he said.

Thomas More and John Fisher were canonized in 1935, and they share the same feast. Thomas More would have been a good candidate for canonization even if he had not been martyred, because he lived such a good and holy life.

OTHER SAINTS OF THE SAME NAME:

St. Thomas the Apostle, died about 72. "Doubting Thomas," patron of architects and masons. Feast, December 21.

St. Thomas à Becket, 1117–1170. Archbishop. Like St. Thomas More, he was Chancellor to the King of England and was martyred for defending the Church. Feast, December 29.

St. Thomas Aquinas, 1125–1274. Great theologian. Feast, March 7.

St. Thomas of Hereford, 1219–1282. Bishop of Hereford. Feast, October 2.

Defender of the Faith

ST. ROBERT BELLARMINE, 1542–1621
Feast: May 13

EQUIVALENTS: Robard, Roberto, Robin, Rupert, Hodge.
FEMININE: Roberta, Robertine, Robertina

Father Robert Bellarmine, S.J., newly ordained, walked toward the Church of St. Michael's in Louvain, where he was scheduled to give a sermon. A number of other persons were walking in the same direction. A man much taller than the slightly built priest fell in beside him and struck up a conversation.

"I see you are on your way to hear the priest who is preaching at St. Michael's," said the stranger. "Well, you have a treat in store for you if you have never heard him before. He is really an excellent speaker. I wonder where he came from, how old he is, and who his teachers were."

Robert Bellarmine gave a noncommittal answer, and the man continued: "The priest towers over that pulpit. He must be a big man. People are saying that a giant has come to Louvain to teach the word of God."

Robert Bellarmine smiled. He always stood on a stool when he preached.

"Well, I think I will hurry on," the man said. "The church will be crowded and I want to make sure I get in."

"Yes, run along," said Robert Bellarmine. "I am sure there will be room for a little fellow like me."

Robert Francis Romulus Bellarmine was born near Florence, Italy, on October 4, 1542, the son of Vincent Bellarmine and Cynthia Cervini, half-sister to Pope Marcellus II. His health was poor from childhood. While still a young boy, he knew Virgil by heart, wrote good Latin verses, and played the violin. Also as a boy, he liked to take part in debates and in public discussions, especially on controversial subjects. He was deeply devout. When he was seventeen the rector of the Jesuit college at Montepulciano, which Robert attended, described him as "the best of our school, and not far from the kingdom of heaven."

In 1560 Robert went to Rome and joined the Jesuits. He spent three years in Rome studying philosophy. Then he was sent to teach in his native Florence and in Mondovi. In the latter place, he found that he was expected to teach Greek, along with many other subjects. He knew no Greek, so he studied every night to master the grammar he was to teach the boys the next day. He was a born teacher and was successful from the start. He loved young people and was opposed to the harsh discipline which was practiced in almost all schools at that time. "We are all only boys," he said, "and our one hope of salvation is for each of us to keep the heart and manner of a boy." In addition to teaching, Robert preached sermons which attracted large crowds.

He was sent to Padua to receive his theological training and was then sent to Louvain so that he might become acquainted with the heresies raging throughout northern Europe. The Protestant Revolt had taken place earlier in the century, and Europe was seething with religious conflict. Whole nations had broken away from the Church and others were in danger of doing so. This called for vigorous action from the Church. Those taking part in the "Counter Reformation" had two huge tasks: (1) to defend the Church against the attacks of its enemies; (2) to work for much-needed reforms within the Church. The Jesuits were in the forefront of the Counter Reformation, and Robert Bellarmine was to be one of their ablest spokesmen. In Louvain, he heard and answered the arguments of Lutherans, Calvinists, Anglicans, and other heretics.

Robert was only twenty-seven and not yet a priest when he

preached his first sermon in the Church of St. Michael in Louvain. He was conscious of his youth, of the fact that many great speakers had occupied the pulpit before him, and of the fact that many learned men were listening to him. He began by apologizing for his youth and his lack of experience. Then he preached a sermon which held his listeners spellbound.

In 1570 Robert went to Ghent to be ordained and then returned to Louvain as a professor in the university. He was the first Jesuit to hold such a post. While teaching courses in the *Summa* of St. Thomas Aquinas and other difficult subjects, he continued his preaching. Protestants as well as Catholics flocked to St. Michael's to hear him. His topics were usually controversial; that is, he attacked the false doctrines of the Protestants or defended Catholic doctrines against the attacks of heretics. His sermons were well reasoned and polite. He was always careful not to hurt or humble an opponent. This was unusual in those days when it was common for opponents to apply to each other such epithets as: ass, fool, devil, dung hill, and even worse names. Some Catholics criticized Bellarmine for his gentleness toward his opponents, but he won many converts including Protestant ministers.

In 1576 Bellarmine was assigned to the recently created chair of controversies in the Roman college. Here for about twelve years he lectured against the heresies that were sweeping over Europe. He was so successful that similar chairs were established in other Catholic universities. His lectures, published under the title *De Controversis* in four large volumes, ran through thirty editions in twenty years.

The lectures of Bellarmine made such an impression in England that Queen Elizabeth founded a chair in Oxford University and another in Cambridge for the sole purpose of answering him. She also made it an offense punishable by death for an Englisman to have in his possession any writing of this Jesuit. This resulted in a huge "under the counter" sale. A London bookseller said: "I have made more money out of this Jesuit than all our doctors put together."

In 1589 Bellarmine was sent on a diplomatic mission to France where there was a war over the throne. In 1592 he was made rector of the Roman College. In 1594 he became the Jesuit provincial of Naples. Three years after that he became the theologian to Pope Clement VIII for whom he wrote two catechisms still in general use in Italy. In 1598, to his dismay, he was made a Cardinal by Clement VIII because "the Church of God has not his equal for learning." As a cardinal he kept up all his former austerities. He lived on bread and garlic, the food of the poor. He would not have a fire even in the middle of winter. He took the hangings from his room to clothe poor people, saying: "The walls won't catch cold."

In 1602 he was appointed Archbishop of Capua. Although he had no previous experience administering a diocese, he threw himself into the work with great zeal. He instituted all the reforms that had been decreed by the Council of Trent. He traveled all about his diocese, preaching constantly, teaching the children their catechism, helping those in need, and winning the love of all classes.

After three years as archbishop Cardinal Bellarmine was called back to Rome. He was made head of the Vatican Library and took part in all the important affairs of the Holy See. An important adversary of these years was King James I of England who was an advocate of the "divine right of kings." Bellarmine, an enemy of tyranny, said that the people, as creatures of God, had certain rights which no king should take away from them. King James ordered the works of Bellarmine to be burned publicly. This made the works very popular among enemies of the king, especially the Puritans.

Cardinal Bellarmine was a strong champion of papal infallibility long before that doctrine had been declared a dogma of the Church. He insisted that the pope was supreme in all spiritual matters. But he said that the pope had only an indirect and not a direct control over temporal rulers. For this he incurred the displeasure of Pope Sixtus V. This pope was about to put the first volume of *De Controversis* on the Index when he died. The next pope, Gregory XIV, gave the work special approbation.

In this limited space it is not possible to list all the activities of Robert Bellarmine. He wrote a Hebrew grammar and a number of spiritual books including *The Art of a Happy Death*. He was the spiritual director of Aloysius Gonzaga during that young saint's last year on earth. He worked for the beatification of Philip Neri, whom he had known personally. The Feast of the Stigmata of St. Francis of Assisi (September 17) was placed on the Church's calendar through the efforts of Bellarmine. St. Francis de Sales was aided by Bellarmine in founding the Congregation of the Visitation. The list could go on and on.

It would be expected that a man as prominent and as articulate as Robert Bellarmine should have many enemies. His enemies included Protestants of every denomination, all those who believed in the divine right of kings, Catholics who thought he was too soft with his opponents, and some of his own brethren who thought they saw defects in his methods. Even a pope, as we have seen, called his work into question. Being human, Robert Bellarmine would have preferred to have every man his friend. But he followed the course which he thought God had set for him, and he bore the misunderstandings and the enmity with patience.

Cardinal Bellarmine was in his seventy-ninth year when he was permitted to retire because his health, never robust, was failing. His few remaining months were spent preparing for the end which came on the Feast of the Stigmata of St. Francis, September 17, 1621. This was the feast he had helped establish. He was born on one feast of St. Francis, and he died on the other.

Robert Bellarmine was canonized in 1930 and made a Doctor of the Church in 1931 by Pope Pius XI who called him "a star of the first magnitude in the heaven of the Church." The title "Doctor of the Church" is conferred upon a few saints in special recognition of the fact that they combined great learning with great sanctity.

OTHER SAINTS OF THE SAME NAME:

St. Rupert (or Robert) of Salzburg, died about 718. Missionary bishop who evangelized Bavaria and Austria. Feast, March 27.

St. Robert of Citeaux, 1018–1110. Benedictine monk and reformer. Feast, April 29.

St. Robert, died 1159. Cistercian abbot of Newminster, England. Feast, June 7.

BL. PHILIP HOWARD, 1557–1595

Feast: October 19

BL. WILLIAM HOWARD, 1611–1680

Feast: June 20

EQUIVALENTS OF PHILIP: Filipe, Fillipo, Lipo. FEMININE: Filipa, Lipa, Philippa, Philippina, Philippine, Pippa

EQUIVALENTS OF WILLIAM: Guillaume, Wilhelm, Will, Willin, Willum, Quillen. FEMININE: Helmina, Wileen, Wilette, Wilhelmina, Willa, Willabel, Willabella, Williamanna, Williamina, Wilma

---

The Howard family of sixteenth and seventeenth century England was a famous family indeed. It contained great nobles (the Duke of Norfolk, the Earl of Arundel, the Viscount Stafford), a Cardinal (Philip Thomas), a noted poet (Henry), and England's first great art collector (Thomas). The family produced outstanding military and naval officers. And it produced the two martyrs named above, both of whom have been beatified.

Philip Howard, Earl of Arundel, was born at Arundel House in London. His father had yielded to pressure and had left the Catholic Church to join the Church of England. Philip, therefore, was reared and educated as a Protestant. He married Anne, Countess of Surrey.

Philip went to the court of Queen Elizabeth and for a time completely neglected his wife for the dissolute life of the court. In 1581 he heard the disputations of Blessed Edmund Campion and was greatly impressed. He returned to his wife and tried to make amends

146

for his past behavior. In 1584 he and his wife were received into the Church by Father William Weston, S.J.

The people at court, including Queen Elizabeth, soon noticed the change in Philip's way of living. They discovered that he had joined the despised "papists." Philip saw that he was in danger, and he determined to flee. He wrote a letter to Elizabeth explaining why he was leaving and then boarded a ship with his wife. But all Philip's movements had been watched. He was captured at sea, brought back to England, and confined to the Tower of London. When the Spanish Armada sailed against England, all Catholics were suspected of being Spanish agents. Philip was brought to trial. On forged evidence he was convicted of high treason and sentenced to death. For some reason the death sentence was not carried out. Philip languished in prison for another six years. He asked to see his wife and his son who had been born since his imprisonment. He was told that not only might he see them but he might have his complete freedom provided he would attend Protestant services. He refused. Philip died October 19, 1595, and there was some suspicion that he had been poisoned. He was thirty-eight years old.

Ten of Philip's thirty-eight years had been spent in prison. He spent much of this time in writing and in translating devotional works. As if his close confinement were not enough, he fasted three days a week and got up at five o'clock every morning for prayers. When he was expecting to be executed he wrote this statement: "The Catholic and Roman faith, which I hold, is the only cause (as far as I can any way imagine) why either I have been thus long imprisoned or why I am now ready to be executed."

In the stone walls of the Tower of London it is still possible to see two inscriptions carved by Philip and one referring to him after his death by a fellow prisoner. Philip Howard's relics are at Arundel.

Philip showed that he would die before he would renounce his faith, and there is little doubt that his imprisonment hastened his death. The Church, therefore, lists him as a martyr.

Philip's son Thomas, the art collector, succeeded his martyred father as Earl of Arundel. Thomas did not have the great courage and faith of his father; he renounced the Catholic Church and became a member of the Church of England. Thomas' fifth son, William, remained a Catholic, however, and eventually followed the example of his grandfather.

William suffered from the unjust laws that had been passed against Catholics. He had to pay the excessive taxes that were levied, but he did not suffer personal persecution in his younger days. King Charles I came to the throne when William was only fourteen. Charles, who was rather favorably disposed toward Catholics, seems to have taken a liking to William. On his coronation day, Charles made William a knight of the Bath. The king also sent William on several important missions to the continent where he was able to acquire items for the art collection that had been started by his father. In 1637 Sir William married Mary Stafford, the Catholic sister of the last Baron Stafford. Three years later Charles transferred the barony to William and immediately afterward made him a viscount. He was now entitled to sit in the House of Lords.

Viscount Stafford defended Charles I in the Great Rebellion which ended in 1649 with the execution of Charles by the followers of Oliver Cromwell. He paid dearly for this during the years that Oliver Cromwell ruled England. His rights and property were restored when Charles II came to power in 1660. The next sixteen or seventeen years must have been happy ones for William. He spent much time with his wife and with their many children. During this period he conducted his nephew, Philip Thomas Howard, to Rome to receive the cardinal's hat.

In 1678 a disreputable character named Titus Oates appeared before the House of Commons and said that he had discovered a terrible "Popish Plot." He said that the pope, the Society of Jesus, and their confederates had hatched a plot to assassinate the king and take over the government of England. The chief positions in the papal-dominated government, according to Oates, had already been assigned to Catholic peers; financial matters were to be directed by William Howard.

Under questioning, Oates and his perjured witnesses repeatedly contradicted themselves. But the enemies of the Church were bent upon using any means to gain their ends. Public sentiment was lashed to a fever pitch, and the people demanded death for those who had been named by Oates.

King Charles II did not for a minute believe the accusations of Titus Oates, but he did not have the power to stop the persecution that had been ordered by Parliament.

William Howard and four other Catholic peers named by Oates were arrested in October, 1678, and imprisoned in the Tower of London. As the months dragged by and nothing treasonable could be proved against the five, a face-saving device was sought. One of the group must be put to death to prevent the whole affair from becoming ridiculous. William Howard was the one selected. His trial before the House of Lords began on November 30, 1680, his sixty-ninth birthday. William was denied the aid of counsel. He conducted his own defense very capably, but he was doomed from the start. When the vote was taken, fifty-five peers voted guilty and only thirty-one voted innocent. William was amazed. He had not thought that the nobles of the realm could be so blinded by prejudice.

To the nobles who had condemned him William said: "God's will be done, and your Lordships' . . . God forgive those who have sworn falsely against me." After a pause he continued: "My Lords, I do here, in the presence of Almighty God, declare that I have no malice in my heart against those who have condemned me. But I have one humble request to make; that for the short time I have yet to live I may be allowed to see my wife and children and friends."

The request was granted. The Lords also petitioned the king to allow the prisoner to be beheaded. The usual penalty for traitors was hanging, drawing, and quartering. The king granted the request without hesitation; he would have freed William if this had been within his power.

Viscount Stafford spent his last days in preparation for death. He wrote letters to his two daughters on the continent who were nuns. He wrote to his niece, the countess of Arundel; to her husband he bequeathed the sword which the Howards had wielded in defense of the English crown. He was told that December 29 was the day appointed for his execution. To his wife he said: "This is the day which the Lord hath made, let us then rejoice."

December 29, feast of St. Thomas à Becket, was a cold bleak day. About ten o'clock in the morning Viscount Stafford was summoned to the courtyard. He accepted a cloak which was offered to him. "I may perhaps shake from the cold," he whispered to his friends, "but not, please God, from fear."

At Tower Hill, the place of execution, William Howard made a brief speech in which he said he was innocent of any crime. Many in the crowd said: "We believe you, my Lord, we believe you." He reaffirmed his attachment to the Catholic Church and to the king. He added that he died for the faith and for that alone. Then he knelt before the block, kissed it, saying: "Lord Jesus, receive my soul," and laid his head on the block. The executioner hesitated. The viscount asked what was the matter, and the man said: "Do you forgive me?" The answer came quickly: "I do." Then the ax fell.

William Howard, Viscount Stafford, one of twenty-four innocent men to die because of the "Plot," was beatified on December 15, 1929, by Pope Pius XI.

OTHER SAINTS NAMED PHILIP:

St. Philip, third century martyr. Public official of Alexandria, Egypt; father of St. Eugenia. Feast, September 13.

St. Philip Neri, 1515–1595. Apostle of Rome; founder of the Oratorians, a congregation of secular priests. Feast, May 26.

Bl. Philippine Duchesne, 1769–1852. Associate of St. Madeline Sophie Barat, and first superior of the Religious of the Sacred Heart in the United States. Feast, November 17.

OTHER SAINTS NAMED WILLIAM:

St. William of Tours, died 1154. Archbishop. Feast, June 8.

St. William of Toulouse, died 1242. Dominican priest, martyr. Feast, May 29.

Apostle of Organized Charity

ST. VINCENT DE PAUL, 1576–1660
Feast: July 19

EQUIVALENTS: Vicente, Vincens, Vincenti, Vance. FEMININE:
Vincentia

Vincent de Paul, who was ordained at the age of twenty-four, was intelligent and attractive and could have risen high in a material way if he had chosen to do so. In seventeenth-century France it was possible for an ambitious priest to gain position in the world. The Council of Trent had moved to bring the clergy under more rigid discipline, but in France there was considerable lag before the decrees of the Council went into effect. Priests were not as closely supervised by their bishops as they are today. A young priest was free to seek his own post. Vincent de Paul could have lived a life of ease as chaplain to a wealthy family or perhaps to the royal family itself. He probably could have become a bishop, and there was a considerable income attached to most bishoprics. It is to his credit that he turned his back on a life of ease and devoted himself to the poor and the downtrodden.

As a young priest Vincent had his share of ambition, and he seems to have given little thought to the poor. He had received his seminary training through the sacrifices of his mother and father who lived on a small farm in southwestern France. After his ordination he set up a school for the sons of the nobility and gentry. With the money received from the tuition he continued his own higher education. By the time he was thirty he had come a long way on the path of learning and was trying to become a bishop. In those days the pope usually heeded the recommendations of the king when he appointed bishops, and the king, in turn, usually listened to the advice of his nobles. Through a friend who was a noble, Vincent thought he had a good chance of securing the king's recommendation. For some reason the appointment did not come through. Vincent was no doubt disappointed, but he probably consoled himself with the thought that he was still young and there would be other opportunities.

Thus, at thirty, we find that Vincent was a good man but ambitious and inclined to be worldly. There was nothing about him to suggest that he would become a great saint.

A turning point came in his life when he was left a legacy. His right to the inheritance was challenged, so Vincent went to law and won his case. The money was in Marseilles, and he went there to receive it. Instead of returning to southwestern France by land, he decided to go by sea. His ship was captured by Barbary pirates. The captain of the captured ship was cruelly murdered because he had resisted the pirates. Vincent and the others were put in irons and taken to the Barbary coast where they were sold as slaves.

Vincent was sold first to a fisherman, then to a physician, and then to a renegade Christian farmer who had three wives. During his two years of captivity Vincent never ceased to ask our Blessed Lady for deliverance. His master was impressed by Vincent's faith and decided to return to Europe and to the practice of his religion. Vincent and his former master secured a ship and escaped across the Mediterranean Sea to France.

The two years as a slave had brought about a big change in Vincent. His hardships had made him more compassionate toward the sufferings of others.

Shortly after this, another event had a profound effect upon Vincent. A learned theologian whom he knew was so afflicted by temptations against faith that he could not offer Mass or recite the Divine Office or even come near a church without being tempted to blasphemy, or to a denial of the very existence of God. Besides this, he suffered terrible temptations of the flesh. This sorely tried priest came to Vincent for help. Vincent made every effort to help him, but all in vain. At length Vincent asked God to relieve his friend and to let him suffer the temptations instead.

Soon the priest came to Vincent with the joyful announcement that the temptations had left him. But Vincent had the temptations now. He suffered terribly for four years and wasted away in the fight. Then Vincent prayed: "Dear God, if you will take away these temptations I will spend the rest of my life working for the poor." The temptations stopped at once, and Vincent's lifework had begun.

It had taken two years of physical slavery and four years of spiritual agony to prepare the soul of Vincent for the work that God wanted him to do.

During the years of spiritual struggle Vincent made the acquaintance of a priest, Pierre de Berulle, who became his spiritual director. Vincent said of Pierre that "he was endowed with such learning and holiness that his like could not be found." It was upon the advice of de Berulle that Vincent accepted his next three offices. For a year, Vincent was parish priest in Clichy, a suburb of Paris. Then for four years he labored on the estate of the noble de Gondi family. This did not mean a life of ease for Vincent. The de Gondi estate was extensive. Many people lived on it. Vincent was the spiritual head of something resembling a modern county.

Soon after Vincent accepted this new post he was called to attend a peasant who lay dying. He was shocked to find that the man had been poorly instructed in his religion and had been making bad confessions for years. The man said his soul would have been lost if it had not been for Vincent. As Vincent moved about the estate he was appalled by the ignorance he found. He secured permission from Madame de Gondi to have missions given for the benefit of her dependents and to provide them with regular religious instruction. But who would give the missions and the religious instruction? Where were the priests who would devote themselves entirely to the service of the poor? To meet the need for such priests, Vincent organized, with the approval of the Archbishop of Paris, the Congregation of the Mission. The work of this congregation was twofold: working among the poor and training future priests in seminaries. Today, the members of this order are commonly called the Vincentians. The de Gondis gave Vincent the financial help he needed to start his congregation.

After four years Vincent left the de Gondis and became a parish priest at Chatillon-des-Dombes. At Mass one Sunday Vincent told his congregation about a family whose members were sick and very much in need. That afternoon he called on the family. He found that the parishioners had responded generously. The family had more food than they could use before it would spoil. Vincent saw that some kind of system was needed. He found, too, that other families in the neighborhood needed assistance. To answer these needs he organized the Confraternity of the Ladies of Charity and a little later a corresponding Confraternity of Charity for men.

The first Ladies of Charity were middle class women for whom Vincent drew up a plan of action. Each group of ladies had three officers: a president, a vice-president, and a treasurer. These officers were to visit poor families, see what they needed, and supply what was lacking. The officers were the responsible agents, but they were to enlist whatever other help was needed. There was to be no indiscriminate giving.

The men's Confraternity helped find jobs for the poor, gave advice, and provided religious instruction for those who needed it. (Two hundred years later when Frederik Ozanam organized the St. Vincent de Paul Society, he used this Confraternity as a model.)

Almost since the beginning of mankind there have been people in need of charitable contributions. Always this charity had been given on a hit-or-miss basis. St. Vincent de Paul was one of the very first to organize it. Wherever the work of the two Confraternities spread, the practice of street begging became unnecessary and was forbidden by civil authority.

When this work was well launched Vincent went back to the de Gondis. The Duke de Gondi was in charge of the galleys, or warships. These ships were propelled by galley slaves who rowed in unison. Vincent became interested in the plight of these miserable men. He persuaded the Duke to provide hospitals and medical care for them and to improve the conditions in the prisons from which they came. Vincent himself often visited the galleys, consoling the men and hearing their confessions.

In 1625 the first home of the Congregation of the Mission was opened and Vincent left the de Gondis to live there. In 1632 the Congregation obtained a permanent home at St. Lazare in Paris. Here Vincent made his headquarters for the remainder of his life.

The Ladies of Charity in Paris were mostly wealthy women and members of the nobility. Their social obligations often prevented them from visiting the poor families in person, so they sent their servants instead. This was not very satisfactory; also the work among the poor had grown to such proportions that the Ladies could no longer take care of it all. Vincent was convinced that there should be an organization of women who could give all their time to this work. With the help of Louise de Marillac (St. Louise), a wealthy and distinguished widow, he started the Daughters of Charity in 1633. The young women who were admitted to this organization were to work among the poor and to strive for great personal holiness. There was no idea of a religious institute at first. This idea developed gradually. The blue habit and white cornet that were eventually adopted by the Daughters of Charity of St. Vincent de Paul are now known throughout the world.

In 1633, during the Thirty Years' War, eastern France was invaded and pillaged by mercenary troops. The results were poverty, hunger, and disease. Vincent organized what would now be called "war relief" and did much to alleviate suffering. Some of his missionary priests and some of his Daughters lost their lives while fighting pestilence.

In 1634 Vincent organized the Confraternity of the Hotel Dieu to care for the sick in hospitals.

One night as Vincent was walking along a street in Paris he saw a man crippling a helpless child. He was doing this so that the child would be more pitiable and so would receive more money from his begging. Vincent's heart could not stand such terrible injustice, and so he started a home for foundlings, with the Daughters of Charity in charge.

He also started a home for the aged. In this home the husband and wife were not compelled to separate in order to receive care, as was the case in most homes at that time.

There is scarcely a work of charity that is known today that was not undertaken by St. Vincent more than three centuries ago. He cared for the poor and the sick, for abandoned infants, for orphans, for prisoners. He arranged vocational training for boys and girls. In the care of the aged he was far ahead of his time, as he was in war relief. He organized his charities so that the people who needed assistance would continue to get it.

Vincent's work was inspired by Christian ideals. Always the souls of the afflicted were cared for along with their bodies. Those who did the work were taught to recognize the poor, the sick, and the helpless as the suffering members of Jesus Christ.

Where did Vincent get the money for his many charities? The men and women who belonged to the Confraternities of Charity collected funds. The king, queen, and nobles contributed. Civic organizations lent aid. Ordinary people in all walks of life sent in their contributions. Vincent made use of the newspapers and magazines to make his needs known, and the readers responded generously.

Toward the end of his life Vincent suffered much from ill health. In the autumn of 1661 he died calmly in his chair. He was 84 years old. He was beatified in 1729 and canonized in 1737. In 1885 Pope Leo XIII proclaimed him patron of all charitable societies.

OTHER SAINTS OF THE SAME NAME:

St. Vincent Kadlubek, died 1223. Bishop of Cracow. Feast, March 8.
St. Vincent Ferrer, 1350–1419. Dominican miracle worker. Feast, April 5.
St. Vincent Maria Strombi, 1745–1824. Passionist, Bishop of Tolentino. Feast, January 1.

ST. ROSE OF LIMA, 1586–1617
Feast: August 30

EQUIVALENTS: Rosa, Rosalia, Rosalie, Rosalind, Rosamund, Roseline, Rosetta, Rosette, Rosina, Rosita, Rosalyn, Rosel, Roselle, Rosemarie, Rosemary, Rhoda

---

Rose of Lima, the first canonized saint in all America, is extraordinary even for a saint. She is tremendous.

Rose was a beautiful, joyous creature who seemed born to have her own way and to live in luxury. But she always followed God's way rather than her own, and she lived a life of poverty and incredible penance. Her whole life was penitential and expiatory, from her earliest years till her last breath. She had an intense love for our Lord, an overwhelming sense of the evil of sin, and a consuming desire to save sinners from hell. She could not be the missionary she longed to be, so she turned to penance instead, saying: "As I cannot do any good, is it not just that I should suffer whatever I am capable of suffering?"

She was born at Lima, the capital of Peru, in 1586. She was of Spanish extraction, her parents being Gaspar and Maria de Flores, decent people of moderate means. She was christened Isabel but was commonly called Rose, a name she later took in Confirmation.

From her earliest years Rose chose the path of suffering. At the age of three she injured her finger badly and endured the suffering in silence without telling her parents. When the injury was discovered, a physician found it necessary to remove a fingernail. She endured the operation wide-eyed but tearless.

As Rose reached her teens, her father lost most of his money in a gold-mining venture. The family, which included eleven children, was impoverished. Rose helped to support the family by selling flowers from her own garden and by doing embroidery work. After the day's work she spent hours in prayer and in acts of penance.

Maria de Flores hoped that her beautiful daughter would marry into one of the wealthy and prominent families of Peru. She arranged it so that many prospective mothers-in-law had the opportunity of seeing and admiring Rose. The girl, however, felt that God had called her to a life of virginity. When she was about seventeen, she retired to a hut in the garden to work, pray, and do penance. When she was twenty she joined the Third Order of St. Dominic. There was no Dominican convent in Lima, so she continued to live in the hut in the garden.

Rose, with other Dominican Tertiaries, engaged in many works of charity. She chose for herself the care of the most neglected and abandoned women, whether Indian, Negro, or Spanish. She sought them out, brought them to her family's house, and cared for them regardless of their condition. Cancers, ulcers, and hideous sores were dressed personally by Rose. Indian women were likely to be the most abandoned, and Rose gave much of her time to them. All of this was most disgusting to Maria de Flores, but God inspired Rose with ways of overcoming her mother's objections. Almost all the women died while in Rose's care; there was seldom the consolation of sending them away cured.

The girl's rosy cheeks and fair complexion faded, and she became pale and emaciated. When she was going to church with her mother one day, she heard someone remark about her changed appearance and the sanctity which it seemed to indicate. She was horrified because she was afraid such words might encourage spiritual pride. She begged God to restore her youthful freshness, so that she might work and fast in secret. Her prayer was answered.

For years Rose received Communion three times a week. She would have liked to receive daily, but custom forbade a girl to go out — even to church — unless accompanied by an older woman. Her mother could not, or would not, accompany her to church more

out. Rose would not accept a mattress, however, and compromised on plain boards for the duration of her illness.

After this illness Rose left her hut and lived at the home of friends. Her austerities were mitigated for a time, by order of her confessor. Rose knew that the Lent of 1617 would be her last on earth, and so she secured permission to resume her penances. She knew that she would die on the feast of St. Bartholomew and that during her last illness she would suffer such torments as she had never endured before.

Toward the end of July, 1617, Rose visited her hut, where her mother heard her singing more joyously than ever. On July 31 she became intensely ill. A week later she suffered parching thirst, but the doctor forbade water. On the night of August 23, Rose asked that the wooden cross be placed in her bed so that she might die on it.

During her illness she was observed in periods of ecstasy. Upon coming out of one, she told her confessor that she could tell him about the wonders that God has prepared in heaven for His saints. After saying farewell and asking God to comfort her mother, Rose said three times, "Jesus, be with me," and expired. It was a few minutes after midnight on the feast of St. Bartholomew.

Strangely, the mother did not give way to tears. Instead she was filled with great joy and hurried to another room to conceal this feeling. The whole house was filled with joy, and so was the town. By common consent there was no mourning.

So many miracles followed immediately upon the death of Rose that the people of Lima demanded her immediate canonization. But a recent papal ruling required fifty years between death and canonization. She was canonized in 1671, the first person in all America to be so honored.

OTHER SAINTS OF THE SAME NAME:

St. Rose Elizabeth, d. about 1130. Hermitess. Feast, December 13.
St. Rosalia, 1130–1160. Patroness of Palermo, Italy. Feast, September 4.
St. Rose of Viterbo, 1235–1253. Franciscan tertiary. Feast, March 6.
St. Roseline, d. 1329. Prioress of a Carthusian convent. Feast, January 17.

ST. ISAAC JOGUES, S.J., 1607–1646, and
ST. CHARLES GARNIER, S.J., 1606–1649

Feast: September 26

EQUIVALENTS OF ISAAC: None
EQUIVALENTS OF CHARLES: Cahil, Carel, Carleton, Carlo, Carlos, Charlet, Charlot, Carl, Carol, Carroll, Carlton, Karl, Karol.
FEMININE: Carol, Caroline, Carolyn, Carola, Carry, Charlotte, Charlene

A fleet that sailed from France in the year 1636 carried a small band of newly ordained Jesuits who had volunteered to work in the wilderness of North America. These well-educated, cultured Frenchmen were leaving home, family, safety, and comfort to work among the savages of New France. They knew they faced great hardships and possible martyrdom. Father Isaac Jogues and Father Charles Garnier were two members of this band.

Isaac Jogues was born at Orleans in 1607, of a solid middle class family. Charles Garnier was born in Paris in 1605. Both young men had to overcome strong parental opposition before they could enter the Society of Jesus. Both men had great devotion to the Blessed Mother, and Garnier had made a vow to uphold her Immaculate Conception until death. This was more than 200 years before the doctrine of the Immaculate Conception was defined.

When the fleet docked at Quebec, capital of New France, Garnier and others were sent at once to the mission which the Jesuits had established among the Hurons, at the end of Georgian Bay. There they joined Father John Brebeuf, S.J., who for a time had been the only missioner at this outpost. A few months later, Father Jogues also came to the Huron mission. One of the first tasks of these missionaries was to learn the very difficult Huron language. Father Garnier amazed even the Indians themselves by learning the language within six months.

Although the Hurons were enemies of the Iroquois and allies of the French, this fact did not guarantee the French missionaries a warm welcome. The Hurons were savages, steeped in superstition. Moreover, the medicine men did not wish to give up their hold on the people, and so they used every opportunity to discredit the priests. The Hurons lived in great filth, and this filth brought about frequent epidemics, for which the priests were blamed. Adult conversions were rare at first; the missionaries baptized mostly dying persons, especially dying children. This made the Hurons even more suspicious. "Every time they pour water on a person, that person dies," they said.

A council of twenty-eight Huron villages was called, and it was decided that the missionaries must die. Father Brebeuf invited the Indians to a farewell feast. Then he spoke to them eloquently of life and death. The Indians were so impressed that they decided to spare the Father and his companions. They were safe for the time being, but the threat of death hung over them constantly.

Using the Georgian Bay missions as a base, the Jesuits ranged far afield, among many tribes besides the Hurons. Father Jogues and Father Garnier traveled together among the Petans. Father Jogues and another companion went as far as Sault Ste. Marie and were the first white men to reach this point, a thousand miles from the Atlantic coast. Father Garnier paid several visits to the Tobacco nation. He was turned away at first but his persistence was to pay off, and in time he would be invited to make his home among the Tobacco Indians.

The first adult was baptized in 1637, more than eighty were baptized in 1639, and sixty in 1641. This was not spectacular progress, but it was encouraging.

Father Jogues volunteered to go to Quebec on an important errand in the summer of 1642. He took along a party of forty, including several lay helpers and a number of Indians, both Christian and non-Christian. When the party was near Three Rivers, on the return trip, it was attacked by a band of Mohawks, fiercest of the Five Nations that comprised the Iroquois confederation.

Captors and prisoners reached the Mohawk village of Ossernon (now Auriesville, N. Y.) on the eve of the Feast of the Assumption, 1642. Days and weeks of torture followed. The prisoners were beaten till they fell to the ground, then they were propped up and beaten again. Indian women chewed away parts of their fingers. One Indian woman sawed off Father Jogues's thumb with a clam shell. They were staked to the ground, and Indian children threw hot coals on their naked flesh. Rene Goupil, a lay assistant to Father Jogues, made the Sign of the Cross on the forehead of a child and for this he was tomahawked on September 29. He was saying the Rosary when he was struck. Father Jogues gave him absolution as he died.

The Dutch at Fort Orange (now Albany, N. Y.) had been supplying the Indians with guns and fire water so that they would harass the French, but the plight of Father Jogues aroused their sympathy. They smuggled him aboard a boat and took him to the safety of New Amsterdam on Manhattan Island. From there he was able to book passage for France on a small ship that barely withstood the winter gales.

On Christmas Day, 1642, Father Jogues reached the Jesuit college at Rennes and told the superior that he had come from New France.

"Then perhaps you can tell me something about Father Jogues," said the superior. "We heard that he had been captured by Indians."

The visitor held out his mangled hands and said: "I am Jogues."

Father Jogues thought that he would never be able to say Mass again because his hands were so badly mangled. However, Pope Urban VII gave him special permission to do so, saying: "It would be unjust if a martyr of Christ should not drink the blood of Christ."

Father Jogues could have remained in France, but he was burning with a desire to get back to the Indians. When he arrived in Quebec, Governor Montmagny asked him if he would undertake a peace mission to the Iroquois. The Five Nations, armed with guns from the Dutch, had become exceedingly powerful and planned to eliminate the other Indians and the French from the eastern part of North America. No doubt they eventually planned to turn on the English, too, and then the Dutch. Father Jogues was to try to persuade them to live in peace with their neighbors and avoid useless bloodshed. The priest gladly accepted the mission and was received with honor by the very people who had tortured him the year before. The negotiations went well and Jogues went back to Quebec to report that his mission had been successful. He left behind him in Ossernon a box of religious objects, because he planned to return to the village.

The Mohawks had a bad crop, and this was followed by an epidemic. They blamed these things on evil spirits in the box. When Father Jogues returned with a layman, Jean Lalande, the two were taken prisoners. The Mohawks debated as to the course they should follow. Some were for honoring the peace and freeing the prisoners. While the debate went on, a young brave took matters into his own hands and tomahawked Father Jogues as he was entering a cabin. He died instantly. His head was cut off and placed on a pole facing the route by which he had come. The next day Jean Lalande was also tomahawked and beheaded. This was in late October, 1646.

The martyrdom of Father Jogues sealed the fate of the Hurons who now had twenty-four Jesuits working among them and were gradually becoming a Christian nation. The Iroquois wiped out one Huron village after another. Father Antony Daniel, S.J., was killed by Indian arrows on July 4, 1648. Father Brebeuf and his companion, Father Gabriel Lalemant, S.J., were captured March 16, 1649, and died after undergoing unspeakable tortures.

Father Jogues and Father Garnier had crossed the ocean together in 1636, but their paths had been different. Father Jogues's journeys had carried him thousands of miles, even back to France for a short time. Father Garnier had never left the mission country. Father Jogues had shown his love of God by bravely enduring terrible tortures. Father Garnier showed his by his zeal, his patience, and his mortifications. Merely living in the wilderness and eating the scanty fare of the Indians would have been great penance, but he did more. He slept on the bare ground even when a more comfortable bed was available. He wore a girdle with iron points which dug into his skin. He scourged himself with a wire whip on which were sharp points.

Because he was of a slight build and seemingly frail, his superior asked him if he wished to give up the life of a missionary. Three days before his death Father Garnier replied that he would give it up, if necessary, in the spirit of obedience, "but otherwise, I will never come down from the cross on which His goodness has placed me."

Before the end of 1649 the Iroquois penetrated as far as the Tobacco nation and fell on the village where Father Garnier had his mission. The result was a slaughter. Father Garnier, unmindful of his own fate, hurried about giving absolution to the Christians and baptizing the children. He was shot down by the musket of an Iroquois. He tried to reach a dying man whom he thought he could help, but he did not have strength enough to make it. He was killed by a hatchet blow that penetrated to the brain. This was on the eve of the Feast of the Immaculate Conception.

Father Noel Chabanel, the companion of Father Garnier, was absent from the mission when the massacre took place. When he heard the news he started back. On the way he was killed by a Huron apostate.

The eight martyrs mentioned in this sketch were canonized in 1930. They are SS. John de Brebeuf, Isaac Jogues, Antony Daniel, Gabriel Lalemant, Charles Garnier, Noel Chabanel, Rene Goupil, and Jean Lalande. They are the first North American saints. A great shrine at Midland, Ontario, honors the five who were martyred in Canada, and another great shrine at Auriesville, New York, honors the three who were martyred there. The saintly Mohawk girl, Venerable Kateri Tekakwitha, is also honored at Auriesville, because she was born there. This reminds us that the Iroquois later came to include many Catholics, and one of these may some day be declared a saint.

OTHER SAINTS NAMED ISAAC:

St. Isaac of Constantinople, died 410. Abbot, founder of the Dalmatian monastery in Constantinople. Feast, May 30.

St. Isaac of Spoleto, died 550. Hermit on Monte Luco in Italy. Feast, April 11.

St. Isaac of Cordova, died 852. Martyred by Mohammedans in Cordova, Spain. Feast, June 3.

OTHER SAINTS NAMED CHARLES:

Bl. Charles of Blois, 1320–1364. Prince and soldier. Feast, September 29.

St. Charles Borromeo, 1538–1584. Cardinal, Archbishop of Milan, reformer. Feast, November 4.

Bl. Charles of Sezze, 1613–1670. Franciscan lay brother remarkable for simplicity and charity. Feast, January 19.

Bl. Charles Lwanga, died 1886. Negro page to a wicked native king, martyred in Uganda, Africa. Feast, June 3.

Saint of the Sacred Heart

ST. MARGARET MARY, 1647–1690
Feast: October 17

EQUIVALENTS: Gredel, Greta, Grita, Gretchen, Madge, Magda, Maisie, Margery, Marjorie, Marguerite, Pearl

Love of God had grown cold in seventeenth-century France. The great religious fervor of the Middle Ages was gone. The religious unity of the Western world had been shattered by the Protestant Revolt. Thousands of French people who remained in the Church were affected by the teachings of a Catholic bishop named Jansen whose writings had brought about a sort of Puritanism within the Church. As a result of these and other developments there was no longer the great love of God in France that there had once been.

God could have let the world suffer the results of its own indifference. But, in His great mercy, He intervened to rekindle the love of the people for Him. He offered the Sacred Heart of Jesus, overflowing with love for us, as a symbol to the people. As His instruments he used a humble nun, St. Margaret Mary Alacoque, and her adviser, Blessed Claude de la Columbiere. (It is worth noting that St. John Eudes, who preached devotion to the Hearts of Jesus and Mary, also lived in France at this time.)

Margaret Alacoque was born at Lautecour, a small town in Burgundy, on July 22, 1647. She was the fifth of seven children of Claude and Philiberte Alacoque. When she was eight years old her father died, and she was sent to a boarding school conducted by the Urbanists. She was attracted by the life of the nuns, and they were so impressed by her piety that they obtained permission for her to make her First Communion at the age of nine, which was early in those days.

When Margaret was ten she was stricken with a kind of rheumatic ailment that rendered her helpless and caused her intense pain. In the course of her illness she was taken back to the family home at Lautecour. She suffered from this illness for four years, during which time her thoughts turned more and more toward God. She was cured of the disease — miraculously it seemed — after she promised to become a daughter of Mary, a nun.

She was cured of her illness only to have another kind of suffering thrust upon her. The family estate came under the management of an in-law. This arrangement was necessary because Margaret's mother, Philiberte, was physically weak, lacking in initiative, and unskilled in business matters. The result was that Margaret and Philiberte were treated worse than servants in their own house. "The heaviest of my crosses," Margaret said later, "was my inability to lighten those laid upon my mother." Philiberte looked forward to the day when her eldest son would take over the management of the estate. But the young man died. Then her second son died, and the third one became a priest.

Margaret grew up to become a very attractive young lady. She was small, slight of build, and graceful. The fine features of her lovely face were set off by a pair of hazel eyes under heavy but beautifully arched eyebrows. She was quick in her movements, sensitive and affectionate, charming and gay.

Philiberte urged Margaret to marry so that the two of them could escape what the older woman considered an intolerable situation in the home. To please her mother Margaret entered upon a social life which, to her surprise, she began to enjoy.

When Margaret was about twenty-two she was confirmed and took the name Mary. This reminded her that she had not kept her promise to enter a convent. This was a dark period in Margaret's life. The social activities she once enjoyed were no longer satisfying. She felt that God was calling her to enter the convent, but she could not leave her ailing mother. The situation in the home was still as bad as ever. In addition to all this, her mother was accusing her of selfishness and indifference because she had turned down several proposals of marriage.

Things took a turn for the better eventually. Margaret's brother Chrysostom — the fourth oldest boy in the family — came of age, married a fine woman, and took over management of the estate. To the immense relief of Margaret he said that he was able and willing to take care of the mother. On June 20, 1671, Margaret entered the Visitation Convent in the village of Paray-le-Monial.

As a novice, Margaret Mary made more than the usual number of mistakes. She broke dishes right and left in her eagerness to handle them carefully. She was so anxious to serve a sick sister properly that she fell down the stairs with a tray. She was sweeping a corridor when the community bell rang; so eager was she to answer promptly that she left a broom and a pile of dust in front of the chapel door, where it promptly fell under the eye of the Mother Superior. A pair of donkeys ran all over the vegetable garden while she was supposed to be keeping them out of it.

On the other hand, Margaret was able to kneel for hours at a time when the Blessed Sacrament was exposed, totally oblivious of her surroundings. Her awkwardness in practical matters, combined with her great piety, caused her superior and the older sisters to wonder if she were in the right place. Her profession was delayed, and this caused Margaret Mary great sorrow.

Margaret Mary had been in the convent only two and a half years, and was still considered a newcomer, when she received the first revelation concerning the Sacred Heart. On December 27, 1673 — the Feast of St. John the Beloved Disciple — she was kneeling at the grill before the Blessed Sacrament exposed. Suddenly she felt herself suffused by the presence of God. She heard our Lord inviting her to take the place that St. John occupied at the Last Supper. Jesus told her that the love of His Heart must spread, and that she should be the instrument by which it would be done.

This was the first in a long series of revelations to Margaret Mary.

In all, there were to be about forty revelations, four of which, including the first, were to be major ones.

When Margaret Mary told her superior, Mother de Saumaise, about her mystical experience she was given a sharp reprimand for her presumption. Overwrought by all that had happened, Margaret became desperately ill. Mother de Saumaise said: "If God cures you, I will take it as a sign that all you experience comes from Him, and I will allow you to do what our Lord wants in honor of His Sacred Heart."

Margaret was cured, but this did not end her troubles. The superior decided to have her questioned by a group of theologians. These priests announced that Margaret was the victim of a delusion.

The revelations went on, but few in the community believed Margaret. For two years she suffered a lack of understanding from the sisters, from her superior, and from her confessor.

Our Lord told Margaret Mary that His Heart was to be honored under the form of a Heart of flesh. He showed her His Heart on a throne of flames and surrounded by thorns with a cross above it. He said that in return for His great love for mankind He received for the most part nothing but indifference. He asked her to make up for this ingratitude as best she could by receiving Communion frequently especially on the First Friday of each month and by an hour's vigil every Thursday night before the Blessed Sacrament in memory of His agony and desertion at Gethsemani.

While making these requests our Lord also told Margaret Mary that she was to "do nothing without the approval of those who guide you," and those who guided her did not believe in the revelations. This caused Margaret Mary great suffering.

At the end of two years a learned Jesuit priest, Claude Colombière, came to the small Jesuit house at Paray-le-Monial. Father Colombière became the confessor of the Visitation nuns. He had been slated to go to the University of Paris as a professor, but someone had persuaded his superior that he needed humbling, so instead of going to Paris he was "buried" in this obscure town. Thus Margaret Mary secured the understanding adviser she so badly needed.

While Father Colombière was still in Paray-le-Monial the final revelation, often called the Great Apparition, took place. This was during the Octave of Corpus Christi, 1675. Our Lord showed Margaret Mary His Heart and said: "Behold the Heart which has so loved men that it has spared nothing, even exhausting and consuming itself in testimony of its love. Instead of gratitude I receive from most only indifference."

He asked that a feast of reparation to His Heart be established on the Friday after the octave of Corpus Christi.

By way of encouraging His servants in the practice of devotion to the Sacred Heart, our Lord said: "I promise that My Heart shall abundantly shed the gifts of its divine love upon those who render it this homage and induce others to render it."

Claude Colombière did not stay at Paray long, but he was there long enough to be convinced that Margaret Mary's experiences were genuine. He became an ardent preacher of devotion to the Sacred Heart and deserves the title "Apostle of the Sacred Heart." After leaving Paray, Father Colombière went to England where he spent two years as the chaplain of the Queen. King Charles II of England died a Catholic, and perhaps his acquaintance with Father Colombière had something to do with this.

In 1677 Margaret Mary had one of the greatest trials of her life. Our Lord asked her to offer herself as a victim for the shortcomings of some of the nuns in her community and for their ingratitude toward the Sacred Heart. So the sister of only five years' standing had to kneel before her sisters in religion and tell them that she was appointed to be victim for their failings.

In June, 1678, Margaret Mary wrote to Mother de Saumaise, her former superior: ". . . my whole life, body and soul, is nothing but a cross. Yet I cannot complain, nor do I desire any other consolation than that of not having any in this world and of living hidden away in Jesus Christ crucified, suffering and unknown. . . ."

In 1681 Claude Colombière came back to Paray for the sake of his health. He had a few more conferences with Margaret Mary before he died. He has been beatified and we honor him as Blessed Claude Colombière. A private journal that he had written was read aloud to the community, and for the first time all the sisters learned the true story of the revelations. The experience was embarrassing for Margaret Mary, but after that there was little or no opposition to her within the community.

Margaret Mary served for a year as novice mistress (1684–1685). During this time she was permitted to introduce devotion to the Sacred Heart among her charges. The first real triumph of the devotion took place on June 21, 1689, when the Feast of the Sacred Heart was observed for the first time in the Visitation convent at Paray. The Jesuit Father Rolin was in Paray at the time. He helped spread the devotion to the other Visitation convents in France and to the various houses of the Society of Jesus.

Margaret Mary wrote: "I shall die happy now that the Sacred Heart of my Saviour is beginning to be known."

Early in 1690 she was heard to say: "I shall not live much longer, since I no longer suffer." She died in October of that year.

No other life shows so clearly the sanctifying power of suffering combined with great love of God.

The feast of the Sacred Heart was extended to the whole world in 1856 by Pope Pius IX. The same pope beatified Margaret Mary in 1864. She was canonized in 1920.

OTHER SAINTS OF THE SAME NAME:

St. Margaret of Antioch. Martyr of the fourth century. Feast, July 20.
St. Margaret, Queen of Scotland, died 1093. Feast, June 10.
St. Margaret of Hungary, died 1270. Feast, January 26.
St. Margaret of Cortona, 1247–1297. Penitent who became a Franciscan. Feast, February 22.

ST. GERARD MAJELLA, 1726–1755
Feast: October 16

EQUIVALENTS: Gerald, Geraud, Gerhard, Giraud

More and more mothers are turning to St. Gerard Majella as their special patron. Women who have been childless for years have prayed to St. Gerard and have been rewarded with healthy children. Women who have been warned of serious danger to themselves and their unborn children have called upon this saint in full confidence and have had the happiness of holding normal children in their arms. Mothers have learned to rely upon St. Gerard in all their problems regarding the bearing or rearing of children. It would seem that God has reserved a special role for St. Gerard in our days when mothers are so much in need of his help.

This saint who is the Patron of Mothers never married. He found his vocation in being a lay brother. Pope Pius IX tells us that Gerard is "a perfect model for those of his own condition, the lay brothers."

Gerard was born at Muro, fifty miles south of Naples, on April 6, 1726. He was frail, and his parents had him baptized the day he was born. His mother testified after his death: "My child's only happiness was in church, on his knees before the Blessed Sacrament." She said that he would stay there for hours forgetting that it was time for dinner. "In the house, he prayed all day. He was born for Heaven."

When Gerard was twelve his father died. He left school and became an apprentice to a tailor. The tailor himself was kind to Gerard, but the journeyman took a strange dislike to the inoffensive boy and showed his anger by blows and curses. Gerard bore the treatment with patience.

Gerard learned his trade very well and then applied for admittance to the Capuchins. They refused him because of his poor health. He then became a servant for the Bishop of Lacedogna, a man exceedingly hard to please. Gerard served the Bishop faithfully and without complaint till the latter died in 1745. Then he set up his own tailor shop. One third of his earnings went to his mother and his three sisters; one third went to the poor; what remained after he took out his own meager expenses went in stipends for Masses for the souls in Purgatory. He spent several hours of every night in prayer in the cathedral.

When Gerard was twenty-three a mission was given in Muro by some priests of the newly founded society of the Most Holy Redeemer. Gerard offered himself to these Redemptorists as a lay brother. Again he was refused because of his poor health. He persisted. Finally, Father Cafaro sent him to the Redemptorist house at Iliceto with the note: "I send you a useless brother."

This "useless" lay brother was soon doing the work of four men. He worked so hard that it was said of him: "Either he is a fool or a great saint." The founder of the Redemptorists, Alphonsus Liguori, now St. Alphonsus, knew which he was and shortened his novitiate. When Gerard made the usual vows of a religious he added one of his own: Whenever he had a choice of two or more possible courses, he would choose the way he considered most pleasing to God.

Gerard advanced rapidly in sanctity. His prayer life was continual and his spirit of obedience was perfect. One day Gerard was praying before the tabernacle and a priest who was nearby heard him cry out: "Lord, let me go, I pray Thee! I have work that I must do!"

During the three years that Gerard was a lay brother he worked as a tailor and sickroom attendant, he begged for the house, and he traveled with the missionary priests. He was of great assistance to the priests in bringing sinners to repentance. On at least twenty occasions he did this by revealing to the sinners the secrets of their consciences.

It was also during these three years that a number of supernatural phenomena took place. Sometimes while he was meditating he rose several feet above the ground. He knew about the murder of the Archpriest of Muro at the very time it happened fifty miles away. Several times he was seen and spoken to in two places at the same time. He restored life to a boy who had fallen from a high cliff. He blessed the scanty wheat supply of a poor family and it lasted till the next harvest.

The rector once looked for Gerard in his cell and could not find him. Later he saw Gerard in church and asked him where he had been.

"In my cell," Gerard replied.

"What do you mean? I looked in your cell twice and I didn't see you."

Gerard then said reluctantly: "I was in the cell but I was in retreat and wanted to meditate without being disturbed. I asked God to make me invisible."

"Well, I forgive you this time," said the rector. "But don't say that kind of prayer again."

No person has ever been canonized because of marvels that were performed through him. Gerard is no exception. It was not because of the marvels that Gerard was canonized but because of his great holiness.

In 1754 Neira Caggiano, a girl whom Gerard had befriended, determined to destroy the reputation of her benefactor. In a letter to Alphonsus Liguori she accused Gerard of sins of impurity with the younger daughter of a family at whose house Gerard sometimes stayed on his missionary journeys. Alphonsus called Gerard before him, but Gerard did not deny the charge. Alphonsus could not believe that Gerard was guilty but he was forced to take action. He forbade Gerard to receive Holy Communion and ordered him to leave the monastery. Gerard's friends pleaded with him to deny the charge, but Gerard merely said: "God will provide." Those words were the motto of his entire life. Some time later Neira became dangerously ill and retracted the false story. Gerard had not been depressed in the time of trial, and he was not elated in the hour of his vindication. In both cases he felt that the will of God had been done.

Gerard was always in poor health and when he was seized by violent hemorrhages of the lungs it was evident that he did not have long to live. He had this sign placed on the door of the room where he lay on his deathbed: "The will of God is done here, as God wills it and as long as He wills it." He died on the day and at the hour he had foretold, just before midnight, October 15, 1755. Thousands came to view the body of the "saint" who had helped them so much. After his death miracles attributed to his intercession were reported from all over Italy. He was beatified in 1893 and canonized in 1904.

St. Gerard has been invoked as the patron of workingmen, of vocations, and of good confessions. But he is known principally for his intercession in behalf of mothers and children.

During his life there were two examples of his remarkable power to help mothers. As he was leaving the Pirofalo home one day, the young daughter ran to give him a handkerchief he had forgotten. He said: "Keep it. It will be useful some day." Years later when the girl had married and was in danger of death from childbirth she called for the handkerchief. Almost immediately she delivered a healthy baby. On another occasion the prayers of Gerard were requested by a mother when she and her unborn child were in danger. Both the mother and the child came through the danger safely.

The devotion of mothers to St. Gerard increased greatly after his death. A witness at his beatification testified that Gerard was known as the "Saint of happy delivery." Many hospitals have dedicated their maternity wards to him and distribute St. Gerard medals and leaflets to mothers awaiting delivery. Many mothers have named their children after their patron.

Various reasons have been brought forth to explain why God has given St. Gerard such power to help mothers. Perhaps the best explanation is his complete trust in God, a virtue needed by every mother.

OTHER SAINTS OF THE SAME NAME:

St. Gerard, 935–994. Bishop of Toul in France. Feast, April 23.

St. Gerard of Brogne, d. 959. Abbot of Brogne in Belgium. Feast, October 3.

St. Gerard, d. 1046. Martyr-bishop of Chzonad, apostle of the Hungarians. Feast, September 24.

Model of Reparation

BL. JULIE BILLIART, 1751–1816
Feast: April 8

EQUIVALENTS: Julia, Juliana, Jullienne, Juliette, Juliet

Twenty-two-year-old Julie Billiart was sewing in the kitchen of the family home in the village of Cuvilly, France, and talking with her father who was sitting nearby. Suddenly the quiet of the winter night was shattered as a stone came crashing through the window. Then Julie was horrified to see a gun barrel come through the window, pointed in the direction of her father. A piercing shot rang out.

This shot from an unknown enemy fortunately missed Jean-Francois Billiart, but it marked a turning point in the life of Julie. The shot, which was fired in the year 1774, was such a shock to her nervous system that she suffered in all her limbs. By 1782 she was a helpless cripple and she remained so until 1804. She suffered for thirty years, and for twenty-two of these thirty years she was almost completely helpless.

Julie had been so well known for her piety and for her charity, even before she was stricken, that the townspeople called her "The saint of Cuvilly." Now, she looked upon her afflictions as an extra gift to offer to God. Through her sufferings she offered reparation to the Sacred Heart of Jesus for all the sins of the world, especially for those committed against the Sacrament of the Altar.

The French Revolution broke out in 1789 and reached its height in the Reign of Terror of 1793–1794. Churches and convents were destroyed, and priests and religious put to death or sent into exile. Freethinkers ridiculed the existence of God. Sixteen nuns from the nearby Carmelite convent — all friends of Julie — were marched to the guillotine. Julie escaped a like fate only because friends hid her in a cart under some straw while a mob ransacked the house where she had been hiding. She changed residences frequently to avoid annoyance to her friends and betrayal by enemies of the Church. The frequent movings added to the pain that she would have been suffering anyway. Her malady was so aggravated that for several months she almost completely lost her power of speech.

In 1795, Julie wrote to a friend: "You wish me to speak of my wretched body. It is not worth the trouble, but, since you wish it, I will tell you that it is worth nothing, nothing at all. My days, thanks be to God, are full of suffering, and my nights are sometimes worse. But, my dear good friend, what are my sufferings compared with the love God has for me? Yes, I confess I am indeed happy when the good God gives me the grace to suffer much. Then I give a little share to all my good friends in the Faith, through the infinite merits of our good Saviour."

Her physical pain was far less acute than the pain of being deprived of Mass and Holy Communion, while enduring spiritual desolation. Julie had been permitted to make her First Communion at the age of nine, a very unusual privilege in those days, and at the age of twenty she had been permitted to receive Communion daily. But now, during the Revolution, priests were being hunted down like animals, and it was seldom that she could hear Mass or receive the sacraments.

During this dangerous period, Julie had a vision of the future Institute of Notre Dame. She saw Jesus on Calvary; gathered around the foot of His cross were a group of Sisters whose faces were so distinct that she recognized them years later when she met them. Before the vision faded, Julie heard a voice say: "Behold the spiritual daughters whom I give to you in the Institute which will be marked by my Cross." Often during the dark years that followed, Julie was strengthened by the memory of this vision.

At the Hotel de Blin, a hospital in Amiens where Julie was taken for safety during the Terror, she met Marie Louise Francoise Blin de Bourdon who was to be associated with her in all her future work. In 1797 Julie and Marie Louise moved to Bettencourt, and there they met Father Joseph Varin who was to encourage them in the founding of the Institute of Notre Dame. The persecution was coming to an end, and there was a great need for women who would help in the Christian education of the young. This apostolate had always been dear to the heart of Julie, and she had always engaged in it to the limit of her strength. In August, 1803, Julie and Marie Louise moved to a large house in Amiens and here, with the approval of the bishop, began the Institute of Notre Dame. The Institute was to devote itself primarily to the spiritual care of poor children but also to the Christian education of girls in all classes and to the training of religious teachers. Soon several postulants joined Julie and Marie Louise. An orphanage was opened and evening catechism classes were started. "My daughters," said Julie to the postulants, "think how few priests there are now, and how many poor children are sunk in the grossest ignorance. We must make it our task to win them back!"

In 1804 Pope Pius VII proclaimed a jubilee to celebrate the fact that the religious persecution in France had come to an end. Missions were held all over the country to rekindle the religious fervor that had been dimmed by the Revolution. Julie and her companions helped by teaching women and children to profit by the jubilee.

One of the most arduous workers among the priests giving the missions was Father Enfantin, who had been ordained in a barn during the Reign of Terror. One day Father Enfantin said to Mother Julie: "I am beginning a novena to the Sacred Heart today for a person in whom I am interested. Will you join me in it?"

Julie prayed earnestly for the unknown intention. The fifth day of the novena was the first day of June, month of the Sacred Heart. Toward evening, while Julie was sitting in the garden, Father Enfantin came to her and said: "Mother, if you have any faith, take one step in honor of the Sacred Heart of Jesus."

Instantly Julie took one step.

"Take another," said the priest. And she did.

"And another!"

Julie was completely cured of paralysis from that moment.

Her health restored, Julie threw herself into the work of the Institute with great vigor. Convents were opened at Namur, Ghent, Tournai, and other places until within Julie's lifetime there were ten of them.

There were some serious setbacks. Because of a misunderstanding the Bishop of Amiens virtually expelled Julie from the diocese. She moved to Namur and made her headquarters there. Later, the Bishop of Amiens acknowledged his error and invited Julie to return. This was not practical, and Namur remained the center of the Institute. Some of the houses of the Institute suffered greatly during the closing years of the Napoleonic Wars. The poverty that followed the French Revolution was also a great handicap.

God consoled Mother Julie during these troubles by revealing to her the future expansion of her work. God blessed her with the gift of healing, which she used in the terrible year of 1808 by curing twenty-three sisters who were desperately ill of typhoid. Her associates believed she also had the power of multiplying the necessities of life, a power of great value in those days of grinding poverty.

At the beginning of 1816 Mother Julie was failing in strength. In the evening of Palm Sunday, April 7, she was heard softly saying the *Magnificat*. After she finished it, she did not speak again. She died peacefully the next morning at two o'clock in the presence of the chaplain and a few Sisters.

Mother Julie was beatified on May 13, 1906, by Pope Pius X, who has since been canonized.

Blessed Mother Julie is usually remembered, and rightly, as the foundress of the Institute of Notre Dame de Namur. In the last twelve years of her life she performed a tremendous task in establishing the Institute on a firm foundation. In this regard, the Bishop of Namur said after her death: "Mère Julie was one of those souls who do more for the Church in a few years than could be done in a century by hundreds of others, however good, who lacked her apostolic spirit. . . ."

But we must not forget the thirty years during which Julie Billiart was a paralytic, and during which she was a model of reparation. Someone once said: "It is harder to endure than to act, harder to suffer than to do, harder to bear trials than to accomplish things. In action we are often helped by our feelings, carried along by excitement, stimulated by applause. In suffering we have, for the most part, a constant conflict with feeling; the mind is not excited as in action, but on the contrary is depressed by forced inaction."

Julie bore the years of inaction with patience and gave herself entirely to the will of God. She offered all to the Sacred Heart of Jesus in reparation for the sins of the world. She had the true spirit of reparation.

OTHER SAINTS OF THE SAME NAME:

St. Julia of Lisbon, fourth century. Martyr. Feast, October 1.

St. Julia of Saragossa, fourth century. Martyr. Feast, April 16.

St. Julia of Corsica, seventh century. Captive of Mohammedans. Feast, May 22.

St. Julia of Cornillon, 1192–1258. Instrument used by God to bring about the celebration of the Feast of Corpus Christi. Feast, April 5.

ST. CATHERINE LABOURÉ, 1806–1876
Feast: November 28

EQUIVALENTS: Catharine, Cathryn, Kate, Kitty, Karen, Karin, Kasia, Kathleen, Kathryn

---

The bell in the village church in Fain-les-Moutiers, France, rang out on May 3, 1806. The villagers heard the bell as they worked in their fields, in their homes, or in their shops. Without pausing in their work they reflected that within a few minutes there would be a new Christian in the village: the one-day-old daughter of Pierre and Louise Madeleine Labouré. The event seemed worthy of no more than passing notice. This was the ninth Labouré baby to be baptized. Within a few years there would be two more.

If the ringing of the bell attracted little attention, it was at least more attention than Catherine Labouré would receive during the remainder of her life. She was to live and die in obscurity: ignored, overlooked, held in low esteem. Her mission was to be a great one, but she was to accomplish it in secret.

Zoë, as Catherine was called within the family, was only nine and a half years old when her mother died. One day soon after that, the family servant saw her standing on a table, reaching up to embrace a statue of the Blessed Virgin. "It is you then," Zoë said, "who are going to be my mother."

There were only three girls in the family, while there were eight boys. For a time, Marie Louise, the eldest girl, managed the household for her father, while Zoë and her younger sister lived with an aunt. After two years Marie Louise went off to join the Daughters

184

of Charity of St. Vincent de Paul, and the two younger girls returned home. At the age of twelve Zoë was put in charge of the house. She had the help of one servant and of her younger sister, Antoinine. When Zoë was fifteen the servant left and was not replaced. In addition to the household work, Zoë often carried meals to her father and his hired men in the fields. Despite the hard work, she walked a mile and a half to Mass every morning, and she fasted two days a week. Her education was completely neglected; she was the only one of the eleven Labouré children who did not go to school.

One day, apparently in a dream, Zoë attended a Mass said by a priest she had never seen before. As he came down from the altar he looked at her with piercing eyes and beckoned to her. Frightened, she ran from the church. On the way home she stopped in to visit an invalid. There, she saw the same elderly, white-haired priest.

"My child," said the priest, "it is a good deed to look after the sick. You are running away from me now, but one day you will be glad to come to me. God has plans for you. Do not forget."

The significance of this dream did not become apparent till later.

Zoë had a strong desire to become, like her sister, a Daughter of Charity, but her father did not wish to give up a second daughter to the society. When she was twenty-two, he sent her to visit her married brother Charles who owned a restaurant in Paris. He thought that this would take her thoughts away from the religious life. She spent a year in Paris but found the life intolerable. Next, she went to visit another brother, Hubert, at Chatillon-sur-Seine. Hubert's wife, who conducted a fashionable school for young ladies, took a liking to Zoë. She taught Zoë the rudiments of reading and writing and encouraged her religious vocation.

One day, in Chatillon, Zoë visited a hospice under the care of the Daughters of Charity. While she waited in the parlor, she was startled by a portrait on the wall.

"Who is that?" she asked the Sister who came to see her.

"That is our founder, St. Vincent de Paul."

This was the priest Zoë had seen in the dream five years earlier! After that Zoë was more certain than ever of her vocation, and with the help of her sister-in-law she won her father's reluctant consent. She became a postulant in the House of the Daughters of Charity at Chantillon in January, 1830. After her probationary period, she was transferred to the novitiate of the Daughters of Charity at 132 (now 140) Rue du Bac in Paris. When she received her habit, she went back to her baptismal name and became Sister Catherine. In April and May, the Sisters made a novena in honor of St. Vincent. During this time Sister Catherine saw several visions of St. Vincent's heart. On Trinity Sunday, 1830, she had a vision of Christ the King. She told her confessor, Father Jean Marie Aladel, but he thought her visions were imaginary.

On July 18, 1830, the eve of the Feast of St. Vincent de Paul, Sister Catherine retired with a prayer that St. Vincent would obtain for her the privilege of seeing our Lady. At 11:30 she was awakened by a child who, in a voice of authority, told her to come to the chapel at once because the Blessed Virgin was waiting for her. Sister Catherine dressed quickly and hurried to the chapel which was ablaze with light. Led by the child, she went to the sanctuary. The child cried: "There is the Blessed Virgin!"

Catherine looked in the direction indicated and saw our Lady, clad in white, advance to the foot of the altar. She sat in the chair ordinarily occupied by the priest while giving a conference to the Sisters.

Catherine rushed forward and threw herself to her knees. She rested her clasped hands on the knees of the Blessed Virgin. It was "the sweetest joy of my life," she said later, "a delight beyond expression."

"My child," the Blessed Mother said, "God wishes you to undertake a mission. For it you will have much to suffer, but you will overcome that by recalling that you do so for the glory of God. . . ."

She talked with Catherine for about two hours, telling her many things that were for her ears alone, but also some things for the world at large. She said that the times were evil and that France and the whole world would suffer great calamities, but the two societies founded by St. Vincent — the Daughters of Charity and the Vincentian Fathers — would remain unharmed and would grow. She was quite specific in some of her forecasts, and Catherine understood that some of the calamities would take place soon and others in about forty years.

"My eyes are ever upon you," our Lady said to Catherine. "I shall obtain many graces for you. Special graces will be given to all who ask for them, but people must pray."

Catherine said nothing about the vision to her companions. She told only Father Aladel and pledged him to secrecy. He was inclined to disregard her story at first, but he was somewhat shaken when a revolution broke out in Paris a few days later and everything happened as Catherine said our Lady had foretold. Churches were profaned, convents were pillaged, priests were subjected to great indignities. The mother house in the Rue du Bac shook with gunfire and was surrounded by an angry mob, but, true to our Lady's word, it remained unharmed. (The other events foretold by our Lady, including the killing of the Archbishop of Paris, were to take place during the War of the Commune, 1871.)

On November 27, 1830, our Lady again appeared to Catherine in the chapel. She stood on a globe with shafts of light streaming down from gems on her fingers. Catherine understood that the globe represented France, the world, and each individual person. The lights represented graces which went to all who asked for them. From some of the gems there were no lights because some people failed to ask for graces. An oval frame enclosed our Lady, and around the top of the frame were the words: "O Mary, conceived without sin, pray for us who have recourse to thee." Then the picture turned around and Catherine saw on the reverse side a capital M with a cross above it; below the M were two hearts, one encircled by a crown of thorns, the other pierced by a sword. Catherine heard a voice tell her to have a medal struck on this model, promising great graces to all who wore it. This or a similar vision was repeated several times up to September, 1831.

Father Aladel did not know what to do. He did not have the authority to have a medal struck. Besides, it was to say "O Mary, conceived without sin . . ." and the Immaculate Conception was not then declared a dogma of the Church. (The promulgation of this doctrine was to come twenty-four years later.) He prayed for divine guidance and consulted the Archbishop of Paris. In June, 1832, the medals were struck and a few were distributed in Paris. The medal brought about such amazing results that it was soon in great demand. It became known as the Miraculous Medal. Everyone knew that the Blessed Virgin had revealed the medal to a Daughter of Charity, but only Father Aladel knew her name. Even the sisters with whom Catherine lived and worked did not know that she was the favored one, although they often speculated upon the subject.

A second specific request of our Lady was that a Confraternity of Children of Mary be established. "Tell him who is in charge of you, though he is not your superior, that before long he will be entrusted with the care of the community in a special way." Five years later Father Aladel was appointed Assistant to the Superior-General of the Vincentians. He made use of his new authority to organize the Children of Mary. In 1847 Pope Pius IX authorized the organization as a Confraternity with all the indulgences. Sister Catherine knew that the organization was spreading throughout Europe and the world, but she did not betray her joy.

Catherine Labouré, the chosen messenger of the Blessed Virgin Mary, was almost entirely unknown outside her community, and within the community she was considered a person of rather mediocre talents. The description of her in the archives reads: "Catherine Labouré. Strong. Of medium height. Can read and write after a fashion. Seems to have good character. Her mind and powers of judgment are not outstanding; she is pious. Tries hard to be virtuous." It was thought that she had talent enough to cook for the old men in the Hospice d'Enghien in Paris and she was sent there in 1831. She remained there until her death in 1876. The installation of the new cook took place without attracting much attention. The old men had been quick enough to complain when they did not like the food, but under Sister Catherine there was nothing to complain about, and they took the food for granted.

Sister Catherine found time for other things besides cooking. She performed many services for the old men. She took charge of the linen room and did wonders with her mending. The hen run and the dairy also came under her care, and she kept the accounts of these for thirty years. The spelling is strange in these accounts, but the handwriting is balanced and regular. Because she was so often seen in the back yard with the hens she became known by the somewhat scornful title: "Sister of the hen run."

In her later years she suffered from coughing spells and from painful arthritis. On every feast of the Blessed Virgin, she became ill or suffered in some manner. During the last sixteen years of her life she had a superior who was overly strict with her and reproached her for matters for which she was not responsible. Sister Catherine bore all such things with meekness and humility. The Blessed Virgin had said to her: "You will have much to suffer, but you will overcome that by realizing that you do so for the love of God. . . ."

But her greatest suffering came because the third request of the Blessed Virgin had not been carried out. In addition to the Miraculous Medal and the Children of Mary, our Lady wished a statue of herself holding the world in her hands and looking up as if she were offering it to God. She had appeared in this position during several apparitions.

Father Aladel moved slowly in the matter. He had some preliminary drawings made, but he died in 1865 before work on the statue could begin. Sister had to begin all over again with her new spiritual director, Father Chinchon. In 1876, he was moved to another post, and the statue still had not been made. Sister Catherine was miserable. She was now seventy years old and did not feel that she could start again with a third spiritual director. She first asked permission of the Blessed Mother and then sobbingly told her story to her superior, who had previously been so unsympathetic. It was the first time she had disclosed her secret to anyone except her spiritual adviser. The superior, her eyes now opened, gave her consent and ordered the work to go ahead at full speed. A model of the statue was made. Catherine trembled with joy when she saw it, but she also said: "Oh, but Our Lady was so much more beautiful than that!" The statue was completed and placed above the high altar where our Lady had appeared.

Sister Catherine's last duty had been performed. She had said that she would not live to see 1877, and she died on December 31, 1876. Today, her incorrupt body lies in state under the statue of the Virgin Most Powerful, the statue which she called the "torment" of her life.

On Sunday, July 27, 1947, the bells rang out from the dome of St. Peter's to celebrate the fact that Catherine Labouré was being added to the Church's roll of saints. The bells of Rome's 400 other churches took up the joyful clamor which reverberated from the city's seven hills.

And in the little village of Fain-les-Moutiers another bell rang, the same little bell which had announced Catherine Labouré's baptism in 1806.

OTHER SAINTS OF THE SAME NAME:

St. Catherine of Alexandria, 282–307. Virgin and martyr; patroness of philosophers and needleworkers. Feast, November 25.

St. Catherine of Sweden, 1331–1381. Daughter of St. Bridget of Sweden, friend of St. Catherine of Siena; she carried on her mother's work in founding a monastery in Vadstena. Feast, March 24.

St. Catherine of Siena, 1347–1380. Great mystic, instrumental in bringing about the return of the popes from Avignon to Rome. Feast, April 30.

St. Catherine of Genoa, 1447–1510. Widow who received revelations concerning purgatory. Feast, September 14.

ST. JOHN BOSCO, 1815–1889

Feast: January 31

EQUIVALENTS: Giovanni, Hansel, Ian, Ivan, Jan, Janek, Jesse, Jonathan, Johan, Johann, Juan, Shawn

---

"Oh look, an acrobat is going to do his tricks!" said one of the boys in the group that was walking toward the church.

"Yes," said John Bosco, who was 16 at the time. "He shouldn't be doing that so close to the church when it's time for services. I hope he won't draw anyone away from the instructions."

"But why shouldn't we stop and see his stunts?" asked another boy. "We have already gone to Mass today."

One after another the boys approved the idea. John saw that argument would be useless, so he went up to the acrobat.

"If you will wait till services are over, I'll challenge you to a contest in anything you wish."

The acrobat laughed at the idea of a mere boy challenging him, a professional. "All right," he said, "if you have any money to put up I'll accept your challenge."

John was a poor boy, barely able to pay his tuition, but his companions had enough money among them. And so the acrobat waited while the boys went off to instructions.

After instructions, John's classmates and others who were coming from the church gathered to see the contest. The first event was a half mile race to the turn in the road and back to the starting point. As the two approached the finish line the acrobat was ahead but it was obvious that he was winded. John, on the other hand, was breathing easily. He took a sudden spurt and crossed well ahead of his rival. The acrobat then challenged John to jump the stream at the edge of town. The acrobat jumped it, but John jumped farther.

And so it went in one event after another. Finally, in desperation, the acrobat staked everything on a tree climbing contest. "The winner will be the one who can climb to the highest point in that elm tree," he said. John agreed.

The acrobat climbed up and up till he reached a point where the tree swayed and cracked under his weight. No one could go higher without crashing to the ground. He laughed triumphantly when he reached the ground.

John nimbly climbed the tree until he had reached the point achieved by the other. It was true that no one could go higher. But suddenly those below him gasped in amazement. John was standing on his hands in the treetop. His feet were higher than the mark made by the acrobat.

Grudgingly, the acrobat handed John a large sum of money.

John refused to accept it. "Let's make a bargain," he said. "We'll call everything square if you agree not to perform your tricks while services are going on."

"Well, now, you're a real sport," said the man. "I happen to need that money very badly."

This story is typical of John Bosco. He was a boy, and later a man, of many accomplishments. He had great personal charm and great physical strength. He was an athlete, acrobat, juggler, tight rope walker, and ventriloquist. He used all these accomplishments in the service of God and especially for leading boys closer to God.

John Bosco's mother, Margaret, had married a widower with a nine-year-old son, Anthony. In 1813 her first son, Joseph, was born, and John was born in 1815. Two years later the father died. The Boscos had been poor even before this, but now they found it almost impossible to make a living from their small farm in northern Italy. From the moment he was able to do anything, John was made to work by his half brother, Anthony, who considered himself the head of the family. Anthony was ill-natured and resentful because he thought Margaret treated her own children better than she treated him.

In spite of her poverty, Margaret tried to help neighbors who were even less fortunate. John often went with her on her errands of mercy. While she took care of a sick person inside a poor cottage, he waited outside and gathered the children around him, teaching them the prayers that his mother had taught him.

When he was nine years old John had a dream in which he saw himself surrounded by a gang of fighting and blaspheming children. He tried to quiet them by arguing with them. When this failed, he went at them with his fists. Then a mysterious lady appeared and said to him: "Softly, softly . . . if you wish to win them! Take your shepherd's staff and lead them to pasture." As she spoke, the children were transformed into wild beasts and then into lambs. From that time, John realized that his vocation was to help poor boys, and that he was to do it with gentleness and love. He would begin with the boys in his own village.

John Bosco's work was cut out for him. There were few schools in Italy in those days, and poor boys found it almost impossible to secure an education. Jobs were also scarce and boys who did not live on a farm had little to do with their time. As a result they were constantly getting into trouble and were in grave danger of losing their souls. To make matters worse, the government of a large part of Italy was in the control of men who were enemies of religion and opposed even to having it taught.

When he was only nine, John began preparing himself for his vocation. He practiced juggling and tumbling and tightrope walking. He gave performances for the children of the neighborhood. Each performance began and ended with a prayer. During the "intermission" he gave his version of the Sunday sermon; not everyone walked the six miles to Mass as the Boscos did. As John's performances improved, his audiences became larger and larger.

Before long John knew that he wished to be a priest. Every time he mentioned this, his half brother, Anthony, would scoff. "And where do you think you're going to get the money for your education?" he would ask.

When Anthony decided one day to take his share of the family goods and set out for himself, there was peace in the family. John was able to attend school at Castelnuova, three miles away. By this time he was fifteen years old and the largest boy in his class. He was sneered at by some of the teachers who thought a boy who was that big and only a beginner must be very stupid. When he handed in perfect work he was accused of copying.

During this period, when he was very much discouraged, John Bosco had another dream in which the Blessed Virgin appeared to him and asked him to look after her flock of sheep. "There," she said, "I give it into your charge." After this he was sure that, despite all the difficulties, he would become a priest.

Somehow, Margaret Bosco scraped together money enough to send John to the Franciscan college at Chieri. The incident of the acrobat, told at the beginning of this sketch, took place soon after he started there. John made up for lost time and soon caught up with his classmates. He helped pay for his schooling by working at different jobs, and so he learned many skills that were not taught in school.

After graduating from the school in Chieri, John Bosco attended the diocesan seminary in Turin. On Sundays he gathered about him a number of neglected boys and taught them their catechism. At length he was ordained and became Don Bosco. (Italians call their priests "Don" as we call ours "Father.")

His first assignment was as chaplain of a girls' orphanage, but in his free time he sought out the boys who wandered the streets. In time, the boys came to seek him. A large classroom in the orphanage was set aside for the boys, and a place outdoors for recreation grounds. When the number of boys reached 300, the wealthy lady who supported the orphanage said they would have to leave. Three hundred noisy, lively boys were simply too much, she said.

For the next several years Don Bosco and his boys constantly moved their meeting place. Nobody, it seemed, wanted them for long. They were too noisy; they picked the flowers; they wore off the grass. When they were forced to move Don Bosco smiled and said to his boys: "Well, cabbages are made better by transplanting."

At last he rented a shed in a slum district of Turin. It wasn't much, but it looked wonderful to Don Bosco and his boys. Here at last they had a home. The new home was named the Oratory of St. Francis de Sales, because Don Bosco had a great devotion to this saint.

About this time the lady who supported the orphanage told him he would have to resign as chaplain if he did not give up his work with boys. With the bishop's permission, he resigned.

The boys set to work to convert the shed into a room that could be used as a chapel, classroom, study hall, and recreation center. They lowered the dirt floor so they would be able to stand upright. They built kneelers, benches, and tables.

Just when things were looking up for Don Bosco, he collapsed. The doctors said there was no hope for him. His boys, including boys who had seldom prayed in their lives, stormed heaven for him. They prayed; they begged prayers of others; they made sacrifices, and they promised to reform their lives if God would spare their priest. God listened to their prayers, and Don Bosco recovered.

He asked his mother to come and join him. He said he needed a mother for the boys. She came, but at what sacrifice! Margaret was getting along in years, and she had raised her own family. Now she had a "family" of several hundred boys. Moreover, she loved the country, and now she must live in the slums of a large city. Don Bosco rented the house that was on the same property with the shed and lived there with his mother and some of the boys. In time he was able to buy both the shed and the house.

Don Bosco proceeded to overcome every obstacle. Many of the boys could not study their catechism because they were illiterate. He taught them to read and write. He taught them trades so they would be able to make an honest living. There were not enough teachers, so he trained the older boys to teach the younger ones.

Thirty boys who had no homes were allowed to live in the house or in the shed. A chapel was built between the shed and house. Soon the house and shed were torn down and replaced by clean substantial buildings. This inspired a change in the whole neighborhood. Shacks were torn down and replaced by decent houses. But the spiritual change in the neighborhood was even greater than the physical change.

The Oratory of St. Francis de Sales soon became too small for the 800 boys enrolled. By 1849 Don Bosco had two more oratories in other sections of Turin.

How was Don Bosco able to accomplish so much? People who saw the wonderful work he was doing with boys helped him with their services and with donations. Skeptics, heretics, and atheists were among his contributors. The boys helped too. Many of them found jobs, thanks to the training they had received at the oratory, and they contributed part of their wages. And sometimes the money came in ways that seemed miraculous.

But the enemies of religion were Don Bosco's enemies. Once while he was teaching, a shot came through a window and pierced his cassock. "A pity — it was my best cassock," he said. He visited a dying man and was offered a glass of wine. He guessed, correctly, that the wine was poisoned, to the great confusion of the family. He was attacked on the street several times and saved himself by the use of his fists.

One night when Don Bosco was returning home through the worst part of the city, a big gray dog appeared to be following him. He called, and the dog came and allowed himself to be petted. He took Don Bosco as far as his door and then left. The dog came again and again when Don Bosco was going on errands that involved danger. Several times he fought off attackers. The priest gave the dog the name of Grigio — Italian for gray. On one occasion Grigio threw himself across the doorway and refused to allow Don Bosco to leave the house. Later the priest learned that some men had been waiting near his house to shoot him as he came out.

Don Bosco needed help in his work, so he started a religious society for men which he called Salesian after St. Francis de Sales. By the time he died there were 768 Salesians and today there are more than 9000 priests and brothers in the society. He also started a society of sisters under the title of Our Lady Help of Christians. Today these sisters have more than 600 houses throughout the world. A third society, composed of lay people, is called the Salesian Co-operators. Members of this organization are pledged to help the work of the Salesians.

The work that Don Bosco accomplished is amazing. In his spare moments he wrote about seventy books and pamphlets. He also had a reputation as a church builder. His first little church was followed by a much larger one. Then he built a large basilica in the poor quarter of Turin. Pope St. Pius X commissioned him to raise the money to construct a Church of the Sacred Heart in Rome. He preached throughout Italy and France, and the money came pouring in. The church was dedicated on May 14, 1887, and he said Mass in it shortly afterward.

At the end of 1888 Don Bosco was worn out from all his labors. He became gradually weaker and passed away on January 31, 1889. The whole city of Turin turned out to honor him when his remains were taken to their last resting place. He was beatified on June 2, 1929, and canonized on November 28, 1933, by Pope Pius XI who had personally seen this saint's great work in Turin.

OTHER SAINTS OF THE SAME NAME:

St. John the Baptist, Precursor of Our Lord. Feast, June 24.
St. John the Beloved Apostle. Feast, December 27.
St. John Chrysostom, 344–407. Golden tongued orator, Doctor of the Church. Feast, January 27.
St. John de Brebeuf, d. 1645. North American Martyr. Feast, March 16.
St. John Baptist Vianney, 1786–1859. Curé of Ars. Feast, August 9.

ST. BERNADETTE SOUBIROUS,
1844–1879
Feast: April 16

EQUIVALENTS: Bernarda, Barnarde, Bernardina, Bernardine.
MASCULINE: Bernal, Bernard, Bernardino, Bernardo

Almost everyone in the Christian world knows that the Blessed Virgin appeared several times to little Bernadette Soubirous in Lourdes, France, in 1858. The detailed story of the apparitions has been told often and well. There is no need to repeat that story here. This sketch will deal with Bernadette herself.

Bernadette was the eldest child of François and Louise Soubirous, who ran a mill in Lourdes. She was born January 7, 1844, and the next day she was baptized Marie Bernarde, after St. Bernard, the famous doctor of the Church who was known for his devotion to the Blessed Virgin. The family always referred to her by the pet name Bernadette, the name by which the world knows her today.

The mill which the Soubirous managed had once been prosperous and should have kept the family in good circumstances. But François and Louise proved to be poor managers and the profits fell to nothing. In 1845 they could no longer pay the rent for the mill, and they were evicted. Both father and mother worked at any kind of an odd job in an effort to support the family, but jobs were few and paid little. Time after time they were forced out on the street because they could not pay their rent. In 1856 a cousin, Andre Sajoux, allowed them to live rent free in a miserable little room which had once been a cell of the city jail. There were four children by this time. Bernadette was twelve and a half.

Bernadette was a round-faced, bright-eyed, ebony haired girl. When she was seven she developed the asthma which was to plague her the rest of her life. She suffered in the cholera epidemic of 1854 and this apparently stunted her growth. She never grew taller than four feet seven inches.

As if the family had not been sufficiently afflicted, François was arrested on suspicion of stealing two bags of flour. He spent seven days in jail while awaiting trial. The case was dismissed for lack of evidence, but the stigma remained. The Soubirous now knew bitter disgrace as well as grinding poverty.

In September, 1857, Marie Lagues Araveant asked that Bernadette be allowed to come and stay with her at Bartes. Bernadette would help Marie with the children, and in return she would be sent to school and would be taught her catechism. Louise readily agreed to this; it would get Bernadette away from the miserable home in Lourdes, and the girl would secure some of the education she had missed. But at Bartes, Bernadette worked all day long and was never sent to school. After several hours of housework she went out and watched the sheep until nightfall. Marie did try to teach Bernadette some catechism in the evenings. But Bernadette was tired after such a long day of work, and the catechism was in French, while Bernadette spoke a *patois* that was more Spanish than French. (The Blessed Virgin would speak to Bernadette in this *patois*.) Sometimes Marie would throw down the catechism and box the girl's ears. "You are too stupid to learn anything," she would say. Bernadette bore all this with quiet resignation.

In January, 1858, Bernadette was allowed to return home. She was fourteen and looked twelve. She could neither read nor write, and she knew practically no catechism. She had not received her First Communion.

This was the girl whom the Blessed Virgin selected from all the people on earth for a very special mission.

The apparitions began on February 11, 1858. Bernadette had gone with her sister and a friend to gather wood with which to heat their cold room. The other girls had run ahead of Bernadette. When she reached a little millstream at the point where it emptied into the river, she stooped to remove her stockings so she could wade across. She heard the sound of wind and looked up, but the trees were not moving. She began to remove her stockings again, and once more she heard the sound. Frightened, she stood straight up. She looked in the direction of the large rock on the other side of the millstream.

"I saw at one of the openings of the rock a bush," Bernadette said later, "one only, moving as if it were very windy. Almost at the same time there came out of the interior of the grotto a golden colored cloud, and soon after a Lady, young and beautiful, exceedingly beautiful, the like of whom I had never seen, came and placed herself at the entrance of the opening above the bush. She looked at me immediately, smiled at me, and signaled me to advance, as if she had been my mother. All fear had left me, but I seemed to know no longer where I was. I rubbed my eyes, I shut them, I opened them, but the Lady was still there continuing to smile at me and making me understand that I was not mistaken. Without thinking of what I was doing, I took my rosary into my hands and went to my knees. The Lady made a sign of approval with her head and took into her hands a rosary which hung on her right arm. When I attempted to begin the Rosary and tried to lift my hand to my forehead, my arm remained paralyzed, and it was only after the Lady had signed herself that I could do the same. The Lady let me pray all alone; she passed the beads of her rosary through her fingers, but she said nothing. Only at the end of each decade did she say the 'Gloria' with me.

"When the recitation of the Rosary was finished, the Lady returned to the interior of the rock, and the golden cloud disappeared with her."

That was the beginning. The Lady kept appearing to Bernadette until she had appeared eighteen times in all. Large crowds accompanied the girl to the grotto. They could not see the Lady, but they could see Bernadette in ecstasy, and they were sure that she was seeing something. They referred to Bernadette as "the saint" and tried to touch her. They even tried to get her to bless them and she would exclaim: "I cannot bless. I am not a priest." The local officials were afraid of the crowds that Bernadette was drawing and they did not for a minute believe that apparitions were taking place in "this enlightened nineteenth century." They badgered Bernadette and tried to cross her up in her testimony, but her story remained consistent. They threatened to arrest the family, and this frightened François who had already spent a week in jail. He forbade his daughter to go to the grotto and she obeyed, until one day an unseen force made her go. Her parents took this as a sign and did not interfere again.

The Lady told Bernadette some things that were for the girl's ears alone. She asked for prayers and penance. She revealed a spring through which many marvelous cures have been worked. And she identified herself by saying: "I am the Immaculate Conception." This was just a little more than three years after Pope Pius IX had promulgated the doctrine of the Immaculate Conception. On July 16 the Lady smiled a tender farewell and Bernadette did not see her again.

"I do not promise to make you happy in this life but in the other," the Blessed Virgin told Bernadette in one of the early apparitions. The girl's life had not been happy before the apparitions; it was even less happy afterward.

Pilgrims came to Lourdes in large numbers, and all tried to see Bernadette. She felt that she was constantly on display "like some kind of animal." Largely to get her away from the crowds, her pastor, Father Peyramale, advised that she go to live with the Sisters of Charity and Christian Instruction. She did so in January, 1860, when she was sixteen years old. She helped in the kitchen, the workroom, and the infirmary.

This change did not bring about the desired privacy. No matter what she was doing the bell would ring and she would be called to the parlor to tell the story of the apparitions. She went through this so often that sometimes her eyes would fill with tears at the thought of going through the ordeal again. But she would brush away the tears and greet the visitors graciously. She took lessons in French and was soon able to talk without the aid of an interpreter.

The interviews fatigued Bernadette and aggravated her already bad health. One day, in 1862, her condition became so poor that she was given the Last Sacraments. Later, she recovered to the point where she could go about her tasks again.

Later that month Bishop Forcase of Nevers, where the mother house of the Sisters was located, came for a visit. He came across Bernadette grating carrots. That evening he sent for her and asked her what she intended to do with herself. He told her that she could not remain with the Sisters forever because she was not a Sister.

"I don't think I should be a Sister," she said. "I have no dowry and I cannot do anything."

"You need not worry about the dowry, and I think you underestimate your talents. You are good at something."

"Good for what?"

"This morning I saw you grating carrots."

With this encouragement, Bernadette asked to be admitted to the novitiate. Her entrance was put off two years because of her bad health. She was to leave for the mother house at Nevers on July 4, 1866. She paid a last visit to the grotto crying: "O Mother, my Mother, how can I leave you?" She stopped for a few minutes at the new mill the family had acquired. The family gathered in silence. Bernadette hugged and kissed them all, and then rushed to the waiting carriage.

All the first day at the mother house, Bernadette wept from homesickness. Later, she always went out of her way to comfort girls who were entering the convent.

On July 27, 1866, Bernadette put on the habit of the Sisters of Charity and took the name Sister Marie Bernarde, her baptismal name.

Soon after this, the Mother Superior called together the entire convent and had Bernadette tell the story of the apparitions. Then, the Mother Superior said that the apparitions must never be referred to again. This pleased Bernadette, but streams of distinguished visitors kept coming to the door. Mother Superior could not refuse them permission to see Bernadette, and so the ordeal went on.

The other Sisters may not have referred to the apparitions, but they did not forget them. They regarded Bernadette as a saint. Every scrap that fell from her scissors was picked up and treasured. When her hair was cut, the hair that fell to the floor was picked up and saved. Sisters tried to touch her robe and kiss her veil when she passed. They tried to walk next to her when she was coming down the stairs. They even prayed to get sick so they would be under her care in the infirmary. All of this did not escape Bernadette's notice and was a very great trial to her.

The Mother Superior and her assistant, who was also the novice mistress, saw all the adulation and were sure that it must be going to Bernadette's head. They decided that she needed humbling and they humbled her at every opportunity. One of the other young nuns recalled saying to herself: "What a mercy I am not Sister Marie Bernarde." Bernadette herself never complained. "The novice mistress knows what she is about," Bernadette said. "I do have lots of pride."

In the latter part of October, 1866, Bernadette seemed at the point of death. She received the Last Sacraments again. Bishop Forcase came to the convent and admitted her to the vows of the Congregation. That same year, on the Feast of the Immaculate Conception, her mother died. Bernadette had not seen her mother since that last day at the mill.

On October 30, 1867, Bernadette made her profession again with the other Sisters of the novitiate. The young nuns were given letters assigning them to various houses of the Community. But there was no letter for Bernadette. Bishop Forcase asked the reason for this.

The novice mistress answered: "It has not been possible to assign her an obedience. She is good for nothing."

When the bishop called Bernadette, she said: "That is just what I told you at Lourdes, your Excellency, and you answered that it would not make any difference."

"If you like, your Excellency," Mother Superior broke in, "we can keep her out of charity and employ her in the infirmary. As she is almost always sick, it will be just the place for her. She can begin by keeping it clean, and if we are able to teach her, perhaps she will be able to make up cough mixtures later on."

Bernadette admitted, some time later, that this public humiliation was very bitter to her. But at the time she did not allow her feelings to show.

Her health became worse as the years went on. Her asthma was worse, and a large tumor formed on her knee. The pain was almost unendurable. But she wrote in her notebook that her interior sufferings were even worse than her physical sufferings.

During Holy Week, 1878, her suffering became more intense than ever. Easter brought no relief. Tuesday night she sank into a half stupor from which she roused at times to cry, "Begone, Satan!"

In the morning, she could no longer breathe while lying down. She was placed in a chair, and she clutched a crucifix to her heart. The Sisters knelt around her and recited the prayers for the dying. After a time she raised herself in her chair and asked for water. Her lips were moistened. She made the Sign of the Cross. Then she sank back. It was about three o'clock in the afternoon, April 16, 1879.

As she bowed her head and died her last words were: "Holy Mary, Mother of God, pray for me — a poor sinner, a poor sinner."

On December 8, 1933, the poor little peasant girl of Lourdes was inscribed on the Church's great roll of saints.

OTHER SAINTS OF THE SAME NAME:

St. Bernard of Clairvaux, 1090–1153. Rich man who became a poor monk devoted to our Lady and renowned for the almost irresistible power of his preaching. Feast, August 20.

St. Bernard of Parma, died 1133. Abbot, cardinal, remarkable for reforming zeal and for defense of the authority of the pope. Feast, December 4.

St. Bernardino of Siena, 1380–1444. Franciscan priest, zealous in giving missions in Italy, noted for his spirit of penance and for devotion to care of the sick. Feast, May 20.

ST. FRANCES XAVIER CABRINI,
1850–1917

Feast: December 22

EQUIVALENTS: Francesca, France, Francella, Franchette, Francine, Franchon, Fran, Franny

---

Little Frances Cabrini was making paper boats and floating them on a deep swift-flowing canal. Millions of children have played the same way, but there was something different about the way she did it. Frances filled each paper boat with violets, and the violets were "missionaries" that she was sending across the seas to spread the word of Christ throughout the world. Young as she was, Frances' thoughts were constantly on the missions where she hoped to go some day.

As she leaned over to set one of her boats on its course, she fell into the swift current and almost drowned. To her dying day she was not able to say who pulled her safely to the bank and concluded it must have been her guardian angel. The incident gave her a fear of water that lasted throughout her life but did not in the least deter her from traveling thousands of miles by sea in the course of her amazing missionary career.

The thirteenth child of Agostino and Stella Cabrini was born July 15, 1850, in Lodi, in northern Italy. She was baptized Maria Francesca. Later, her love of the missions influenced her to add Xavier to her name and to make St. Francis Xavier her special patron. Frances' education and upbringing were left largely to an older sister, Rosa, who had been a school teacher. At thirteen Frances went to a convent school at Arluno. She applied twice to be admitted

to religious life but was rejected because her health was considered
too frail. She attended normal school and taught for a short time.

Monsignor Serrati, provost of the little town of Codogno, persuaded her to come there to straighten out the affairs of a badly
managed orphanage. The orphanage was in charge of a woman
named Antonia Tondi who had put up the money to found it. The
Bishop of Lodi had induced Antonia Tondi and two of her helpers
to adopt a semireligious habit, in the vain hope that this would
bring about a more regular life. After Frances was at the orphanage
a short time she and five of the orphan girls were also invested with
the habit. Three years later she took her vows. Then, at the direction
of Monsignor Serrati, she sat in the sanctuary and received the
vows of the five girls who had entered with her. She was now the
superior of the little community. Antonia Tondi did not like this
arrangement; she brought suit and won back the money she had
donated for the orphanage and the building itself.

Frances and seven young Sisters, including the former cook of
the orphanage, had to find a new home. Monsignor Serrati bought
them an abandoned Franciscan friary. A rule was drawn up, and
the community was named the Institute of the Missionary Sisters
of the Sacred Heart. A statue of the Sacred Heart was the most
prominent object on the premises and the work of the foundation
was entrusted to the Sacred Heart.

Young women were attracted to the institute in ever increasing
numbers. In a short time several houses had been established. In
1887 Mother Cabrini went to Rome to seek papal approbation of
the rule under which the Sisters lived and permission to establish
a house in the Eternal City. The cardinal who received her was
astonished at the audacity of the second request. "You are not needed
in Rome, where we have so many congregations already," he said.
"Go back to Codogno where you are needed." Her persistence won
out, however, and the cardinal ended up by asking her to found two
houses in Rome, a kindergarten and a school for the poor.

While in Rome, Mother Cabrini met Bishop J. B. Scalabrini, a
founder of the Missionaries of St. Charles Borromeo for Italian

Emigrants. He told her about the sad plight of the Italians who had emigrated to America. These people were largely unskilled workers with little or no education. In America, they were given the roughest, hardest kind of work at very low pay. Because they could speak no English they were scorned by native Americans. They did not even have a sense of unity among themselves, because Italy had not been a united nation for long; they had divided into little groups according to dialect and local loyalty. Worst of all, they were in danger of losing their faith, because they lacked priests and teachers who could speak their language. Mother Cabrini listened to the sad story with sympathy but she did not think she was personally involved; her field, she felt, was China and the Far East. She changed her mind a short time later when she had an audience with Pope Leo XIII and told him of her ambitions. His reply was: "Not to the East, but to the West." She took this as a command, and her lifework had begun.

Bishop Scalabrini promised Mother Cabrini that he would make the necessary arrangements with Archbishop Corrigan of New York, and soon afterward he told her that she could go. Mother Cabrini and five companions landed in New York on March 31, 1889. There had been a series of misunderstandings, however, and Archbishop Corrigan was not ready for Mother Cabrini. He had no house for her and no money. The situation looked so hopeless that he said: "Go back to Italy on the first ship." But she said that she had come at the pope's command and was going to stay. She produced her written authorization. Archbishop Corrigan agreed that she could stay, but he warned her that he would not be able to give her much help.

Without friends and without money, Mother Cabrini had nothing but faith, hope, and courage with which to start her great works of charity. These assets were sufficient. The little Italian immigrant proved irresistible. She begged from the rich to help the poor; she encouraged those who had a little more to help those who had a little less. Miraculously, it seemed, her work spread from New York to New Orleans, to Denver, to the west coast, and to places in between.

She had a gift for finding Italian immigrants. She went to the places where they worked — mines, mills, forests, stone quarries — and inspired them to improve their spiritual and material conditions. She urged them to hold fast to the Catholic faith, to expend their energies in helping themselves, and never to lose courage. Busy as she was, she never lost her peace of mind or her tranquillity.

In 1892 Mother Cabrini founded a hospital for Italian immigrants in New York City. It was the fourth centenary of the discovery of America, so she named the institution Columbus Hospital, in honor of "the first Italian emigrant to America." This was a title in which all Italians, regardless of their birthplace, could take pride. Even anticlerical Italians felt they could contribute to a hospital with such a title. A year later she made plans to purchase an abandoned hotel in Chicago and to convert it into another Columbus Hospital. On the morning she was to make the down payment, she and another sister used bits of knotted string to obtain the exact measurements of the property. It was well that they did so, because the sellers tried to cheat them out of a valuable section of the land. Mother Cabrini produced the strings and insisted upon getting all that had been promised to her.

The exterior walls of the old hotel were sound, but much remodeling had to be done inside. The contractors tried to defraud Mother Cabrini by doing more work than was necessary and by charging exorbitant prices. When she came back from one of her numerous trips and found out what was going on, she fired the contractors and dared them to sue her. Then she became her own contractor, hiring the workers and supervising them. In doing so, she reduced the time that had been estimated for the construction from twelve months to eight months.

Mother Cabrini did not confine herself to the United States. She went to Central America and sought out Italian immigrants there. She went on to South America where she crossed the rugged Andes Mountains on a mule! She went to Europe where she visited the houses of the institute in Italy and extended the work to Spain, England, and France. Her foundations on both sides of the Atlantic included kindergartens, schools, colleges, day nurseries, orphanages, free clinics, and hospitals.

She became convinced that she could do more effective work in the United States if she became a citizen. She made application and became a citizen in 1909.

Her health had never been good, yet she never spared herself. Her only "rests" came during her ocean voyages, but she spent most of the time on shipboard writing letters to the sisters in her charge. She spent the last five years of her life in the United States. On December 22, 1917, she was stricken in Chicago, at Columbus Hospital, while wrapping Christmas gifts for poor children of the neighborhood. She died the same day.

The funeral Mass for Mother Cabrini was celebrated in Chicago by Archbishop George Mundelein. She was buried at West Park, New York, a fact she had predicted years before. Her body is now enshrined in the chapel of Mother Cabrini High School on Fort Washington Avenue in New York City.

Ordinarily, fifty years must pass after a person's death before the process of beatification and canonization can begin. Pope Pius XI, who had known Mother Cabrini personally, dispensed with this law in her case. She was beatified November 13, 1938. On this occasion the Pontifical Mass in St. Peter's was celebrated by Cardinal Mundelein who had celebrated the funeral Mass only twenty-one years before. Frances Xavier Cabrini was canonized July 7, 1947. She is the first citizen of the United States to be so honored.

ANOTHER SAINT OF THE SAME NAME:

St. Frances of Rome, 1384–1440. Model wife and mother, favored by the visible presence of her guardian angel. Feast, March 9.

Saint of the Little Way

ST. THÉRÈSE OF LISIEUX, 1873–1897
Feast: October 3

EQUIVALENTS: Teresa, Teresita, Terry, Flora, Floretta, Florella, Florita, Floris, Flossie

---

Thérèse of Lisieux lived less than twenty-five years and at the time of her death only a handful of people knew that she had ever existed. Today, the whole world knows her; she is a canonized saint, and she is the patroness of all missionaries.

As we read the stories of the saints we are impressed by the great things some of them have done. They have braved every danger to bring the word of God to heathen lands. Great preachers among them have talked to audiences numbering in the thousands. Bishops, kings, and popes have called in certain saints as advisers. Saints have led great armies. Many saints have been put to death for their faith. But Thérèse shows us that it is not necessary to do spectacular deeds in order to become a saint. She achieved great heights of sanctity without ever leaving her convent. Her method consisted in doing little things well. For that reason, she called it the Little Way.

Both parents of Thérèse Martin had, in their youth, wished to become religious; both had been rejected, without apparent reason, by superiors of the congregations to which they had applied. They found God's will in marriage and raised their family in the town of Alençon, in northern France. Five of their seven children lived to be adults and all five became religious. The youngest, Thérèse, was born January 2, 1873. Her mother died when she was only three

210

years old. From her earliest days Thérèse had just one ambition: to become a saint.

By special permission of the bishop, Thérèse was allowed to enter the Carmel of Lisieux at the age of fifteen. Her two older sisters were already in the Carmel. Thérèse received the religious habit on January 10, 1889, and the black veil on September 24, 1890.

Sister Thérèse spent nine years in the Carmel of Lisieux, growing spiritually while she wasted away physically. Those who lived with her saw her do nothing extraordinary. It was the custom for the superior, upon the death of a sister, to write an account of the life of the deceased and send it on to the other houses of the order. During her last illness Thérèse heard a sister remark: "Whatever will Mother write about Sister Thérèse? She has done nothing worth mentioning." Thérèse was happy when she heard these words; she had never wished to attract attention to herself.

Outwardly, Thérèse's life was much like that of the other nuns in the Carmel. She sang in choir, swept the cloister, worked in the sacristy cleaning the sacred vessels and mending the vestments. She helped tend the sick. She did a little painting. Later, when ordered by her superiors to do so, she wrote *The Story of a Soul*, her autobiography. In 1893, when she was only twenty years old, she was appointed to assist the novice mistress and became mistress in all but name.

What made Thérèse a great saint? There were many other sisters in the same Carmel with Thérèse, and outwardly they led exactly the same kind of life she did. There were hundreds of other cloistered nuns in various parts of the world. Why, of all these, does Thérèse stand out?

It is not possible to give complete answers to these questions. The Church canonizes persons who, while they were on this earth, achieved a great amount of union with God. The details of this union are known only to the person himself and to God.

Thérèse tried to tell the story of her soul in her autobiography, and the book is rated as a great spiritual classic, but we may be sure the words are only a pale reflection of her experience. A biographer of

Thérèse, as of other saints, can only play about the fringes of her life. He can tell the known facts, but he cannot present a photograph of her soul.

Thérèse herself tells us that her Little Way had three parts: (1) All that she had to offer to God were "little things," but she offered them all to Him, without exception, and she offered them with the utmost love. (2) She aimed to be childlike in her relations with God; she realized that "unless you become as little children you shall not enter into the kingdom of heaven." (3) She had great devotion to the Holy Face of the suffering Christ. This devotion accounts for her heroic acceptance of suffering.

And Thérèse did suffer, physically, mentally, and spiritually. Her health had never been robust and it declined rapidly after she entered Carmel. She was not permitted to fast but no other exceptions to the austere Carmelite rule were made for her. "A soul of such mettle," said the prioress, "must not be treated like a child. Dispensations are not meant for her." It was often exceedingly difficult for the frail girl to follow this rigorous life, but she did not allow anyone to guess how difficult it was. On days when she was ill she concealed the fact and kept to her daily routine. She remembered the Face of her crucified Lord which seemed to be watching her and begging for sacrifices.

Thérèse suffered abnormally from the cold, and it was cold much of the time in the unheated Carmel. This torture went on day and night, for months at a time. But Thérèse never mentioned the fact until she was on her deathbed.

She was harshly treated by the Mother Prioress and received many undeserved rebukes from her. This treatment caused Thérèse great mental suffering but she accepted it meekly. "Having nothing to reproach myself with, I offer gladly to God this small injustice. Then, humbling myself, I think how easily I might have deserved the reproach."

Her spiritual sufferings were even greater than her physical and mental sufferings. She suffered constant temptations against faith, and experienced prolonged stretches of spiritual dryness. She asked nothing but to give herself completely to God, and she received no encouragement, no response, from Him. She received no consolation even from Holy Communion. "Is this not to be expected," she said, "since I do not desire to receive Our Lord for my own satisfaction but to please Him?" She had a spirit of self-sacrifice that refused to be discouraged.

There are trials concerning charity even in the quiet of a cloistered convent, because human nature is human nature everywhere. Sister Thérèse had an astounding amount of charity. Henri Gheon, in Secrets of the Saints tells us: "There was a certain nun whom Thérèse found disagreeable in every way. Not content with overcoming a natural antipathy, she set herself to treat her just as she would one of whom she was very fond. Whenever they met, Thérèse prayed for her; she did whatever services she could; if the nun was vexatious, Thérèse gave her a charming smile and changed the subject; and all so convincingly that the nun asked one day, 'Sister Thérèse, won't you tell me why you are so drawn to me?' Presumably, Thérèse was able to satisfy her curiosity without offending and without lying."

In the face of supernatural heroism of this sort, it is hard to think of Thérèse's way as the "Little Way." It was certainly not an easy way. Pope Pius X — who has himself been canonized — said to one who was surprised at his devotion to St. Thérèse: "If you think her way so easy, go and do likewise."

Thérèse yearned to be a missionary and to extend the kingdom of God, but she never went beyond the walls of Carmel. She prayed incessantly for the missionaries and today is one of their patrons.

The last eighteen months of her life were a time of intensified physical suffering and spiritual trials. She seems to have been given the gift of prophecy during this time, and three of her statements have become famous: "I have never given the good God aught but love, and it will be with love that He will repay. After my death I will let fall a shower of roses." "I will spend my heaven doing good upon earth." "My Little Way is the way of spiritual childhood, the way of trust and absolute self-surrender."

In June, 1897, Thérèse was confined to her bed. At her request she remained in her own cell instead of being taken to the relative comfort of the infirmary. After August 16 she was so ill that she could no longer receive Holy Communion. She died on September 30.

Immediately, the Shower of Roses began falling, and it has been falling ever since. Sometimes it is not too easy to get the miracles that are needed for beatification and canonization. In Thérèse's case this was no problem at all. Accounts kept at Lisieux tell of marvels of healing, conversion, forewarning, actual visions. After these accounts had filled seven large volumes they were described as "only a drop in the torrent." Only a small proportion were accepted as miracles, because a miracle is hard to prove, but there were so many miracles that Pope Benedict XV exempted her cause from the delay of fifty years required by Canon Law. She was beatified in 1923 and canonized two years later.

Thérèse's Little Way has universal appeal: trust God blindly no matter what happens, use the little events of every day life as the material of sanctification; offer all to God with great love; labor in obscurity; in suffering think of the Holy Face.

Pope Benedict XV proposed St. Thérèse to everyone for imitation: "There is a call to the faithful of every nation, no matter what may be their age, sex, or state of life, to enter wholeheartedly into the Little Way which led Sister Thérèse to the summit of heroic virtue."

ANOTHER SAINT OF THE SAME NAME:

St. Teresa of Avila, 1515–1583. Great reformer of the Carmelites. Feast, October 15.

ST. MARIA GORETTI, 1890–1902

Feast: July 6

EQUIVALENTS: Mae, Manette, Maire, Manon, Marian, Mariana, Mariane, Maribel, Marie, Mariella, Marien, Marilyn, Marion, Marsia, Mary, Maureen, Mayme, Minna, Minnie, Miriam, Moira, Molly. (For equivalents that belong exclusively to the Blessed Virgin, see "Other Saints of the Same Name" at the end of this sketch.)

Maria Goretti met her violent death in 1902 and was canonized in the Holy Year of 1950. She is thus a saint of our own twentieth century. The Holy Spirit, who guides the Church in such matters, undoubtedly wishes to bring St. Maria to the attention of the modern world. To a world that has all but forgotten the virtue of purity, the Holy Spirit presents a saint who died in defense of purity.

The story of Maria's life is rather easily told because it was such a short life. She was not yet twelve years old when she died.

Maria was born October 16, 1890, the third of seven children. Her parents were poor peasants who lived near Corinaldo, in the Province of Ancona, in Italy. The family moved twice and eventually found themselves in the village of Ferriere di Conca, not far from Anzio. Maria's father, Luigi, formed a partnership with a man named Serenelli, who also shared a house with him. Serenelli had two sons.

Maria was eight and a half when the family moved to Ferriere de Conca. When she was ten, her father was stricken with malaria and died. The mother had to take care of the family and the father's work at the same time. Maria cheerfully helped her mother in every way possible and did more than her share of the household chores.

215

Because of their poverty, and because Maria was needed at home, she had no chance to go to school and therefore never learned to read or write. She was remarkably pious and trudged miles on foot for the privilege of hearing Mass. She made her First Communion in 1901, when she was eleven. This was the usual age for First Communion in the days before Pope St. Pius X.

Maria's unusual beauty attracted the attention of Alessandro, the younger Serenelli boy, who at twenty was wild and undisciplined. She spurned his advances, and this only made him more determined. Once he made a serious assault upon her, but she escaped. He warned her that if she told her mother or anyone else about the incident, he would kill her. Maria kept quiet but probably not because of the threat. She simply did not wish to cause trouble between the two families.

On July 5, 1902, Maria found herself in the house alone with Alessandro. The young man brought out a dagger and threatened Maria with death if she would not yield to his advances. Thinking more of Alessandro's spiritual welfare than of her own danger, she cried: "No, no, no! God does not wish it. If you do that, you'll commit a sin, you'll go to hell."

She struggled and tried to call for help, gasping that she would be killed rather than submit. The infuriated Alessandro struck at her with his dagger. As he kept striking, she fell to the floor in a pool of blood. Alessandro plunged the knife into her back and fled.

Maria was found soon after that and taken in a horse-drawn ambulance over seven and a half miles of bad roads to the hospital. She lived for twenty-four hours. During that time she became a Child of Mary, received the Last Sacraments, and forgave her murderer. She died on the afternoon of July 6, 1902.

Alessandro was captured and nearly lynched. He was tried and sentenced to thirty years of hard labor. For a long time he was surly, brutal, and unrepentant. Then he had a dream in which he saw Maria Goretti gathering flowers and offering them to him. From that time, he was a changed man. He became such a model prisoner that he was released three years before his term expired. The first thing he did was to visit Maria's mother and beg her forgiveness.

People regarded Maria as a saint and prayed for her intercession. Miracles were attributed to her intercession. She was beatified by Pope Pius XII in 1947 and canonized by him in 1950. Both Maria's mother and her murderer were still alive when she was canonized. The crowd in St. Peter's Square was the largest that had ever assembled for a canonization.

Maria Goretti is listed on the rolls of the Church as a martyr because she died in defense of a Christian virtue. Cardinal Salotti, however, says that she would have been a saint even if she had not been a martyr because her everyday life was so holy.

OTHER SAINTS OF THE SAME NAME:

The Blessed Virgin Mary, d. about A.D. 45. Mother of Jesus, Queen of all Saints. Her singular prerogatives as well as her various feasts and shrines are the sources of many names that are borne by her devoted clients. Some of these are: Alma, Ancilla, Annunciata, Carmel, Carmela, Carmelita, Concepta, Concetta, Concha, Conchita, Consuela, Consolata, Dolora, Dolorita, Doloris, Loretta, Loretto, Immaculata, Imogene, Lorentine, Madonna, Donna, Merced, Mercedes, Regina, Rosaria, Rosario, Rosarita, Sharon, Stella.

St. Mary of Egypt, d. 430. Penitent who lived in the desert. Feast, April 2.

St. Mary Ann of Quito, 1618–1645. Patroness of Ecuador. In 1950 she became the second native of the Americas to be canonized. Feast, May 26.

ST. BENEDICT THE MOOR, 1526–1589
Feast: April 4

EQUIVALENTS: Benedicto, Benito, Bennett.
FEMININE: Benedicta, Benita

St. Benedict the Moor has been made patron of North American Negroes. The choice is most appropriate. The Negroes of North America are the descendants of Africans who were brought to these shores as slaves, and Benedict was an African whose parents were slaves. His parents belonged to a wealthy landowner in Sicily. Benedict was given his freedom, but he had no chance to secure an education. He was such a devout child that when he was only ten years old he was known as "the holy Moor."

Benedict lived for a time as a hermit, and then he joined the Franciscans at Palermo. Despite the fact that he could neither read nor write he was elected superior. Later he was made novice master. His power to read men's hearts and his great sympathy made him the ideal choice for this position. Nevertheless, he was glad when he was released from this position and allowed to become cook. In the kitchen, however, he did not find the seclusion for which he longed. His reputation for sanctity and for miracles brought a steady stream of visitors. He never refused to see those who asked for him, but he shrank from all marks of respect. Throughout his life he continued the austerities of his hermit days. When he was in chapel his face often shone with an unearthly light.

He died at the age of sixty-three after a short illness. In addition to being patron of the Negroes of North America, he is also patron of the city of Palermo.

ST. VERONICA GIULIANI, 1660–1727
Feast: July 9

EQUIVALENTS: Verenice, Venise, Vera, Veron, Veronique

Ursula Giuliani was born at Mercatello in the Duchy of Urbion, Italy. She showed marvelous signs of sanctity from the beginning. As a result of a vision of our Lady, she made a vow to become a nun. When her father opposed this she fell ill and only became well when he gave his consent. She entered the Capuchin Poor Clares in 1667, taking the name Veronica in honor of the Passion, to which she had great devotion. After her profession her absorption in the Passion deepened. She had a vision of our Lord bearing his cross, and she began to have acute pain over her heart. In 1693 she had another vision in which the chalice of Christ's sufferings was offered to her. She accepted it after a great struggle with herself. After that something of the sufferings of Christ were reproduced in her body and soul. The imprint of the crown of thorns appeared on her head and she also had the impress of the five sacred wounds. By order of the bishop, she submitted to medical treatment but obtained no relief.

While having these supernatural experiences Veronica remained a practical woman of affairs. She was novice mistress for thirty-four years, and in 1716 she was elected abbess. While holding that position she had the convent enlarged and she improved the convent water supply by having a system of pipes installed.

Long before her death Veronica told her confessor that the instruments of our Lord's passion were imprinted on her heart. A post mortem, performed in the presence of the bishop, mayor, and many other witnesses, showed that this was true.

ST. LEONARD OF PORT MAURICE, 1676–1751

Feast: November 26

EQUIVALENTS: Lenn, Leonardo, Maurice, Morris.
FEMININE: Maura

Paul Jerome Casanova was born in Port Maurice on the Italian Riviera and received his education from the Jesuit Fathers in Rome. He entered the Franciscans when he was twenty-one, taking the name Leonard. He was ordained in 1703. He was assigned to the Franciscan monastery at Florence and for a time was superior of the monastery. Leonard was known best for his missionary efforts throughout Italy. His sermons frequently had to be given in the open air because no church would hold the vast crowds that came to hear him. He made his missionary journeys on foot, as St. Francis had done.

Leonard constantly preached the Way of the Cross, a devotion not very well known at that time. He set up the stations at every place he preached. In 1750 one of his ambitions was realized when Pope Benedict XIV permitted him to set up the stations of the cross in the Colosseum. He also encouraged exposition of the Blessed Sacrament, devotion to the Sacred Heart, and devotion to the Immaculate Conception, all of which were far less widespread then than they are today. He made great efforts to have the Immaculate Conception defined as a dogma of faith. This came about a century after his death.

In spite of his missionary activity Leonard found time to write many letters, sermons, and devotional treatises. He is highly regarded as an ascetic writer.

ST. CLEMENT HOFBAUER, 1751–1820
Feast: March 15

EQUIVALENTS: Clemence, Clemente.
FEMININE: Clementina, Clementine

John Hofbauer, a native of Austria, was the ninth of twelve children of a grazier and butcher. As a boy, he longed to be a priest but the family did not have enough money to send him to a seminary. At the age of fifteen he was apprenticed to a baker. With this experience he was able to work in the bakery of a monastery at Bruck. While there he managed to secure some education. He became a hermit until the emperor did away with hermitages. Then he went back to his profession of baking. Later, he was fortunate enough to find people who would pay for his seminary training. He went to Rome and enrolled in the Redemptorists. Some time before this he had taken the name Clement by which he was known for the rest of his life.

St. Alphonsus, founder of the Redemptorists, was still alive when Clement arrived. He was delighted, because the Redemptorists had never spread beyond Italy. He was confident that Clement would establish the society north of the Alps.

After he was ordained, Clement wished to go to Vienna, but the emperor would permit no religious foundations in Austria. He and another priest and a lay brother went to Warsaw, Poland. They began their labor in the utmost poverty. They slept on tables because they had no beds. They had to borrow their cooking utensils. For the next twenty years they did an amazing amount of work. They preached five sermons every day, three in Polish and two in German. They started an orphanage and collected alms for it. They administered two large parishes. A school for boys was founded. Protestants came into the Church, and Clement was particularly successful in the conversion of Jews. As the community increased, Clement sent missionaries to other countries. Then Napoleon became master of Poland and suppressed religious communities.

Clement went to Vienna in his native Autria and spent his last twelve years there. He was not allowed to found a house of the Redemptorists, so he acted as chaplain to the Ursuline nuns. He was free to preach and to hear confessions and to make sick calls. Through him, fresh vigor was poured into the religious life of Vienna. He did not live to see the Redemptorists established in Austria, but he had perfect confidence. "Scarcely shall I have breathed my last when we shall have houses in abundance," he said. This prophecy was fulfilled. St. Clement is sometimes called the second founder of the Redemptorists because he first planted the congregation north of the Alps.

Patron Saints of
Special Works and Groups

Altar boys	John Berchmans
Boy Scouts	George
Catholic Action	Francis of Assisi
Catholic schools, colleges	Thomas Aquinas
Charitable organizations	Vincent de Paul
Confessors	Alphonsus Liguori
Eucharistic Congresses	Pascal Baylon
Foreign missions	Francis Xavier, Thérèse of Lisieux
Girl Scouts	Agnes
Home missions	Leonard of Port Maurice
Hospitals	Camillus of Lellis, John of God, Gemma Galgani
Immigrants	Frances Cabrini
Interracial understanding	Martin de Porres
Natural sciences	Albert the Great
Negro missions	Peter Claver
Religious instruction	Charles Borromeo, Robert Bellarmine
Retreats and retreatants	Ignatius Loyola

Patron Saints of
Industries and Occupations

Many industries and occupations have patron saints accorded them by long continued popular devotion. Some of the following patrons have been so designated by the Holy See.

Astronomers	Dominic
Athletes	Sebastian
Architects	Barbara
Aviators	Our Lady of Loreto, Joseph of Cupertino
Bakers	Nicholas of Myra
Bankers	Matthew the Apostle, Elizabeth of Hungary
Barbers	Cosmas and Damian
Book industry workers	Peter Celestine

223

Booksellers and publishers	John of God, Bl. James Duckett
Bricklayers	Stephen
Builders	Vincent Ferrer, Blaise, Thomas à Becket
Bus drivers	Christopher
Butchers	Bartholomew, Anthony the Abbot
Cabinet-makers	Anne
Carpenters	Joseph
Comedians	Vitus (Guy)
Cooks	Martha, Lawrence
Customs officers	Matthew the Apostle
Dentists	Apollonia
Doctors of medicine and surgeons	Luke, Cosmas, Damian
Domestic servants	Zita
Farmers	Isidore
Firemen, mathematicians	Barbara
Fishermen	Andrew, Peter
Goldsmiths	Dunstan, Eligius
Grocers	Michael
Gunners	Barbara, Joan of Arc
Hospital administrators	Frances Cabrini
Housewives	Anne, Martha
Hunters	Hubert
Innkeepers and travelers seeking good lodging	Julian the Hospitaller
Jewelers	Eligius, Bernard
Journalists	Francis de Sales
Lawyers and jurists	Ives, Alphonsus Liguori
Librarians	Peter Canisius, Jerome
Merchants	Nicholas of Myra, Francis of Assisi
Miners	Anne
Motorists	Christopher
Mountaineers	Bernard of Menthon
Munitions makers	Barbara
Musicians	Cecilia, Gregory the Great
Night watchmen	Peter of Alcantara
Nurses	Camillus of Lellis, John of God, Agatha
Radio, television, and communications workers (Television, Clare of Assisi)	Gabriel the Archangel
Sailors	Francis of Paola
Soldiers	Sebastian, Martin of Tours
Tax collectors	Matthew the Apostle
Teachers	Thomas Aquinas, John Baptist de la Salle
Workers	Joseph the Worker

Writers   Francis de Sales

X-ray therapy: doctors, technicians, nurses and patients concerned   Michael the Archangel

Patron Saints of Countries

Australia	Our Lady Help of Christians, Francis Xavier, Patrick
Austria	Our Lady, St. Mary
Belgium	Joseph
Brazil	Our Lady of the Immaculate Heart
Canada	Anne, George, the Jesuit Martyrs
Ceylon	Our Lady Immaculate
China	Francis Xavier
Columbia	Joseph
Czechoslovakia	Wenceslaus
Denmark	Anscar
Ecuador	Mary Ann of Quito
England	George, Peter, Edward the Confessor
Finland	Henry of Upsala
France	Louis, Joan of Arc
Germany	Boniface
Greece	Nicholas of Myra
Holland	Willibrord
Hungary	Stephen the King
India	Thomas the Apostle
Ireland	Patrick, Bridget
Italy	Francis of Assisi, Catherine of Siena, and others
Lithuania	Casimir
Mexico	Our Lady of Guadalupe
New Zealand	Our Lady Help of Christians, Francis Xavier, Patrick
Norway	Olaf
Peru	Rose of Lima
Poland	Casimir, Stanislaus
Portugal	Vincent of Saragossa, Elizabeth
Russia	Andrew the Apostle, Nicholas of Myra, Vladimir (Thérèse of Lisieux is invoked for the conversion of Russia)
Scotland	Andrew the Apostle
Switzerland	Nicholas von Flüe

South America	Rose of Lima
Southern Slavs (Yugoslavia)	Cyril and Methodius
Spain	James the Greater (Apostle), Teresa of Avila
Sweden	Bridget
United States of America	The Immaculate Conception
Venezuela	Our Lady of Coromoto
Wales	David

Dioceses and many cities also have patron saints; these are too numerous to list here.

INDEX

The names in *italics* below are derivatives or equivalents. All the others are actual saints' names. The numbers in **bold face** type indicate where a biography of the saint can be found in this book.

Adalbert, 125
Adelaide, 57, **59-62**
Adelaide, abbess, 62
Adelaide of Schaerbeck, 62
Adelbert, 71
Adele, Adelheid, 59
Afra, 133
Agatha, 30, 35, 224
Agnella, 30
Agnes, martyr, 30, **35**, 223
Agnes of Assisi, 36, 84
Agnes of Montepulciano, 36
Agnes of Poitiers, 36
Agnese, Agnesine, 30
Agnita, 30
Aileen, 52
Albert of Bergamo, 94
Albert the Great, 58, **91-93**, 223
Albert of Louvain, 94
Albert of Montecorvino, 94
Alberta, Alberto, 91
Albertina, Albertine, Albertino, 91
Albertus, 91
Albrette, 91
Alice, Alicia, 59
Alix, 59
Alma, 217
Aloysius Gonzaga, 145
Alphonsus Liguori, 175, 176, 221, 223, 224
Ambrose, 44
Ancela, 131
Ancilla, 217
Andrew, Apostle, 12, 17, 224, 225
Andrew Avellino, 131
Angela of Foligno, 135
Angela Merici, 130, **131-135**
Angela of Prague, 135
Angele, Angeline, 131
Angelica, Angelique, 131
Angelita, 131
Angelo, 128

Aniela, Anjela, 131
Anita, Anitra, 3
Ann, Anna, 3
Ann of St. Bartholomew, 6
Anna Maria Taigi, 6
Annabel, Annabelle, 3
Anne, mother of BVM, 1, **3-6**, 224, 225
Anne of Constantinople, 6
Annette, 3
Annina, 3
Annunciata, 217
Anscar, 225
Anthony of the Desert, 89, 90, 224
Anthony of Padua, 57, 58, **88-90**
Antoine, Anton, 88
Antoinetta, Antoinette, Antonetta, 88
Antonia, Antonio, 88
Antonina, Antonita, 88
Antonio Maria Claret, 90
Antonius of Florence, 90
Antony, 88
Antony Daniel, 165, 166
Anusia, 3
Appolina, 224
Augustine, 2, 22, 41 ff., 88

Bab, 30
Babette, 95
Babora, 30
Barbara, 30, 35, 223, 224
Barbe, 30
Barcia, 30
Barnarde, 198
Bartholomew, 161, 224
Bella, Belle, 95
Benedict, 57
Benedict the Moor, **218**
Benedicta, Benedicto, 218
Benita, Benito, 218
Bennett, 218
Bernadette Soubirous, 130, **198-204**
Bernal, 198

Bernard, Bernarda, Bernardo, 198
Bernard of Clairvaux, 204, 224
Bernard of Menthon, 224
Bernard of Parma, 204
Bernardina, Bernardine, Bernardino, 198
Bernardino of Siena, 204
Bess, Beth, 95
Betsy, Betta, Betty, 95
Birgitta, 105
Blaise, 224
Boniface, 57, 225
Bride, 105
Bridget of Sweden, 57, 105–110, 226
Brigetta, 105
Brigid, 105
Brigid of Kildare, 110, 225
Bruno, 57, 123

Cahil, 162
Camillus of Lellis, 223, 224
Carel, 162
Carl, 162
Carleton, Carlton, 162
Carlo, Carlos, 162
Carmel, Carmela, Carmelita, 217
Carol, Carola, 162
Caroline, Carolyn, 162
Carroll, 162
Carry, 162
Casimir, 225
Catharine, 184
Catherine of Alexandria, 112, 190
Catherine of Genoa, 190
Catherine Laboure, 130, 184–189
Catherine of Siena, 160, 190, 225
Catherine of Sweden, 190
Cathryn, 184
Cecilia, 30, 34–35, 224
Cecily, 30
Celia, Celie, 30
Celine, 30, 52
Charlene, 162
Charles of Blois, 167
Charles Borromeo, 167, 223
Charles Garnier, 130, 162–167
Charles Lwanga, 167
Charles of Sezze, 167
Charlet, Charlot, 162
Charlotte, 162
Chiara, 83
Christopher, 224
Cisily, 30
Claire, Clarice, 83
Clara, 83
Clare of Assisi, 58, 81, 83–87

Clare Isabella Fornari, 87
Clare of Rimini, 87
Clareta, Clarita, 83
Claribel, Claribelle, 83
Clarinda, Clarine, 83
Clarissa, 83
Claude de la Colombiere, 168, 171 ff
Claus, 117
Clemence, Clemente, 221
Clement Hofbauer, 221–222
Clementina, Clementine, 221
Clovis, 101
Colin, 117
Concepta, Concetta, 217
Concha, Conchita, 217
Consolata, 217
Consuela, 217
Cosmas, 223, 224
Cyril, 57, 226

Damian, 223, 224
Danette, Danita, 128
Daniel of Morocco, 128
Daniela, 128
Danil, Dannel, 128
David, 226
Diago, Diego, 12
Dionysius, 106
Dolly, 30
Dolora, Doloris, Dolorita, 217
Dominic, 75, 91, 158, 223
Domnus, 128
Donna, 30, 217
Dora, Doris, 30
Doretta, 30
Doria, 30
Dorice, 30
Dorothea, 30
Dorothea of Venice, 36
Dorothy, girl martyr, 30, 36
Dorothy of Alexandria, 36
Dotty, 30
Dunstan, 224

Edmund Campion, 146
Edmund of Canterbury, 71
Edsel, Edson, 63
Eduard, Edvard, 63
Edward the Confessor, 57, 63–66, 225
Edward the Martyr, 66
Edwarda, Edwardina, Edwardine, 63
Edwina, 63
Eileen, 52
Elaine, 52
Eleanor, 52

Elena, 52
Eligius, 224
Elisa, 95
Elizabeth, cousin of BVM, 7, 57, 58
Elizabeth Bichier des Ages, 100
Elizabeth of Hungary, 81, **95–100**, 104, 223
Elizabeth of Portugal, 100, 225
Ella, Ellen, 52
Elna, 95
Elsa, 95
English Martyrs of the Oates Plot, 150
Enrico, 124
Etienne, Etiennette, 125
Etta, 124
Eugene, Eugenio, Eugenius, 55
Eugenia, Eugenie, 55
Eveline, Evelyn, 52

Felicita, 30
Felicity, **30–34**
Filipa, Filipe, 146
Fillipo, 146
Flora, Florella, Floretta, 210
Floris, 210
Florita, 210
Flossie, 210
Fran, France, 78, **205**
Franc, 78
Francella, 78, 205
Frances of Rome, 209
Frances Xavier Cabrini, 130, **205–209**, 223, 224
Francesca, Francesco, 78, 205
Franchette, 78, 205
Franchon, 78, 205
Francine, 78, 205
Francis of Assisi, 57, 58, **78–82**, 83 ff, 88, 89, 97, 132, 145, 223, 224, 225
Francis Borgia, 82, 131
Francis de Sales, 82, 116, 145, 195, 224, 225
Francis of Paola, 224
Francis Xavier, 82, 131, 205, 223, 225
Franco, 78
Francois, 78
Frank, 78
Franklin, 78
Franny, 78, 205
Franz, 78

Gabriel the Archangel, 7, 51, 224
Gabriel Lalemant, 165, 166
Gemma Galgani, 223
Gene, 55

Geneva, Genever, 54
Genevieve, **54**
Georg, Geort, 52
Georganna, Georgina, Georgine, 52
George, **52**, 223, 225
Georgetta, Georgette, 52
Gerald, 174
Gerard of Brogne, 178
Gerard of Chzonad, 178
Gerard Majella, 130, **174–177**
Gerard of Toul, 178
Geraud, Giraud, 174
Gerhard, 174
Germain, 54
Germanus, 47
Gibson, 127
Gilbert of Sempringham, **127**
Gilberto, 127
Giorgio, 52
Giovanni, 191
Gisbert, 127
Giuseppa, Giuseppe, 7
Grace, 3
Gredel, 168
Gregoire, Gregor, Gregorio, 125
Gregory the Great, **125–126**, 224
Greta, Grita, 168
Gretchen, 168
Guillaume, 146
Guinevere, 54
Gwen, 54

Hal, 124
Hanna, 3
Hansel, 191
Harriet, 124
Harry, 124
Hatty, 124
Hawkins, 124
Heinrich, 124
Helen, 52
Helena, **52–53**
Helene, 52
Helmina, 146
Helsa, 95
Hendrick, 124
Henning, 124
Henrietta, Henriette, 124
Henry the Emperor, **124**
Henry of Upsala, 225
Hodge, 141
Honora, 52
Hubert, 224
Hugh of Cluny, 72
Hugh of Grenoble, 72

Hugh of Lincoln, 57, **67–70**
Hugh of Montaigu, 72
Hugo, 67
Hugolino, 128
Hugues, 67
Hutchin, 67

Iago, 12
Ian, 191
Ignatius of Loyola, 131, 223
Ilsa, Ilse, 52
Immaculata, 217
Imogene, 217
Ines, Inez, 30
Isaac of Constantinople, 167
Isaac of Cordova, 167
Isaac Jogues, 130, **162–167**
Isaac of Spoleto, 167
Isabeau, 95
Isabel, Isabella, **95**
Isidore, 224
Ivan, 191
Ives, 224

Jacob, 12
Jacqueline, 12
Jacques, 12
Jacquetta, Jacquette, 12
Jaculin, 12
Jago, 12
Jamek, 12
James Duckett, 224
James the Greater, 1, **12–15**, 16, 106, 226
James the Less, 15
James of the Marches, 15
James Philippi, 15
Jamine, 12
Jamnik, 12
Jan, 191
Jane, 111
Jane de Chantal, 116
Janek, 191
Janet, 111
Janice, 111
Jean, Jeanne, 111
Jean Lalande, 165, 166
Jeanette, 111
Jeanne de Valois, 116
Jenifer, 54, 111
Jenny, 111
Jerome, 224
Jesse, 191
Jessica, 111
Jesuit Martyrs, 225
Joachim, father of BVM, 1, **3–6**

Joachim of Siena, 6
Joachima, 3
Joachima, widow, 6
Joan of Arc, 51, 58, 108, **111–116**, 224, 225
Joanna, 111
Joaquin, Joaquina, 3
Johan, Johann, 191
Johanna, 111
John the Apostle, 1, 12, 17, 19, 197
John the Baptist, 114, 197
John Baptist de la Salle, 224
John Baptist Vianney, 197
John Berchmans, 223
John Bosco, 130, **191–197**
John Chrysostom, 197
John de Brebeuf, 162, 165, 166, 197
John Eudes, 168
John Fisher, 131, 139, 140
John of God, 223, 224
Jonathan, 191
Jorge, 52
Joris, 52
Jose, Josef, 7
Joseph, spouse of BVM, 1, **7–10**, 223, 224, 225
Josepha, 7
Joseph Benedict Cottolengo, 11
Joseph of Cupertino, 223
Joseph of Leonessa, 11
Joseph of Oriel, 11
Josephine, 7
Juan, 191
Juana, Juanita, 111
Julia, Juliana, 179
Julia of Cornillon, 183
Julia of Corsica, 183
Julia of Lisbon, 183
Julia of Saragossa, 183
Julian the Hospitaller, 224
Julie Billiart, 129, 130, **179–183**
Julienne, 179
Juliet, Juliette, 179
Jurgen, 52

Karal, 162
Karen, Karin, 184
Karl, 162
Kasia, 184
Kate, 184
Kateri Tekakwitha, 166
Kathleen, 184
Kathryn, 184
Kitty, 184
Klas, Klaus, 117

Lawrence, 224
Lazarus, 26 ff
Lee, 53, 95
Lena, 52
Lenn, 220
Leo I, 53–54
Leo, Franciscan martyr, 128
Leon, 53
Leona, 52, 53
Leonard of Port Maurice, 220, 223
Leonardo, 220
Leonilla, Leonita, 53
Leonora, Leonore, 53
Leora, 52
Lewis, 101
Libby, 95
Lionel, 53
Lipa, Lipo, 146
Lisa, 95
Lizette, 95
Lorentine, 217
Loretta, Loretto, 217
Louis, king of France, 57, 58, 81, 101–
    104, 225
Louis of Anjou, 104
Louis Bertrand, 104
Louis of Cordova, 104
Luce, Lucetta, 30
Lucia, Lucie, 30
Lucile, Lucille, 30
Lucilla, 36
Lucillian, 30
Lucina, 30
Lucy, martyr, 30, 35–36
Lucy the Chaste, 36
Lucy of Scotland, 36
Ludwig, 101
Ludwig of Thuringia, 99
Luigi, 101
Luis, 101
Luke, 27, 224
Luz, 30

Madge, 168
Madonna, 217
Mae, 215
Magda, 168
Maire, 215
Maisie, 168
Manette, 215
Manon, 215
Margaret of Antioch, 112, 173
Margaret of Cortona, 173
Margaret of Hungary, 173
Margaret Mary Alacoque, 129, 168–173

Margaret of Scotland, 173
Margery, 168
Marguerite, 168
Maria Goretti, 130, 215–217
Marian, Marien, Marion, 215
Mariana, Mariane, 215
Maribel, 215
Marie, 215
Mariella, 215
Marilyn, 215
Marius, 37
Marjorie, 168
Mark, 18
Marsia, 215
Marta, Martel, Martella, 26
Marten, Martene, 37
Martha, 1, 26–29, 224
Martha of Edessa, 29
Martha of Persia, 29
Marthine, 26
Marti, Martil, 37
Martin I, 40
Martin de Porres, 40, 223
Martin of Tours, 2, 37–40, 224
Martina, Martino, Martinus, 37
Marvin, 37
Mary, BVM, 3, 4, 5, 7, 8, 9, 10, 13 f,
    80, 81, 93, 112, 113, 115, 125, 129,
    132, 160, 184, 186, 187, 188, 189, 190,
    194, 198, 199, 200, 201, 204, 217, 220,
    223, 225, 226
Mary, sister of Martha, 26 ff
Mary of Egypt, 217
Mary Magdalene, 26
Mary Ann of Quito, 217, 225
Mathilde, Matilde, 123
Matilda, 123–124
Matthew the Apostle, 223, 224
Matty, 26
Maud, Maude, 123
Maura, 220
Maureen, 215
Maurice, 210
Mayme, 215
Merced, Mercedes, 217
Mertin, 37
Methodius, 57, 226
Micha, Michal, 51
Michael, 51, 111, 112, 224, 225
Michaela, 51
Michaud, 51
Michel, Michele, Michelle, 51
Michon, 51
Mickel, Mikel, 51
Miguel, 51

Miles, Myles, 51
Minna, Minnie, 215
Miriam, 215
Misha, 51
Mitchell, 51
Moira, 215
Molly, 215
Mona, 41
Monica, 2, 41–44
Monique, 41
Morris, 210

Nan, Nann, Nanna, Nannette, 3
Nancy, 3
Ned, 63
Nell, 52
Nesta, Netta, 30
Nicholas, Franciscan martyr, 128
Nicholas Bara, or Myra, 122, 223, 224, 225
Nicholas Tolentino, 122
Nicholas von Flüe, 58, 117–122, 225
Niel, 117
Niles, 117
Nina, Ninette, 3
Nita, 30, 111
Noel Chabanel, 166
Nora, Norah, 52

Olaf, 106, 225

Pablo, 21
Pamela, 53
Pancho, 78
Parnell, 16
Pascal Baylon, 223
Paschal, 34
Paton, 45
Patrice, 45
Patricia, 45, 50
Patricia, martyr, 50
Patrick, 2, 45–50, 225
Patrick of Nevers, 50
Patrig, 45
Patrizio, 45
Paul the Apostle, 1, 21–24, 139
Paul of the Cross, 25
Paul the Hermit, 25
Paula, Paulette, 21
Pauline, 21
Paulus, 21
Payton, Peyton, 45
Peadar, Peder, Pedro, 16
Pearce, 16
Pearl, 168

Perpetua, 30–34
Perrin, 16
Perry, 16
Peter, Apostle, 1, 12, 13, 16–20, 24, 224, 225
Peter of Alcantara, 224
Peter Canisius, 20, 224
Peter Celestine, 20, 224
Peter Claver, 223
Peter Julian Eymard, 20
Peter Nolasco, 75
Peter Thomas, 20
Petra, Petronella, 16
Petro, Petrus, 16
Petroc, 16
Philip of Alexandria, 150
Philip Howard, 129, 146–147
Philip Neri, 131, 145, 150
Philippa, Philippina, Philippine, 146
Philippine Duchesne, 150
Pierce, Piers, Pierson, 16
Pierre, 16
Pippa, 146
Pius X, 197, 213, 216
Pudens, 33 f

Quillen, 146

Raimundo, 73
Ramon, 73
Ramona, 73
Raphael, 51
Raymond Nonnatus, 77
Raymond of Penafort, 57, 73–77
Raymund, 73
Regina, 217
Rene Goupil, 164, 166
Revocatus, 31
Rhoda, 157
Ricardo, 67
Rich, 67
Richard, king of West Saxons, 72
Richard of Andria, 72
Richard of Chichester, 57, 67, 70–72
Robard, 141
Robert, Abbot of Newminster, 145
Robert Bellarmine, 130, 141–145, 223
Robert of Citeaux, 145
Roberta, Robertina, Robertine, 141
Roberto, 141
Robin, 141
Rosa, 157
Rosalia, Rosalie, 157
Rosalia, patroness of Palermo, 161
Rosalind, 157

Rosalyn, Roseline, 157
Rosamund, 157
Rosaria, Rosarita, 217
Rosario, 217
Rose Elizabeth, 161
Rose of Lima, 130, 157–161, 225, 226
Rose of Viterbo, 161
Rosel, Roselle, 157
Roseline, 161
Rosemarie, Rosemary, 157
Rosetta, Rosette, 157
Rosina, Rosita, 157
Rupert, 141
Rupert of Salzburg, 145
Rykart, 67

Samuel, 128
Saturninus, 31
Saturus, 31
Seamus, Seumas, 12
Sebastian, 223, 224
Secundulus, 31, 33
Shamus, 12
Sharon, 217
Shawn, 191
Shiela, 30
Simeon, 8
Stanislaus, 225
Stella, 217
Stephana, Stephanie, 125
Stephen of Hungary, 124, 125, 225
Stephen the Martyr, 22, 125, 139, 224
Steven, 125
Susanna of Constantinople, 6

Teresa, Teresita, 210
Teresa of Avila, 10, 214, 226
Terry, 210
Thérèse of Lisieux, 130, 210–214, 223
Thoma, Thomasine, 136
Thomas à Becket, 65, 68, 127, 140, 150, 224
Thomas the Apostle, 140, 225
Thomas Aquinas, 77, 92, 93, 102, 140, 143, 223, 224
Thomas of Hereford, 140

Thomas More, 129, 131, 136–140
Tomas, Tomaz, 136

Ursula, 133

Valerian, 34
Vance, 151
Venise, 219
Vera, 219
Verenice, 219
Veron, 219
Veronica Giuliani, 219
Veronique, 219
Vicente, 151
Vincens, Vincenti, 151
Vincent de Paul, 130, 151–155, 185, 186, 223
Vincent Ferrer, 156, 224
Vincent Kadlubek, 156
Vincent Maria Strombi, 156
Vincent of Saragissa, 225
Vincentia, 151
Vitus (Guy), 224
Vladimir, 225

Wenceslaus, 225
Wileen, 146
Wilette, 146
Wilhelm, 146
Wilhelmina, 146
Will, 146
Willa, Willabel, Willabella, 146
William Howard, 129, 146, 147–150
William of Toulouse, 150
William of Tours, 150
Williamanna, Williamina, 146
Willibrord, 225
Willin, 146
Willum, 146
Wilma, 146
Winifred, 54
Wolfgang, 124

Zita, 224
Zoë, 184